WHAT I, COULDN'T TELL YOU

Matthew Edwards and Jane Funk

WHAT I, COULDN'T TELL YOU

Matthew Edwards and Jane Funk
All Rights Reserved.
Copyright ©2017

Cover and book design by Dave Bricker
ISBN: 978-0-9983569-0-7

Contents

DEDICATION

Matthew, thank you for sharing your most prized possession with me. Without your somber warning in August of 2010, I might not have dedicated my heart to dispossessing your journals from police custody. I prize nothing in this world more than this gift because it holds your written soul. You held nothing back — nothing. By revealing the total truth, you proved your love for me. The ugly truth is a beautiful freedom! I also dedicate these words to Jesus, the Living God, the One who promises to dry every tear, and He who conquered death so that we may also live.

— Matt's mom

PREFACE

Matt died in September, 2010 at age 25 of a heroin/etc. overdose. Matt was not one of those stereotypical seedy types who lurk in alleys by day and leans against brick walls under neon beer signs by night — not Matt. He didn't stick out in the crowd like that; he was an articulate and well-traveled country boy. We came from rural America; I am a career teacher. Matt liked to bow hunt, study music, ride his dirt bike, travel overseas, play cards, discuss politics, read (The Daily Onion, classic poetry, social commentaries, conservative news, Facebook...), play the guitar, and write. He wrote little vignettes — lists of dos and don'ts, random rants, poems, and daily journal entries.

I discovered his collection of writings after he died, and found they were surprisingly full of hope. They tell of the struggles, common yet often unheard, of a hometown junkie. Matt is part of the growing trend changing the faces in morgues and jails. Substantial numbers of middle class, non-metropolitan

Americans now use heroin. Matt is one of those statistics and changing faces.

This book, in part, allows me to set right what I did wrong. Through helping others to understand how addicts and their loved ones feel and behave, I hope to change our natural tendencies to hide and condemn. I would like others to experience not only how trapped my son was, but how gracious he was. Matt's journals provide an opportunity to listen to him directly without assumptions or staging. I found his conversations refreshing and engaging. I find his writings timeless and enlightening. I so wish for one more conversation with him. Have you ever yearned for one last chance to explain something? I believe Matt wants to say one more thing, too. I pray his one-more-thing will rise like smoke to the nostrils of God, embodying the anguish of untold thousands, to find His favor in their defense.

Because of his journal writings, I understand Matt's shame and his need to conceal a very personal battle with a hopeful smile. His suffering is evident in the many personal artifacts I am left with. I have all the funeral cards he saved, the receipts from drug stores and stubs for cash loans, the letters from buddies and girlfriends dating back to 7th grade, his letters to me from summer camps and jail, transcripts from court depositions, scraps of paper with scribbled notes, random poems (like an "Ode to Pimples"), and many electronic messages on Facebook and email.

He collected anything that held a special memory: locks of hair, quarters shot by rifles, concert ticket stubs, and personal effects of people he loved. I have his grandmother's Bible and his father's favorite watch in a box with grandpa's Old-timer knife and papa's dress knife. He kept it all, neatly organized in cigar boxes and other filing systems. I buried Matt with his favorite artifact, his grandpa Chet's dress hat from the 50s. Thankfully, his words did not get buried with him.

This book contains his journals, my own memories and reflections on the events of his life, and his autobiography. Matthew wrote the short autobiography in the winter/early spring of 2010. I can attest to the truthfulness of the whole thing — except for one thing; he ended with a lie. He was lying to himself more than anyone else. He needed to feel successful and continued to tell himself that all would end happily and all suffering would end. When all hope seems lost, a little time on a raft is enough to believe one has survived the ship's sinking. As the saying goes: "I believe we are making real progress here; things are getting worse at a slower rate." In reality he wasn't doing well at all.

During a good streak he may have felt under control, but a week of living clean is not enough. We all like to believe a week of vacation from our job is the equivalent of freedom, but it isn't. Monday comes and we're right back working for the same jerk boss. We are free from that boss when we achieve what we've set out to build upon this little bit of dirt. Our freedom from life-threatening addiction is only realized when one achieves long-term dreams: marriage, family, home, career, etcetera. Addiction shortens the scope of life goals; the future means little when the present is deadly. No one cares about tomorrow's meeting when battling hurricane force winds and a sinking boat. Matt lived day by day, hoping for some clear sailing, but he was only writing from inside the eye of Hurricane Opiates when he crafted his autobiography.

As Matt's mom I am lost on a sea of sadness. There was hope for Matt, but there is no hope for my dilemma. I will have to wait out my time here on Earth — a lifelong sentence. Every day I remember my son: his first tooth, potty training, stuffed animals, favorite toys, favorite meals, first motorcycle, lead roles in drama, high school trips, first job, and first successful hunt. As I motor through the daily landscape, I am reminded of each time we ate a pizza there or how he hit a rabbit while learning to drive around this curve. Looking at children playing at sunset on a sublime beach, driving through a remote forest filled with hunters unloading gear, watching a new and awkward mother hold her child, I envision myself and Matt as the light dims and the shadows shift through the laughter and murmuring voices. But these are other people's lives and I am only an onlooker. I try to imagine Matt there, what he would say, and how he looked when he walked through the same scenery. Then, I go home and walk past the dining room, now a shrine full of his mementos of childhood, adolescence, and adulthood. Without those items I would have no tangible evidence of a great love, a promising child, and the real man he became.

Drug addiction is not the untimely death of an individual; it is the grotesque loss of generational devotion. Senseless death never ends; it only crystalizes each memorable moment in amber; the living can only look through the darkened sap into the moment when a perfect creature died. While looking and contemplating, they lock eyes with death and try to see a reflection.

The most valuable possession any of us has is love. Its momentum drives our economies, mighty and miniscule. We strive to serve who we love — ourselves and others. Even self-love needs an audience of human hearts. Without someone sharing the experience, nothing has flavor, vacations are lonely, and trips to the beach cast shadows and echoes as other children splash and play. A house full of expensive amenities, a vacation on an ethereal shore, a pantry full of fresh herbs, aromatic breads, and succulent meats are each only truly enjoyed in the company of loved ones. I do share with my friends and family, but I promised Matt he would inherit what I had built and that he would be there to enjoy what I had earned. I worked to enjoy and pass on many things to him. The money I had saved for his first house I spent on his funeral, burial, and gravestone. The 40 acres he hunted on will instead go to — well, I'm not sure who wants that. I had even saved grandma's diamond ring for him to give to my future daughter-in-law and mother to my grandkids. I guess I'll give it away; no one but Matt would care to have it. All these things I collected for Matthew.

He still resides in my heart. I want to physically have him somewhere, but how and where do you put all that love after the warm body is cold in the dirt? He resides in his mementos at every evening meal instead; his guitar, passport, and photos hang on the wall looking down at us every, single, last, day, of, my, life. Some might say I need to move on. His childhood clothes and writings will eventually get pitched as no one will care about or remember the man they represent. I'm okay with that. I'm not okay with conveniently forgetting that he is supposed to be here, with us, miserable like us, loving and sharing the struggles. Sadly, he can't share in our little victories and rants against the defeats; he only exists in our dining room, and he gets a bit dusty at times. This is his legacy. It will not conveniently go away. This is my reality.

I wouldn't be a truthful author if I glossed over my sadness and regret, but I have written my thoughts and published Matt's writings so everyone will understand the real dilemma surrounding addiction and the roles each of us plays. Addicts' and their loved ones' response to addiction needs rethinking.

I wish I could go back and read a book like this before Matt died; my action plan would have been considerably different. I wish Matt could have read a diary like this. Reconsidering his decision to continue faking it might have saved our dreams. We write the script for our own dramatic play. Consider how your own actions will define your role in this drama. In your story, will you be a villain, a victim, an unconcerned yet gossipy onlooker, a concerned citizen who makes an anonymous call, a good Samaritan who puts up cash for someone unknown, or a dimwitted teen in a cheap horror movie who keeps reading a book after receiving a creepy call?

If you are fighting against the demon of addiction, read closely. The ending of Matt's story doesn't have to be yours. You'll find hope, support, and understanding in these pages.

If you are contending with a loved one's addiction, start working earnestly to avert the pain that will certainly follow. The human spirit is stronger than you might think. Don't extinguish your candle in the window.

If you are in a position of power, consider the great danger opiates and addictions pose to ourselves, to our loved ones, and to our society. The laws and politics that address drug enforcement and addiction are based on ignorance of the problems. Enlightened leadership is desperately needed.

If you are a lover of good stories, befriend an addict and ask for theirs. Addicts are not so dangerous and odious. You can make a difference simply by listening, learning, and caring.

If you are a clinical researcher, study the emotional and physiological reactions to pharmaceuticals. Publish your findings. The free trade in addictive opiates must be restrained by facts.

And, if you are human, cry aloud with me. Read Matt's story and learn how we can all act on behalf of the innocent.

— Matt's mom

INTRODUCTION TO MATT'S JOURNALS

Matthew started keeping his journals at age 24, after years of addiction. He died at age 25 of a heroin overdose. Though Matt took responsibility for his addiction, it's important to read his story in context. Repeating themes in Matt's story include failures by friends and family, the medical establishment, and the justice system. Though we all know someone touched by addiction, these are taboo topics that ring of conspiracy theory and externalizing blame. We share our experiences battling cancer, raising a dyslexic child, losing weight, and suffering neglect and abuse, yet we feel shame sharing details about an addicted self or loved one. Cancer and abuse are circumstances that come uninvited. The addict actively, consciously seeks to feed his demon. Though it's absurd to think that an addict has any justification to point a finger and say, "it's your fault that I'm doing this to myself," the mechanisms for intervention and treatment are flawed, and fatally compromised by easily available legal opiate pharmaceuticals.

Matt was addicted, but he wanted to explain his predicament. To this end, I am putting our shared experience in black and white, published, and signed. You must decide who is to blame, who is missing from this conversation, and what the repeating themes are.

Matt's story began when he was a high school freshman with infected toenails, a clinical procedure, and a prescription for Vicodin. Later in life, he told me he had felt "touched by God" and wonderfully filled with peace after taking the first pill from that bottle. Outwardly, everything seemed normal after that. High school went on fairly normally with happy involvement in extracurricular activities and classes — except for one constant issue: whenever the phone rang for Matt, he had to talk privately. Curiosity got the better of me by his sophomore year, and I decided to eavesdrop. He stepped out to the backyard to talk, so I walked out the front door and around the house to listen. He was making a drug deal for pills with a boy from school. I knew the boy; his mom was a nurse. I confronted Matt. After several hours of angry and fear filled, shrill arguing from both of us, I decided to call the other mom even though he begged me not to through sobs and tears. He then did the unthinkable: he threatened suicide and walked off down the road. This ended with his cousin Brian driving over, the police coming, and anyone else I could muster up to save him from his emotional breakdown.

I watched more closely after that; signs were appearing. His grades started dropping, his friends started changing, and his healthy pastimes stopped completely. No longer did he ride his dirt bike, shoot his paintball gun, go hunting with Brian, or snow-boarding with me. His attitude became cocky and his time at home was filled with strife. By the time he was a senior, he was living in a neighboring town with my elderly and frail mother, and I could do nothing about it. She liked the help, and refused to negotiate him out and back home.

Living with my mother was another step into daily drug use for Matthew. My mom had an ongoing prescription for Tylenol 3, a codeine-packed pain killer. The bottle was huge — maybe 200 pills — and endless refills were available at a call. Although she knew he was taking her pills, she never told me. But, my sisters did. In fact they complained constantly about Matt to me. He was messy, didn't help much, stole her pills, drank alcohol, and had loud arguments with his grandmother. Still, no one forced him to come back home where I could try to stop the madness. Through all the craziness of high school, he still managed to grad-uate, stay employed, and make friends; the craziness was private.

But the craziness went public after high school. Matthew devel-oped horrible hemorrhoids. He moved to an apartment with a couple of friends, and started classes at a community college. He got fired from his restaurant job. He lost most of his high school friends over swiping their parents' pills and general distancing. He had to sell his beloved Honda due to not maintaining it. He always looked messy, wrinkly, disheveled, and grimy. There were sudden and constant trips to Chicago; a range of older, dodgy friends; money problems. No one could trust a thing he said, and he acted like a little kid by giving laughable excuses for mounting failures. There was one constant — my nagging and lecturing and yelling and disapproval.

For instance, he was on thin ice with his job for calling in sick too often. Still, he decided to drive down to Chicago to "see a close friend who needed his help." I had no idea he was even going there until I received a call: "Mom, do me a favor and call my boss. Tell him I can't make it into work tomorrow because (insert excuse)."

"Matt, where are you?"

"I'm on my way back from Chicago."

"You call him yourself. I don't want to tell him some cockamamie story like that."

"I can't call, Ma. I don't have reception."

"What! I'm talking to you right now!"

"Ma, I don't have reception, so I can't call. Please? Would you just call him and tell him that?"

Of course, I refused. These types of incidents had been occurring throughout the years after high school — but not daily. We still had good times, normal conversations, and family events together here and there. He still came over and helped me cut firewood, haul building materials, babysit his sister, and move stuff around. He still had nice girlfriends, and developed several deep affections.

Then, in all my wisdom, I suggested he get his hemorrhoids removed before he had to be taken off my insurance at age 21. This was the single most devastating step into medically supported addiction for Matt. The operation went well, but he was put on pain meds 4 times a day for 4 weeks. At the end of the month, he complained that he still had pain, so the doctor prescribed them for another month. This went on for 6 months. Then, the doctor performed another procedure to try to fix his pain. This meant more months of complaints followed by prescriptions. Going to the doctor and making a huge issue over something meant pain meds. He had doctors do more and unnecessary procedures and operations to get extended pain prescriptions.

Love struck Matthew during this time. He was working at the local grocery store's wine and liquor warehouse, which he loved. He also fell in love with Paulina — a beautiful, sweet, summer worker from Poland. They spent every free moment together traveling to local lakes and down forest roads, eating local delicacies, and drinking wine at sunset. At summer's end, she returned to Poland but chatted with Matt daily online and by phone. The next summer she did not return as planned, but Matt devised a plan to go visit her in Poland. Time had distanced her feelings, and another man was on her arm, but Matthew was undaunted. He accepted the intruder with sly grace in hopes of winning her heart back. His plan did not go as expected, at least completely. He was able to keep her friendship but lost her confidence.

Thinking she would not abandon a dying friend, he contrived an insane lie — he told her he had cancer in the winter, that his treatment was not working in spring, that he was in constant pain in summer, and that the doctors did not know if they could save him that fall. She accepted his offer to fly over and spend a month touring Poland with her, thinking this might be the last time she would ever see him, and that she really did love him after all. By this time Matthew had plenty of prescriptions and had saved up a great deal of money by working crazy hours and pilfering cash. He went.

His time in Poland was a strange mix of wonderful vistas and reunions with former summer workers, and calculated manipulation to obtain more drugs. He was able to get liquid morphine by lying to kind and sympathetic doctors who believed he really had cancer and pain. Paulina watched him shoot up, catered to his every whim, and poured her mercy out. However, she cringed inwardly as he slurred his words, dressed sloppily, and begged for pity-love.

The trip ended well; the tour was pleasant, but the result was final. Paulina was cemented at friend status, and Matt was crushed. She had her lover and Matt his — opioids.

When Matt returned, he was excited to tell me his memories. He explained each postcard I had received and popped out a present or two for everyone. But he was bent in defeat because he had failed to win back his true love. Life went forward, but his constant quest to find some way to reignite her flame never fully left. He became Matthew the Forlorn and often pined in solitude, returning to all those summer spots to sip wine at sunset alone.

Finally, the truth came out about his supposed cancer. He inadvertently left himself logged in to his email on my computer, and given his history, I read a few of them. The insanity of his ploy then became a point of discussion — open, tangible. Disgusted by his ruse but empathetic to his cause, I approached him with some advice about women, love, and lies. He actually listened to me. Maybe he just did not want to keep up his acting job on a canceled show; I am unsure. But he decided to tell her and beg her forgiveness. This closed the show with a sudden lights-out, and he found himself focusing on his first love again — opiates.

Paulina and I still communicate today. She did love Matt deeply. She just decided that she would not be able to have a stable and healthy relationship with both Matt and opiates. His heart was divided.

Matt no longer told people he had cancer, but he did go doctor shopping for his rectal issues. Quite possibly he did have issues at that point. After at least 3 surgeries — 2 of which were unnecessary procedures involving the removal of a portion of his rectum — he most likely could not function without pain. Complicating a disfigured rectum was his opiate use, which causes serious constipation problems. One day he informed me that he was going to get a colostomy bag because he just couldn't move his bowels without intense pain. I flipped. Calling the doctor, I filled his ear: "I will press charges if you mutilate my son. The kid wants pain meds! Are you stupid? I care about my son; he is not alone. I will take this to court."

The doctor's reply: "He won't leave me alone, and yes, I know he is addicted." Stuttering at my candor and angry tirade, he said he would cancel the operation and put him on the do-not-prescribe list at every emergency room.

Matt was equally angry after receiving the doctor's call and his explanation of why he would not prescribe anything more or schedule any more procedures: "You broke the law, Mom. I am an adult, and you can't discuss my health records with my doctor. I am going to press charges."

"Go for it, Matt. I love you enough to go to court and pay fines to keep you from mutilating yourself for pain meds. And, oh, by the way, I took you off my insurance."

But this was only one doctor in a revolving dry-cleaner's conveyor of lab coats. Matt found more doctors, more contrived medical issues, and many more and varied pills.

Then it happened. Everything imploded. It happened so fast that I can't remember the exact order of events, but the ending was unforgettable. To the best of my memory, this is how his 22nd year ensued:

- He lost his beloved wine and liquor store job over stealing money from the till using a coupon scam.
- He got a job at Walmart, and lost that for calling in too often.
- He was caught stealing a cellphone, was ticketed for drunk driving, and burned his arm with a cigarette lighter (to remove needle marks) all in the same night.
- He lost his beater car.
- He couldn't pay his rent so he broke into my mother's locked and empty house (she was in an assisted living apartment) to have a place to stay.
- The family discovered him there and reinstalled the locks.

- He found another roommate and convinced the landlord to let him stay in the apartment.
- He was evicted from his apartment.
- He got a job at a motel front desk and was asked to leave the same day. I discovered later that my own sister had called the owner and told him about Matt's past. This put Matt into an absolute and deep depression coupled with a sense that everyone hated him.
- He got a job at Kmart and another beater car.
- He moved into a ratty motel efficiency apartment. He became inconsolable, deeply hurt, and reckless.
- He lost his job at Kmart.
- I tried to organize an intervention. My other sister and her husband and son came to his motel to try and persuade him to enter a treatment program, which failed miserably.
- Someone slashed Matt's tires.
- I received a call from the police; Matt was in custody over allegedly planning to rob local pharmacies at gunpoint.

I woke up to the local news headlining Matt's name and describing how the police had been able to uncover his plot to hold up 3 local pharmacies. Steeling myself for what was to come next, I went to work at my teaching job at the school Matthew had graduated from. My fellow teachers avoided me; their whispers and guarded eyes following my bent head as I glided down the halls. I don't think I even felt my feet move. I shut off my mind and went into survival mode.

Phone calls started coming in from everywhere. Family members called to chastise me for being a divorcee and ruining my son. They said these things with pity as if I was just unable to raise a child alone, like all weak women who need a man — "You poor thing. So sorry, Jane." Others offered legal advice on how to get him out of jail because they just couldn't believe it was true. The police called constantly, and one even walked into my home when I was at work. At least he left his business card on my kitchen table. He said he needed to interview me, and he needed all my guns — now. Yes, I was a suspect. Somehow, I was involved because I had hunting guns. After interrogating me, they confiscated all my firearms. They even went to my mom's apartment and took a .22-rifle that had been given to Matt by his deceased grandfather. It was stored there for safekeeping as we didn't want Matt to pawn it. I was unsure why they wanted my guns because Matt was locked in jail, but they said they were going to use them as evidence of his plan.

And what a pitiful plan it was. Being out of his mind on every kind of pain killer and street drug, Matt spent his half-waking hours talking in fantasy dream terms. He was a natural actor and a practiced storyteller, so he used his talent to impress his seedy neighbors. One was an ex-convict. Matt thought he would impress him by claiming he had gang affiliations, criminal intentions, and plenty of firearms and knowledge of employee routines to pull off a pharmaceutical drug heist. He hammed it up for this fellow, and acted the part so convincingly that the man told his girlfriend, who told her boss, who called the police, who arranged for a detective to place a wire on the ex-con, who invited Matt over to retell the story. With great aplomb and enthusiasm, Matt vocalized his fantasy blitz in great detail for the voice recorder and hidden detectives.

Returning to his motel room, he lit up a joint and turned on the TV. Someone knocked at his door. He sauntered lazily over to open it. He was not expecting a whole SWAT team with full-body armor and machine guns to rush in, throw him to the floor, and scream commands, but that is what happened. After hauling him off in a military style paddy wagon, they ransacked his room and found a bunch of needles and drug-smeared tin foil, a broken .22 caliber plastic[1] pistol in the bottom of a box of memorabilia, and a small bag of pot.

I showed up for every court hearing, went to weekly jail visits, tried to find competent lawyers, paid his weekly jail rent, put

---

1. This was their "big piece of evidence" — one of those cheap guns people buy to practice with at a firing range so they can say they know how to hit a target. It was broken, too. Matt probably forgot he even had it.

money in his account for an extra shirt or socks, and exchanged letters back and forth for 4 months. I felt like I was a criminal that whole time. The way I was treated when entering the jail for visits, the way the detectives treated me, and the way my community treated me was beyond distrustful; it was institutionalized scrutiny and legalized invasion of privacy. The justice system looked for every possible lead on stolen goods, firearm access, and drug trafficking.

In the end, law enforcement had to drop the main case because it became apparent that Matthew was simply a drug addict who was talking big. He had no firm plans to commit a robbery. He had no weapons to commit a robbery. He didn't even have a working vehicle to drive to a robbery. However, he got stiff penalties for drug paraphernalia, illegal substances, and theft of a camera or something. The court made it seem like they were doing him a favor by offering him a deal to go on several years of probation instead of trying his case. Thankfully, they commuted his last month of jail time to a 45-day program in a drug rehabilitation center.

Finally, I had my dear son back. He and I spoke adult-to-adult for the first time. It was as if he went away as a teenager and reappeared as a mature and wise man. Because of the rehabilitation center, he began taking personal responsibility for his actions and circumstances — but it also connected him with many other drug addicts serving jail time there. He formed many friendships and future contacts there.

He hated humility counseling, which seems to be a common approach to rehabilitation. They were bent on breaking Matt's pride. He would not move on that one issue. All the other pieces he accepted and embraced, but he would not sit in a room with 30 other people and, round-robin-style, stand up and metaphorically disrobe. I had to attend one of these public humiliation ceremonies. All the residents were there with their parents or spouses seated in a big circle. Starting at one end, each addict had to tell this huge crowd of strangers, friends, and enemies (Matt deeply disliked some residents there) what a miserable retch they had been and how sorry they were for being such a lying, stealing, lazy loser. Then, the parent or spouse got their turn to reinforce how horrible life had been due to "their addict." The patients were always referred to as "the addict," without mentioning their individual names. When Matthew's turn came, he refused to speak. Crossing his arms and looking up, he simply said, "I am not doing this, not here. This is humiliating." His counselor was enraged and made an example of him the next day. He extended his release time by 10 days. Still, I am thankful for the effort they made and the son I once again had.

After release, Matt came to live with me. All that summer we talked and laughed. I told him embarrassing episodes from my life he never knew, and he divulged anything I asked. He admitted things he did, and told me things I didn't know he had done. We cried a lot, and we became very close friends. But unfortunately, he was trapped there. He had lost his driver's license, had monthly fines to pay to the probation system, and he had a bad reputation with local employers. We devised a plan to get him out of town, into an area where he could use public transit or walk, and where he could be around caring people who understood addiction.

That October, we moved him to Oshkosh to stay with his aunt by marriage. His job search started immediately, but his criminal record kept him from obtaining any respectable job in a factory or with local industries. After a few weeks he got a job at a fast-food restaurant, and after a few more weeks, he was paying back his probation and fines. Reports came back from the aunts he was living with that they were quite irritated with him. He wasn't helping out with chores as much as they would like, and he was getting on everyone's nerves for petty reasons.

They demanded he get an apartment by the end of the month. Getting an apartment wasn't easy because Matt had a record, so he could only rent rooms from people who didn't care or didn't run him through a records search. None of the rental agents would accept his application, but he was able to find a room within several miles walking distance of his job. He called me weekly, discussed his predicament constantly, and ranged from hopeful to hopeless every other day. Christmas came and I sent him bags of groceries, sets of new clothes and boots, and all my love. Most all of his former friends reconnected with him, and even Paulina chatted with him regularly. He always seemed to have someone coming down, up, or over to visit. Though Matt had hardly known his father, his father's family even connected with him deeply. Old and new friends appeared everywhere — well almost everywhere. He could not make a real friend in Oshkosh. The place was just too industrial in personality for him.

He made it through that first winter walking everywhere. He also made new doctor connections that started with prescriptions for depression medications and more complaints that his rectum hurt. His probation officer was only interested in collecting his monthly payment, and his aunts were interested in his help with chores.

By the summer of 2009 I realized my son was using drugs again, but I had no idea he was losing control because he wasn't acting like his pre-rehab self. I thought he was just using marijuana and a few pills for anxiety and sleep problems. When he called weekly, he was his adult self, who complained logically, laughed easily, and shared his life honestly — or so I thought. We spoke in depth about his next move, how to escape the misery of Oshkosh, how to deal with difficult people, and how to keep his dreams alive.

This is where Matt's journals start. They tell the rest of the story — his story and the story of many other addicts and their loved ones. Watch for the points of failure in his universal tragedy. Consider what obstacles blocked his struggle to be free from addiction. The addict is responsible for his own self-destructive choices, but observe the roles of friends and family, the pharmaceutical industry, the medical establishment, and the justice system. Consider how each might have thought about Matt's condition in a more enlightened way, and intervened constructively.

Matt's account of what happened will open your eyes to the beautiful human spirit inside the nameless — the addict. Matt never gave up hope even though many people knew of his problem, had an opportunity to help, and turned a blind eye; his spirit never completely failed. And perhaps this is the most important of Matt's messages. Inside the most desperate addict lies a bright human spirit — with hopes and dreams, and full awareness of the sad absurdity of the struggle — a spirit that yearns to give and receive love and laughter, and to be free from the chains of dependency. As easy as it may be to write off an addict as someone who has "given up," Matt's journals suggest that's not the case, and that we shouldn't give up, either.

MATT'S AUTOBIOGRAPHY

Whether it is coke, heroin, or prescription medication, it all happens the same way. You are always unsuspecting your first time, and generally people don't set out trying to use drugs, or drinking themselves completely stupid every single day. Things happen, and sometimes you end up trying things as almost an accident. The whole course of my life was changed by one event—a trip to my local doctor in Crandon, Wisconsin for a minor operation to fix-up an infected toe on my right foot.

The pain was excruciating. For several months before I went to see the doctor my big toe was infected beyond belief. It was black and blue, basically just a big pocket of puss. The slightest touch was enough to send me into almost crying pain. At some points it got so bad that I had to use a walking cane in order to get around. My mother finally took me to the doctor. My toe nail had to be cut; it was in-grown and caused a continuous infection. It simply wouldn't heal on its own. My doctor that day was a

Dr. Bradner, a real old-time doctor — my mother remembers him being her doctor when she was just a child. He was a good man and widely respected in the community. It was March 2001. I had just turned 16 years old. I had never had a drink of alcohol, never had a puff of MJ in my lungs. I did smoke cigarettes but this was very casual. I was not in any way, shape, or form a drug user. I knew that dope was bad. I knew that my father destroyed his entire life with alcohol, and even at this young age I had a healthy fear of drugs and alcohol in general.

When we got to the clinic, both my mom and I were ushered into one of the back examination rooms. Dr. Bradner explained to me that he was going to have to numb my toe with lidocaine, peel back the toe flesh by cutting it with a scalpel, and then cut the nail and remove a section of it right out of the root. "Am I going to feel this Doc?" I said.

"No, we're going to numb you up real good. You shouldn't feel a thing," was his answer. Great, I was ready to go.

My mother went back to the waiting room while Dr. Bradner and his nurse's aide prepared to cut. He gave me some injections and asked me if I felt anything. "I don't think so," was the answer. He began to cut with the scalpel. The first few cuts I didn't feel, but when he got to the nail itself, which was surrounded by nothing but infected flesh, I began to feel. Hell, I began to scream because I could feel everything.

The doctor stopped for a second — "You can feel that?!?"

Ooh yeah, I was screaming, and I was crying. My wailing was so loud that my mother heard it in the waiting room, her instinct kicked in, and she came running back to me. I was holding the nurse's hand, and Bradner told me something to the effect of "Well Matthew, we're already so far in, and your toe is so infected that the lidocaine isn't helping, but I have to continue. This is going to hurt, I'm sorry." By this point Bradner was obviously shaken by my screams — he was pouring sweat, and I could tell that he was very focused on the task at hand, shaken, but confident still. When he finally cut the nail he began to rip it out of its root. I cannot explain this torture; pain shot like flaming gasoline through every fiber in my body — a bullet train of agony that derailed in volcanic lava in the inner cortex of my mind. I had never felt anything like that before, and I'm sure that my screams were enough to unsettle the entire staff, and probably a few patients. All of the sudden this little country clinic where people went for a cold or flu was feeling like a triage unit on some field of war. I'm sure that some people probably thought I had been shot or stabbed, it was that bad.

God, thankfully Bradner finished. At this point my mother was there, and the nurse was released from the pit-bull like grip of my hand. I was panting like a rabid dog, red as a stop light, and Bradner was looking about the same way. My mother was crying. I only remember her crying in front of me a few times in my life — this was one. This was totally different than anyone expected. My mother was asking Bradner what he was going to do for me: "Will you give him antibiotics? Should I give him some aspirin? Maybe you can prescribe Tylenol 3?"

I remember this very clearly. He said, "No, I don't think I'll give him Tylenol 3. Believe it or not those things just make children tired. I'm going to prescribe him something called Vicodin, better for pain, much better." The poor man was so shaken; I haven't seen a doctor like that *ever,* before or since. He looked as if he had just murderously stabbed me and felt remorse for it!

We went to the pharmacy and got my pain medication and some antibiotics: 15 Vicodin and a bottle of antibiotics. Now, the drive from town to my house is 32 miles; takes a modest driver about 40 minutes to get there. I have driven this road more times than anyone can count, but this ride was different. We started the journey when I was still young and innocent. By the time we got home I would never be innocent again. I was completely transformed in that short span of time. I took one Vicodin thinking it was going to be similar to Ibuprofen, but it was not so; this was something else, this was an *opiate,* and I fell deeply in love with it immediately. Changed forever.

My mother went out of the country to lead a class trip. She left me the bottle, and in the care of my grandma I began to take these and just felt so wonderful. I was at school, I had a crush on this girl (you know who you are!), and I felt that I could finally ask her out. I felt invincible. I felt no pain, my mind was clear, my soul felt purified as if by the touch of God himself. I couldn't imagine that this was the beginning of the darkest period for me and any of my friends who were along for the ride.

I suppose, on reflection, that my addiction and morbid compulsion didn't start right away; it was a very gradual thing. I remembered the name on that prescription bottle, and whenever I bumped into it in a friend's parents' medicine cabinet I made sure to swipe a few. This happened only every few months or so, but it was graduating, ever so slowly, into a mushroom cloud of mental and spiritual darkness. Hydros turned to oxies, which turned into morphine, and finally heroin. Along the way, inevitably, you pick up things like cocaine, speed, and grass — the same goes for picking up methods; at some point every opiate user will begin intravenous injecting, and then the real trouble starts. You stay up at night worrying about Hepatitis, necrotic abscesses and AIDS. There is no real way out; if you have access you have problems.

The lowest point for me started in the summer of 2005. I had several good friends, all of them by now were drug people; my true friends had to turn their backs, and I don't blame them at all. I wasn't a person anymore–I was a monster. Great people like Matt D. and Mike D. had had enough, so to fill my contacts I made friends with people like Peanut (who was actually a great guy, but sick people run together in packs, like wolves), Anna, and others who I don't care to mention. Heroin by this time was my gold, but I was just snorting it at the time as the worst was yet to come.

I fell in love with a girl that summer, deeply in love, and at the same time I was using whatever I could get my hands on. I was forced into a corner where I had to try my best to maintain while also following love. This culminated into a fateful trip to Chicago on a heroin run (my first) — the strangest experience for a country boy.

Peanut was my mother's age — a streetwise dude who grew up on the Northwest side of Chicago, just bordering the near west side. The west side of Chicago is a Disneyland for junkies of all persuasion. It's a quagmire of violence, sex, hate, racism and enormous danger. Garfield Park is 98% African American, so for once in my life I stood out, and Peanut had to give me a run down on the rules we would be playing by on that fateful July night.

"I'm going to tell you exactly what to do; when I say turn you turn; if I tell you to punch a guy, you punch him. This is going to be dangerous, but if you listen to me everything will be fine," Peanut said. This was my first visit to Chicago, and I didn't start getting scared until we got to the West Side Proper, and then fear gripped me; I was a very scared man. I was terrified out of my mind. We made our way north on Pulaski until we got to a "spot" (term for Chicago's open air drug markets). At a spot, the way it works is that you ride by with your window half down, then guys running the operation will literally shout at you as you pass by slowly, "rocks" or "blows" (crack and heroin). The operation was sophisticated. Gangs of Vice Lords or Gangster Disciples had certain blocks that they controlled. When you went to a certain block you had to be waved up the block by a guy that was checking everything out. If you didn't get the okay from him, you weren't going to be able to buy anything. Worst case scenario, you may get shot.

The first spot we got to was I guess some friends of Peanut's; we even got out of the car!! I was almost shaking to death, but Peanut was cool: "You don't have to worry about anything here. Reggie runs this block. Reggie and I go way back". So, here we were, just hanging out on the porch of a dilapidated home, Peanut's son Stoney was with us– maybe he was 2 at the time. He was playing with Reggie's son of the same age while ten feet away a group of 10 guys was selling as cars kept coming up. It was insane. I felt insane. I had never seen anything like this, even in the movies. I felt guilty too because I allowed Peanut to bring Stoney with us. I still feel guilty about that to this day. As a 20 year I had no business being there, and Stoney certainly should have been much farther away.

We bought a few "bags" of heroin, which cost $10 a piece. We were going to drive around to a few different spots, try a bag at each spot and then return to the best spot to make a bigger purchase. Peanut opened my bag, put it on a pack of smokes, pushed it toward me and I snorted it as I was still driving the car. Almost instantly I had no fear of where I was. I could have been in Mogadishu. I could have been in the middle of a great battle and it didn't matter. I was more than ready to dance all night long with the Devil.

We went to a few more spots–all this occurred at night, which is the worst time to be in the ghetto. We weren't very impressed and decided that it was getting too late to operate safely, so we parked outside a park on the near north side, which is much safer, and called it a night.

The next morning I woke up and just felt petrified again. I told Peanut that we were going to go to the first spot and make our big purchase. The stuff could have been chalk dust at that point, but I didn't care. It was high time to get out of the city. We went back into the Ghetto, which was all the more scary because now it was daytime and I could see everything. Now I knew what to be afraid about. We saw a dude, flagged him down, and I bought maybe 15 or 20 bags from him. "Let's get out of here Peanut," was all I said.

"One more quick stop," he said. "I have to do a line before we get heading back."

Fine, whatever. Back to the park we went, and by this time Peanut's girlfriend was there. I jumped into the back seat of her car, Peanut being in front with his girlfriend. I remember watching them blow their entire bags in one shot; "Good stuff, good stuff."

I thought that I would have the tolerance to do the same, so I opened up and blew my bag, all at once. The last thing I remember was saying, "Yeah, that is good stuff," and then…lights out.

The next thing I remember was Peanut stabbing me in the shoulder with a pen to wake me up. I had OD'd, and I was in serious trouble. The feeling was something like drinking 3 bottles of vodka in the space of 5 minutes. My field of view was dark and kept closing in. I just wanted to go back to sleep, but Peanut was keeping me up; "Talk to me Matt, talk to me, HEY, wake the fuck up, c'mon, do you like baseball? Let's talk about baseball." He hustled me out of the car and across the street to the park where I was just about put into the fountain. I was in a lot of trouble.....

When you OD on opiates there is a period of time I like to call "the flash." If you "flash out" and no one is around to help you, then you're dead. The important thing is to keep someone awake long enough for the first rush to get out of their system; depending on the person this could be about 45 minutes. Falling asleep means that you quit breathing. I only found out later that the summer of 2005 was unique to the City of Chicago because some operations started cutting their dope with Fentanyl, which is one of the most powerful synthetic opiates known to man. This is something like using Ever-Clear to cut regular vodka — you get a very much more potent product. A lot of junkies died in the city that year, and I was a hair away from becoming a statistic, but Peanut saved my life. I wouldn't be around for him a year later when he was shot to death, only a few blocks from that first spot — a tragedy. I still think about him all the time, and I miss him.

Despite all the things I had seen and all the pain and trouble that is endemic to being a junkie, I still didn't stop. I brought my habit with me to Poland in 2006 and ended up losing the most beautiful and lovely girl I had ever met. I stole money from my workplace, I burned my family and my friends ever more, and upon my return from that Poland trip I degenerated into a suicidal wreck.

Rose was there to witness my downfall. Rose was there to see the madness that I had become. No longer a man, I was closer to a sociopathic mad man. I remember getting messed up and burning an 8 inch by 1 inch section of my inner right arm, just to get the track marks out (Rose also witnessed this, with absolute terror in her eyes — how could anyone do that?). I lost many more friends in this time; even hardened drug buddies of mine were walking away; I was just too crazy for even them.

I couldn't hold a job for more than a few months. I couldn't pay my bills and got kicked out of my apartment, which I really loved. It was a shame to lose that place. By the very end I was so incredibly depressed that I would spend every cent on opiates, just to remove the pain for a short time, which in turn would make me even more depressed for being broke. I was on a collision course. My family even staged an intervention, which I refused on its face. I should have taken the offer because what ended up happening was worse than I could ever imagine.

I was in a little shit apartment on the outskirts of my town. I was very unhappy. I had just lost a great job at Shopko because of my poor attendance among other things. I really wanted to die at this point, but I didn't even have the guts to put a gun to my head, or fill a syringe with liquid DrainO and fire away into oblivion. Next door to me was a hardened criminal type. The guy was a real scum bag. He looked like a "meth skeleton." We made easy friends — 7 years before this I would never have given this shit-head the time of day — that's how incredibly overboard I had gone.

We used to get together and smoke dope. During these times we would be all messed up and talk about all sorts of criminal stuff — just real fantasy type stuff. This guy would tell me about his dirty deeds, being in prison, being on meth, etc. I would gloat about my thief like ways and all of my black adventures. Looking back makes me realize that I would have locked me up if I were a cop.

One of these nights we had been smoking and I started to explain a fantasy plan I had of making a perfect robbery on a local pharmacy, just total madness. It was very unrealistic. I didn't even own a gun, and I had never even hurt another person physically…, but you would never know that by the way I was talking. This guy got a real kick out of it. He went back to his apartment and told his girlfriend, who didn't understand that it was a fantasy, nothing more. She ended up telling her employer, who in turn called the sheriff. The sheriff ended up surprising this guy and compelled him to wear a wire on me the very next night. The police put me under surveillance that day, and at one point they lost me and scrambled cops to a few different pharmacies just in case I popped up with machine guns, armor piercing rounds, bullet proof vests, and what the hell, maybe even a TANK. They didn't know me, and I had no idea I was being watched.

That was indeed a fateful night; probably the best and worst thing to ever happen to me. The guy showed up to my place right after I had gotten home. He brought some MJ with him, and we began to smoke. Little did I know there were 4 detectives and several units of regular police decked out with machine guns, all around the building, just waiting for the go. After we smoked we were just talking gibberish again, but this guy was on a mission. He started, "So, remember that thing you were talking about last night? Well, that sounds pretty cool man. Why don't you tell me how that would go again?"

Like a complete fool I started talking about the fantasy again, with all the dramatic inclusions of bulletproof vests, lots of guns, and a suicidal approach. Not only that, but I just had to brag about literally almost every crime I had committed in the last 3 years. It was such a foolish thing to do. I was singing like a canary. I was downright delusional.

This guy left my place, and about 10 minutes after he left I got a friendly knock at my door. I opened the door only to see 3 detectives and 2 heavily armed deputies; I think the mix was 3 machine guns and 2 pistols, all of them aimed right at my face. I was beyond shocked. I don't think I could even talk, let alone move. I had this feeling, all at once, a very strange feeling that I never had before. It was a feeling of absolutely knowing that whatever happened in my life before that moment and what ever happened after were two completely different things. Nothing as I knew it would ever be the same. It was a revelation that came on all at once, a flood. In that instant I was cured of trouble. That moment did more for me than 45 days of drug treatment, more than 5 months in jail, more than anything. It was very powerful. I knew that I was going to do anything to make sure THAT never, ever happened again....

My ordeal into being a junkie lasted from March 15, 2001 until February 1, 2008, just short of 7 years. It's coming up on the two year anniversary of me being arrested, and I haven't had any problems. I moved to Oshkosh determined to change my life, and I have!! I hold 3 jobs at this point, have never missed my rent or failed to keep my serious commitments. I am learning to heal. Things are still a struggle from time to time, but I'm doing very well. I have my plans all lined up now to go back to Europe. I have made amends with my family and old friends. Just last week I saw Matt D. for the first time in 2 years. I have the opportunity now to really be sorry, to make all the amends I have to make, as well as have a clean view and live the life of a man raised well by his family.

I've been waiting a long time to tell this story, and I feel that all of you deserve to know all this. I have no problem talking about it anymore. I am a changed man, a different man. My road out of all of this is still very long, but I suppose that I will walk it and live my dreams again.

Let this be a warning to all of you; keep your guard up. I take responsibility for the terrible things I did in those 7 years, but

I always remember that it all started with a trip to a local doctor, a single stroke of amazing bad luck, but these things will happen to us all to one degree or another, for our entire life. As bad as all these things were, I thank God for the lesson, and I feel smarter and stronger for all the trouble.

Thank you all who have stood by me, or have come back to me in the time since I've gotten out of jail. Even if you have forgiven me I still have a long way to go to forgive myself, a lot of guilt left to be dealt with. But, I'm finally dealing with it, thank God.

BACK OF NOTEBOOK DIVIDER PAGE

On the back of a divider page in his first notebook, Matt wrote out an explanation of symbols, numbering systems, and other devices.

Matt used a few different devices to track his drug use and quality of life. Some, like the numbering system, he used frequently. Others were small symbols he would begin to use and then abandon. He also made some entries in red or black ink during a period of his struggle to highlight sober days (black) and days when he used drugs (red). Colored entries are not depicted in this book.

Numbers in parenthesis (5.75) are daily ratings of how "Good" or "Bad" the day was. One is the worst — a terrible catastrophe, while 10 is an absolutely magnificent occasion. This is a quick key to identify patterns of mental health, happenings, etc.

⊛: Numbers circled off denote sleep* and what I rely on chemically to sleep. Three is the worst; zero is natural sleep.

⊛–opiates, benzodiazepines

⊖–alcohol and/or marijuana.

⊖–Elavil my anti-depressant

◎–natural sleep, all zero entries will include description of quality of sleep.

*previous night to day of entry.

July, 2009

Long overdue—July 13, Monday, 2009

Well, I feel that it's about time to start a journal. To this point I have played around with the idea, and I suppose in some ways I regret not starting one sooner. Better late than never. For the sake of my future self, I must be honest within these pages; failure to do so will render this endeavor useless—so here goes nothing.

I'm 24, and I feel pretty impotent for my youth. I'm just about half way through a 2-year probation term that has gone by quite easily to this point. I'm working at this Mexican restaurant in Oshkosh as a cook. I'm living independently on $600/month; for that I'm proud. I live as a boarder in a big old room with teal paint. I'm still using opiates, a fact that has impacted my current situation less than it should. I have been able (since July last year) to mitigate the negative effects it has had on my life—quite a surprising fact. My habit eats up my extra money, but my basic bills get paid. I need to kill this part of my personality off if I am to have any hope of reaching my higher goals.

I've recently met Ellen—a strange creature—but something draws me to her nonetheless. Perhaps it is just loneliness—and I think it is nothing more than that. It's been almost 3 years since I've seen Paulina, and I still think about her ... although I know there is no use in it. Anyways, my first impressions of Ellen are of a cold, selfish, scientist (I find myself feeling very uncomfortable thinking about her in this way). I question where our … acquaintance will go. Perhaps she will drop me; I have a feeling it may happen. Or, perhaps she will continue to use me. I allow her to use me now for the simple fact that I believe some of my own wants will be fulfilled along the way. What a terrible way to act. I feel I am destined to be more principled in my interactions with others. I still seek truth in love; it eludes me still, and I feel that it will for some time to come.

My goals today are centered on going back to Eastern Europe—Ukraine—to see Irina, and back to Poland as well. I've been lazy lately; I don't know why. I need to get moving. This is a short-term goal.

I worked for about 5 hours tonight, and it went well, busy, but I'm not dope sick. I had a 10 mg methadone that kept my head and body in line. Up to today, work is going well, better in fact than a few weeks ago when I felt I might have quit altogether. I haven't spoken to my mother in about a month, which sucks. Right now my best friends are Rose, Rob, and Lukasz. I don't have any "real" friends in Oshkosh proper.

Anyways, that's the start to this journal. I will try my best to keep up with the entries, knowing that in years to come I will thank myself.

July 14, Tuesday, 2009

Big day today. It started with my wonderful little runaround with the clinic and then pharmacy people about filling my Vicodin and Valium early. This shit would never happen up north! Hung out with April early this morning—she thinks she may be pregnant. Jenny called me today! The first time I've spoken to her in 7 hears! Wow, what a conversation. 7 years of history, 7 years of life I missed with a girl who impacted me so much in my youth. 2001—a huge year for me. I really grew up and into a life of darkness—not her fault, but she was along for the ride.

Made up with my dealer today. He's a nice guy, except for the fact that he's a junkie, and it makes him into a beast I'm familiar with. I like him personally; he helps me out a lot in ways other dealers would never do, but, of course, the nature of our business makes us all a little ill-behaved from time to time. I feel bad for him; I feel bad for all of us really, this path we've chosen. I need to get out before I become a felon, which will end my dreams forever.

> Intake: Today I've eaten a 10 mg Valium
> and 13 x 5s of Vicodin with some weed and
> 15mg speed mixed in for good measure.

In Matt's journals you will see he posted his intake. For some reason, he wanted to record this more than anything else.

I think maybe he may have needed to see his progression/ digression so he wouldn't forget. As for the names, most are changed to protect privacy. April will become an interesting character later on. Jenny was his high school first love—such a nice girl who has become a real lady and presence in this world. When I first met her, I was like, "Umm, Matt, she has lots of dark makeup. Is she a Goth or something?" However, I came to enjoy her responsible yet fun nature. The breakup with Jenny was sudden and final. Matt ached over it for years, as he was a true love, stick to it, never give up, sort of man. Matt tried to win her back, but to no avail.

— Matt's mom

July 16, Thursday, 2009

I missed my damn journal entry for last night! I was too fucked up after speedballing[2] a couple times through the day. I remember that work pissed me off because Rick was a dick all night. Let's see; I have to document intake here quick:

Intake Yesterday: 30 mg Adderall,

70 mg hydroco, 15 mg diazepam

2. Speedballing is the use of heroin or morphine and cocaine, which produces a different euphoric effect than either of the drugs alone; it is also extremely dangerous due to the cocaine's ability to mask the effects of the heroin and thereby lead the user to take more.

Today was interesting. Kelly called me out of the blue and woke me up, had me over and we got high. I got *really* high for some reason. Probably because I don't smoke much anymore. I came home and slept all the way until I went to work. Ellen was working in the kitchen tonight, and I really wanted to do something with her tonight, but she blew me off. I had to chase her to her car, and then it seemed that she didn't even want to talk to me—strange. Maybe now I get the hint. I feel embarrassed. I hold out hope that she will want to do something here in the future (soon) but am unsure. I think it won't happen, but who knows?

Talked with Craig G. tonight for several hours. He's gotten himself into quite a situation, marooned in OK State. Poor guy, smart, but at loss for romance.

Intake: 70 mg hydroco, 7.5 diazepam, smoked

I had little to no idea Matt was using drugs again. How naive. We spoke on the phone once a week or so, mostly about his job. Also, I trusted this extended family to watch over him. But, they knew and didn't tell me until the month before he died. They knew quite well in fact. I was the only one who didn't.

Looking back, the signs should have told me. He was always having trouble where he worked, and the stories all seemed the same: some jerk boss, coworkers complaining, money missing and not his fault....

I wish I could go back and do things differently. I should have called more often, visited more often, and asked to meet people he knew. I should have made close ties with those people. I should have been *more present.* That presence would not have been judgmental but ratherreflective and loving. Addiction seems to be full of lying and hiding. By being more present, friends and family have the opportunity to help the addict see reality more clearly through loving reflection.

— Matt's mom

July 17, Friday, 2009

Well, boring day. Went to work in a shit mood, ended in a better one. Still can't figure Ellen out; would like to get physical again with her real soon—beyond that, God only knows. People are strange. I'm lonely. As such I'm acting and thinking strange thoughts. I ate the last 10 Vicodin I had tonight, and for the next 2 weeks I have to hustle. I will be fighting the "sickness." Shit, I should be okay if a little bit bored. John is being nicer; his lady is around, and she has a good effect on him. I need another job, and I want a girlfriend like *crazy!* I think I may even hit on some of the younger girls around just for something to do. I really need to get back in touch with

Jesus, let Him guide my way. It's so hard now; I'm distracted only by my own sin. That's it for tonight. Hopefully, something more profound happens tomorrow.

Intake: 85 mg hydroco, 12.5 mg diazepam

John is Matt's landlord/roommate, who should not be confused with John at his work. Matt never really connected with him. John didn't really want a roommate but he needed the money. Matt's rented room was close to the train tracks in a big, old, odd house. The floor levels didn't match from room to room, and there were odd transitions from one room through a bedroom to another — and it had lots of strange colors on the walls. But the price was right for Matt, and he had been turned down for other apartments because he had a police record.

— Matt's mom.

July 18, Saturday, 2009

Boring day. Worked six hours today from 4 to 10 pm. Checked the schedule; it was like a slap in the face—45.5 hours total for the next 2 weeks. Unbelievable. My poverty deepens. Ellen wasn't at work as I thought she would be. Disappointed I couldn't do something w/her tonight. Hung out with Joey after work, smoked a bowl and split a Valium. Had a nice talk.

I'm feeling a tad bit dope sick tonight, but the real pain will start tomorrow I'm thinking. Hope I can score from Cindy, maybe, but I don't have high hopes.

That's it. Uneventful today.

Intake: smoked, 5 mg diazepam

Joey is Matt's dealer. 'Dope sick' is Matt's term for the withdrawal he experienced. From his later writings I believe they were very severe and actually made him vomit.

Cindy was the reason I sent him down to Oshkosh, actually. She was Christian, married, stable, and versed in addiction problems. She had even conquered an addiction herself and had been "clean for years."

About a month before Matt died, he told me something about the whole move-in/drop-off at her house that shocked me. Cindy had ties to family, was older, and was using prescription pain meds for a chronic condition. She and I talked on the phone about where Matt could move so he could work and pay back his fines. Matt and I talked and he didn't much like the idea, but free rent while he got on his feet sounded good.

Other places just weren't an option. He had lost his license and couldn't drive, so our hometown didn't work. It didn't work for the 5 months he lived with me after rehab. But Oshkosh had busses and businesses within walking distance, and it had this family tie who knew how to help addicts — or so I was told. She offered to take Matt in so she could watch over him and transition him into work. She understood that he had just come from being in jail because of addiction related issues. She assured me of her ability to get him back into society drug-free.

When I drove away, kisses and hugs given, Cindy immediately went to her meds, pulled them out, and gave some to Matt. "Here Matt, you want one? I know how it is. If you need something, you can always ask me."

Matt didn't tell me what had transpired until years later when we were driving out of Oshkosh. He wanted to tell me secrets, things I would otherwise not know in case something happened to him because he sensed his end was near. He didn't plan it; he just knew it. He didn't want anything left unsaid. He wanted me to know the truth.

To this day, I have never confronted Cindy about this. Her tears were real. She sincerely mourned his death. What good would it do? She knows. God knows. What's done is done. She needs to keep on living, and I trust God to handle this better than I can.

The question I would like answered is: "Why would *anyone* do this? Coming from an addictive past, did she want to connect, look cool, get his acceptance? Why would she do that?

Could Matt have been lying? I doubt it. It would have gained him nothing. He lied to me plenty, but he always lied with gain in mind. And his disclosure about Cindy was made at a point when he *wanted* to explain himself to me — without being asked. The last weeks of Matt's life were spent trying to amend things, trying to enjoy the sun, trying to find peace. He told me about his first day at Cindy's so I could understand just one more crazy, tragic coincidence in his life.

— Matt's mom

July 19, Sunday, 2009

Well, as expected I woke up dope sick as hell. Decided to make my way to Cindy's place in order to score just enough to get off this sick feeling. Her bottle of Percocet 10/325 was lying right out in the kitchen. I was shocked! I conned her into giving me 3, which would have done me just fine, but no, never enough for me to just make do—I had to get high. I ended up swiping an additional 8.5 tabs. The half one is what killed me because it was the "marker" in the bottle. Lenny went for one for his daughter, discovered that half missing, and then Cindy counted her whole bottle—I almost had a heart attack!! She didn't say anything on the ride home, but she has to know—I feel terrible, but more just nervous that I may have been caught. I gotta stop this madness; it's not worth it at all. I could kill my relationship with these wonderful people, which would be terrible for everyone, just for a few pills.

Talked some more with Chris G. I think he may move to Oshkosh and I could help him. Talked to Ellen too; hope she comes around real soon!

<u>Intake: 95 mg oxycodone, 1 mg Klonopin</u>

July 20, Monday, 2009

Went back to Cindy's today and helped her get her house ready for the realtor. As far as I could tell she didn't realize any issues with my heist yesterday; the bottle was left out in the open again. I was able to boost 3 more tabs, which I really didn't want to do, but it was too tempting to resist. I've really gotta stop with this shit; it's stupid and dangerous, risky in ways that I can't handle. My hopes and dreams die a little more each day when I do this. It's not a position I want myself in, but I return to it nonetheless—irresistible.

Talked to Bill Church today. Found out that Eugene Sr. passed away. He was old and ill. It was his time, but still death haunts me when it happens. I will not be able to attend his funeral on the 27th—for that I am quite sorry. I long to go back north for a visit. I miss my family now; being so lonely here gets to me. I spend time now only with my dealer, who is nice enough, but we will always have a "business" relationship, and I need more than that to be anywhere near happy. I hate the way things are now. The possibility of suicide creeps once again into my thoughts.

I think about all the plans for my life that I've ruined; I think about the failure that I have become. I understand there is still so much time for me to set everything straight, but I feel a lack of will and fortitude within to accomplish anything. Why not just give up? Go to sleep, put these dreams and demons to rest in the same grave. I don't think I have the courage to kill. My threshold for pain is too high, so I will continue to suffer, seeking purpose by accident only, bumping into the next reality. I would like to imagine that this suffering means something, but for the life of me, I cannot see past it and into my own future. I'm back into the hole of addiction. It consumes my every thought now. This is about 80% of all of my problems—God, help me. I will continue to suffer. Tomorrow I will score some morphine I think, shoot it up, get high. Thursday will be a hell of a day when I get paid. I will be buying more of that shit. Fuck.

`Intake: 30 mg oxycodone`

Poetry as it Hits the Page

By Matthew Edwards

Bury these things
Demons as well as dreams
Beneath a common stone

Lay to rest all that's wasted.
That which you neglect to bury
Burn instead

The smoke will rise
Reaching the nostrils of the Almighty
He will sense your sufferings
Sending rains that wash away what you couldn't burn nor bury

> I found this poem scratched on a piece of memo paper. It had none of the typical crossed out words or reworked sections. It is as he named it, something that just hit the page.
>
> — Matt's mom

July 21, Tuesday, 2009

Well, today was actually a really big, good day for me. So much happened! It started when I scored big on the morphine—my dealer came by and fronted me 90 mg! See? What a nice guy. I'll even be able to pay him back via Valium, so good for me. April came by next and got high. I got her a job working for the old dentist. She is thrilled and so am I that I could help her out; makes me feel great when I help other people.

Work was strange, too. I had to go in and take this stupid-ass, piddly test, which was all bullshit. We then proceeded to have a big "meeting" with all the kitchen staff in attendance. Nothing of importance was discussed, but you wouldn't know it from the tone of the whole thing. Mark, the 'boss' so to speak of the kitchen, was doing all he could to put off responsibility for the terrible way this place is run onto all of us. It didn't work. Everyone knows he is worthless. I got stuck there from 2 pm until I had to leave at 8:30. Roger FINALLY QUIT!! Thank God! What a worthless asshole he was. I am so happy I won't have to deal with him any longer, whatever happens. I hope to finally move to the top spot at this restaurant. I feel they don't think I'm capable, but I will prove it to them one way or another. I'm going to talk to them about taking on Roger's responsibilities as soon as I go in tomorrow. I'm worried they may turn me down for that incompetent Trish, worthless too!

On Facebook I saw Kortney Edwards say that Uncle John wants to send me a plane ticket to Cleveland sometime soon. That would be fucking awesome! I would be really happy to explore the family again, maybe scout Cleveland as a new place to live and work, who knows? I'm as free as the wind now, and looking for the next opportunity. I would really like to know my father's side of the family; always wanted to; this may be my chance!

Anyways, it's been a great day, mixed in ways, but cool nonetheless.

<u>Intake: 105 mg morphine IV</u>

July 22, Wednesday, 2009

Wow! What an awesome and amazing day in every way possible. It started with me waking up to the sight and sound of wonderful rain, which we haven't had, it seems, in weeks! April stopped by, ready for her interview with the old dentist. We shared a 15 mg shot of morphine and then found out that doc was sick today, so we decided to make our own fun. We went to April's house and scored some really good weed from her dad's bag. We drove around and got really high. It was so much fun, a really psychedelic experience—I loved every minute. I went shopping with her and then we hooked up with Joey and scored 90 mg. I shot her with 45 of it and she got a really good rush. She turned completely red, like she had a sunburn. I shot my 45 after she left and just sank into a semiconscious euphoria driven by the weed but softened by the incredible hit of morphine I had had.

The time went so quickly. Before I knew it I was at work, which was also awesome. I was treated so well by management. They re-did the schedule, and I got all of Rick's hours! He's fucking gone, and I'm *glad* that I never have to see his mean, ugly ass ever again at work. I feel so much happier at work just because he's gone now. I don't have to deal with his immature, hateful, lazy, lying, stupid personality anymore! I'm going to try and assume his role in the kitchen, move up that ladder in short fashion. I think it's possible, but I'm holding my breath because I can never quite tell what management is thinking or doing. I know I can run that kitchen a thousand times better than Rick ever could. I'm glad he's gone now.

I got home from work and scored another 60 mg. Got a really good rush, but now I'm into Joey for $100; that's way too much, but I'm sure I can deal it down with Valium[3]—I hope, anyways. I have all day off tomorrow. I think I may be able to chill with April again, maybe smoke a little more. Going to shoot some more morphine for sure, but I have to kick my habit down soon, for Rose, for myself.

Intake: smoked great weed, 120 mg morphine IV

Rose was a girl Matt had known since middle school. He was very close friends with her. They always did have a bit of romantic attraction but each seemed to always be involved with someone else when the other was single — strange, as

---

3. Matt had a prescription for Valium that was filled monthly. He'd sometimes trade these or use them as currency.

the two really made a great match. Out of everyone in Matt's life, Rose was his steadiest true friend. In the end, he moved to be closer to her. She made the last weeks of his life the best weeks of his life.

As for Matt's good-day journal posts like this one, they always remind me of Coleridge's "Kubla Khan" or Keats's "La Belle Dame Sans Merci" because the pleasure was just a trap — a trap he willingly entered. Multiplied pain and disillusionment always followed the exuberant pleasure.

— Matt's mom

July 23, Thursday, 2009

Today was a great day, a carbon copy of yesterday except I didn't have to work and got paid—$397 this week, of which $120 was spent on dope. I have to pay my note interest this week for $55, which is also considered an old drug debt, so all-told I've spent $175 on dope, almost half of my total income. And I wonder why I haven't been traveling? This needs to stop.

April got the dentist job today. She is so happy, and I am happy for her. We got really high, again, smoked a lot of good weed, and then shot 45 mg morphine apiece. I can see from reading this journal that my drug use is the centerpiece of my entire lifestyle. Needs to stop before this gets any worse. April really needs to stop because she has so much going for her. She will lose it all again; we'll see.

Average day. A few trips to the dealers, and a burn cruise—another day wasted. My intestines are plugged up really bad today too; it's going to suck going potty when I finally do. A sunny, beautiful summer day of my prime youth, spent getting high and blowing hard-earned cash. Need to stop wasting these wonderful days in my life.

<u>Intake: smoked twice, 105 mg morphine IV</u>

July 24, Friday, 2009

Hung out with April again today. Went on the stereotypical "pill hunt" early this afternoon, and couldn't score. April gets sick after only 20 hours or so; her habit is way bad. She's going to crash here, just like me, but can she handle it? Ended up scoring after work. That was nice, but for the first time in 2 years I have quite noticeable track marks on my right arm, which will certainly prevent me from selling any plasma for the next few weeks, or until I can quit shooting long enough for them to heal. FUCK.

Saw Ellen at work tonight. She was nice, but her typical weird coldness was in full effect. I highly doubt that anymore "sexy time" will occur with her, which kinda sucks. She is pretty hot, but she obviously isn't into me, and I see it.

This other girl, Nicole, has gotten my attention at work lately. She is young for me, only 18, but after checking her Facebook page thoroughly, I have discovered that she is quite wise past her years, and mature in her tastes and experiences. I get the feeling at work that she is attracted to me … and I am to her in the slightest way. I hesitate because she is so very young. My prediction is that we will spend time together this week. I could see a future with her; she's quite intelligent.

Intake: 75 mg morphine IV

July 25, Saturday, 2009

April stopped over yet again this morning, this time just so I could fix her up. I clipped 15 mg from her without her even knowing, so that worked out nicely. Went to work; it was one of the busiest days I've ever worked so far at The Flats. Things kinda broke down there for a while. They really have no clue as to what the fuck is going on there at all, it seems. It was a bad night also because April kinda got a little cold about helpin' me out with the whole drug business. I had to limp over to Joey's and beg for a 30mg with the last $8 I have to my name. Good thing it worked out and I staved off the sickness for a little longer, but, tomorrow I really have no options left except dope sick. I don't think I have any more avenues left to my disposal. I'm broke, and now I wonder if April is gonna come thru with some Suboxone help. Maybe it's better in the long run if she doesn't. I need to kick down—or off for that matter. It would be amazing freedom if I could just get off, get away from all this shit. This worry about being physically sick is just the worst. My tracks from the last week are starting to really show. I need off this shit, fast.

<u>Intake: 45 mg morphine IV</u>

So often, in passing conversations with those who are confronted with addicts, I hear their condemnation and monkey court verdicts. They don't realize how very much the addict wants to be free.

— Matt's mom

July 26, Sunday, 2009

Today was the first time I worked at the restaurant on a Sunday, and then being open only for this EAA bullshit,[4] that's going to seriously test my patience for the next week. Tonight sucked. Tabitha was doing non-essential work all evening and left me to the actual

4. Experimental Aircraft Association: http://www.eaa.org/en/airventure

main shit (just like always). They don't see what I do for them, not one bit. It's a shame. When, oh when, God, will I decide to throw myself back into school? The tipping point is coming soon enough where I will elevate or destroy myself forever.

I remember today as quite depressing. I awoke in a depressed mood and it stuck with me throughout the day, probably because I knew I wouldn't be getting high. I didn't get high today, didn't take a thing. I'm sipping some whiskey now, just because, but no opiates were to be found. This is good; I feel a sense of clarity off of that shit. But, I feel naked at the same time, deeply bored, useless. I need to work harder; really I do, if I'm going to get anywhere at all. I'm not feeling sick yet; tomorrow I will be I'm sure.

Intake: Ø, day one

So, what would you do as this man? How would you face each day? What happens when hope is gone? When the icy droplets of defeat freeze the will to continue, when the storm crusts the branches, when the spirit is ensconced in layers of memories what would you do? You may not feel that your daily existence depends on hope, but consider that hope is tied to faith/hope that your loved ones will answer the phone, that your car will start, that you don't have cancer, that you will eat today, that you will find love, that you will have kids and grandkids and family outings and campfire chats, and a life without daily pain and shame. Life without hope dries a person's soul.

— Matt's mom

July 27, Monday, 2009

Today I got to see Rose!! Wow, it was really awesome; I missed her a lot, but she was only able to hang around for like an hour before continuing to Madison with Levi, her ex-husband. Something very strange happened while she was here: she was pointing out to me just how desolate, ugly, and depressing Oshkosh really is—I guess I always saw it before, but after she mentioned it, well, it really got to me. I was depressed from that point forward. I feel now, I realize, just like I felt in jail, trapped in a cage without the ability to break out and into some other form of freedom—and it *is* this place, these people who do it to me.

When I got here I was so full of optimism, so much looking forward, but now I feel so empty, so sad, so trapped. I have just made the decision today that I will break out of here; I will move again to somewhere nicer, better for me. Rose has mentioned that Madison would be a good choice, and it has sparked my curiosity. One big problem is that I'm still on supervision, at least with a *very* cool agent. I'm hesitant to move anywhere that would place me under a new supervisor because no one could possibly be as cool as Laura. But I can hardly think I will be able to survive here until November, 2010 either. It's a bad position to be in, which is why I feel I need the drugs. It really takes my mind off everything around me, gives me a focus point (albeit, a negative one). What am I going to do? Confused now. Really just want to feel good.

I was just starting to feel really dope sick today, but we popped over to Aunt Cindy's and she wasn't home. With doors unlocked we went inside and I was able to score 3 tabs. Feel bad about it as always, very ashamed, but sometimes I feel as if I haven't a choice. I need to grow some balls and get off this shit; it's stupid. Also, it's now EAA[5], so the restaurant is nuts, which sucks ass! Only 4 more crazy shifts to go!

Intake: 30 mg oxyco oral

Rose was Matt's constant friend from middle school and his heartthrob. They dated in middle school for a bit until we moved. They wrote a bit, lost contact, and then bumped into each other after high school and remained close from then on. She is still, to this day, Matt's biggest fan.

— Matt's mom

5. The Experimental Aircraft Association members meet in Oshkosh every year.

July 28, Tuesday, 2009 rating 5/10

Today I awoke a little on the dope sick side, which actually kinda surprised me because of my dose yesterday; it should have kept me okay until at least the afternoon.

John, my roommate, has been an insufferable dick lately, so I decided it was best to head to Aunt Cindy's for the afternoon. I went mainly to use the phone, but of course the opportunity presented itself to grab a few tabs. So, I did, being quite careful to moderate, taking only 2. Just wanted to feel not so sick and perform well at work, which was accomplished. I used the phone and finally got ahold of mom; she was on some remote lake in Minnesota, right in the boat fishing when she called me back. We talked for a while, and I got her nailed down on me visiting sometime in August, which is just great by me!! I miss home—something to look forward to. I haven't been home in ages! —since March in fact, so it's just great!

Work went well. Jack was in the kitchen, and he made everything run nice and smooth. It was slow compared to what they expected. Good! I get paid the same regardless.

Saw April at work. She gave me a ride home. She swears up and down that she's been sick too, but she hasn't called me in the last few days, so I'm not so sure about all that. I got her on the hook with my pill day on Thursday, so let's see if she comes through for me tomorrow. I really hope so. I need to not be sick just this week.

It's nice in a way not to be so totally fucked up every day. I some-times wonder what I miss.

Hmmm … I think I will begin rating days on a scale of 1–10 (1 being the very, very worst and 10 being the very best) every day from now on in this journal right with the date heading. Today would rate as a very average 5, nothing really good nor bad happening—kinda boring and unimpressive anyways. So, now I'll be doing that. I can't believe I've written this journal now for 2 whole weeks!! It's really great; I love it!

<u>Intake: 20 mg oxyco oral</u>

P.S. I just realized that I was up north in June for my aunt's funeral.

July 29, Wednesday, 2009 (6.5/10)

Woke up dope sick again today without much prospect for anything happening. Though I'd have to wait until tomorrow for my vikes, but then I devised a plan. It took quite a bit, a hell of a lot of walk-ing, but it was a wonderful, sunny day outside, and I got to see a lot of the cool, old warplanes overhead on my walk. Morton's filled my vikes, cost me $30, which I had to advance from Cash in a Flash, but it was well worth it. I got to work just in time, but performed poorly. I don't really know why, but my stomach side hurt, which may be my liver telling me I've taken a bit too much Vicodin/Tylenol at once. Saw April at work for a bit. She tells me she's sick, but I can clearly see that she isn't because she calls if she is sick, and she hasn't called. I guess that means I'll be keeping all these vikes to myself this time!! She doesn't help me get shit anyways—a little weed once in a while, but beyond that nothing. If I can't rely on her to score, she is worthless to me as a partner, so she can fend for herself. I have Joey, who is all I really need. I feel alright now, not really too high, but just dandy anyways. I have tomorrow off. I'm going to try to score some smoke. Hope I can.

I heard that Roger called trying to get his job back today! What an idiot. Glad they won't listen to him. Asshole.

Man, I'm coming off as kind of an ass in this journal entry, but John has been pissing me off a lot. I'm seriously considering moving. This house sucks anyways, with the train and his animals and *him!!* Shit just gets on my nerves, you know? I keep it all inside, never standing up for myself. I've never had to before!! People have just never been so fucking mean-spirited, not back home they weren't. I hope I can avoid changing into one of them anyways.

Talked to Jenny on Facebook. Looks like the 12th of August we'll be hanging out. I'm looking forward to it!

`Intake: 80 mg hydroco oral`

Have you ever lived with someone who just didn't want you there, felt that a bad day on their part meant open irritation to you, or just nitpicked at everything you did? Well, Matt couldn't leave a single spoon in the sink, couldn't be downstairs when this roommate was home (unless he wanted a smarmy comment), was not allowed to keep his food in the kitchen, and was never asked to play cards, meet this guy's friends, or do anything social. When I met him he simply said "hi" and then walked to another room. Matt also said he had little temper tantrums and stormed around the place weekly. I felt sorry for Matt as this was his only refuge from the daily drama he was starring in.

— Matt's mom

July 30, Thursday, 2009 (7/10)

Today was a pretty boring day off, until I met Baldwin and had a truly cultural experience!

I was walking to Joey's trying to get a bag when I happened upon Baldwin, this black guy I had met a few times before, briefly. I saw him every time with a pipe in his hand, so I figured I could get a bag from him—which I did. I took an amazing ride with this guy, and I got to see life from his point of view. Everything was black! I got to see the whole black community in Oshkosh, which I never got to see before. I bought a dime and smoked up with this guy and just talked about shit, history, life, etc. It was very deep and moving. It's something I seek in life; it's something I love.

<u>Intake: 85 mg hydoco oral, smoked</u>

Matt had a very good "filter" for people. He would approach anyone he had a good feeling about without any hesitation. He looked at differences not as points of fear but more as points of curiosity. He wasn't one of those irritating people who say something to you in the grocery store, the kind who look you in the eyes and ask how to pick out a good cantaloupe; he wasn't creepy like that. In fact, he had the best sense for creeps himself; he called it his "creep meter." When someone was "giving off a vibe," Matt could nail it like a polar bear smells a seal miles away. He would notice their stance, gestures, eyes — *something* — and say, "What do you think? My creep meter is pegging right now." And he was usually right on. He had a good sense for people. Baldwin became one of his best friends. He had Matt over to his apartment, introduced him to his family, and spent many nights laughing and playing cribbage. Matt had finally found someone who was real.

Matt's mom

July 31, Friday, 2009 (6/10)

Woke up today with some weed still left. Smoked it and got pretty lazy. My agent made a surprise visit while I was still half stoned!!

I guess I had a decent visit because I didn't end up getting arrested or field any questions out of the ordinary.

Other than that, it was a pretty normal day. I'm writing this late, so it's kind of thin from my memories.

<u>Intake: 80 mg hydroco, smoked</u>

Why are people on probation for drug charges assigned an agent? Why do people on probation pay fines and probation costs? Aren't these agents supposed to provide a service for the money that's paid? I still haven't figured out what Matt or his community got out of paying every month to be on probation. I can't figure out what his probation officer did. She knew Matt was stoned. Matt called me after the visit and told me that the house reeked of pot and that he was obviously stoned. He had obvious tracks on his arm as he had had no time to prepare for the visit with a long-sleeve shirt. So, why didn't she do anything? Matt was stunned, happily, but still stunned. I was unaware at that time that he was using IV drugs but was surprised that she didn't bust him for pot. Oddly, this was the first time he told me he was smoking pot in Oshkosh. I didn't know if I should be relieved he wasn't put in jail or pissed that he was using pot. He was so jubilant that he "had the coolest P.O. in the world," that he just had to share this with mom.

I didn't think it was cool at all. I started asking questions about this supposed court ordered "watch-dog."

Some facts: Matt's probation officer was 22 years old — younger than he was. She was not experienced in criminal justice, not a former drug user, and was overwhelmed with paperwork. If she had written Matt up for using, she would have had to fill out *more* paper work. She was being paid by this man, who had just gotten out of jail a year earlier, to satisfy a court order. All she cared about was whether he got arrested again.

He did get arrested — twice. Once he was bitten by a dog and was taken into custody at the hospital because he hadn't paid one of his fines. His P.O. hadn't passed on the information about the late fine to Matt, even though he had seen her just that week. The fines that landed him back in jail were *3 months* overdue.

The second time, Matt was found unresponsive in a city park. He almost died in the ambulance, and was put in jail after being stabilized. His P.O. was on vacation for 5 days and could not be reached, so Matt just sat there. I finally got ahold of another county probation worker and explained that my son had an addiction problem and needed help. I explained that he had been placed in the county jail and was being held until his P.O. could be reached. "Could you please get my son out of jail and put him in a drug program?" This P.O. simply went to the jail and apologized to Matt for the delay while turning the key to his cell — She signed him out. I was not the only one to call and speak to her, either. Other family members called and pleaded with her to have him placed in rehab. When I spoke to her after the release she assured me that he was "just fine, and had only suffered heat stroke. The doctors said he didn't have a problem and his collapse was not due to drugs."

After his death I was able to get his hospital records, the ones with all the doctors' notes and recommendations. The doctors clearly stated that Matt had severe addictions and gave him medications so that he would not have adverse effects from withdrawal. The record did state that his collapse was not due to drugs as far as anyone could tell, and that it looked like heat stroke. The "heat stroke" was complicated by all the legal prescriptions he had for narcotics. As he had just filled a prescription for Vicodin, and many of his Vicodin were gone, the doctors were suspect of his use. Matt told me all of the above, and the doctors' notes supported him.

I wonder how many other people pay for probation and receive absolutely nothing.

— Matt's mom

AUGUST, 2009

August 1, Saturday, 2009 (5.5/10)

Today was the last day of EAA for me at work. Looking back, the week was kinda slow compared with what they told us would happen; it just was a lot slower than I would have anticipated.

Today I helped Aunt Cindy and her husband paint their house to get it ready for the market. They chose a banana yellow scheme for the outside, which I think is a little loud, but they like it, and that's what matters. I will go again tomorrow, I think.

Got Joey on the phone today; he sounded kinda pissed that I was chillin' with Baldwin the other day. Fuck him! Why should he be angry? Whatever. I'll probably chill with him again. In fact, I aim to score a bag from him tomorrow if at all possible.

Nothing else really happened today. I ate the last of this week's vikes. Have to hustle now until payday, or until next refill.

Intake: 55 mg hydroco, 30 mg oxyco oral

Waking up every day just to hustle to feel normal — so tiring for Matt. Addicts are not what they look like to the world; their lazy eyes and untucked shirts are from the stress of this crazy cycle. They get too tired to even care how they look like to others anymore. How could they care when they feel so very alone in their battle?

If you are an addict, know you are not alone. I care.

— Hugs, Matt's mom

August 2, Sunday, 2009 rating 6.5/10

Semi-eventful day today. Saw Baldwin on my walk up to Aunt Cindy's to help finish painting. Of course, we rolled and scored a dime bag of smoke, so I went to Cindy's place sorta high. Her step-son, Ned, was, I guess, dying to get high, so I let him smoke some of the very little that I had. He ended up bumming me smokes for the rest of the day! At one point Lenny pulled me aside and told me not to smoke with Eric, so I didn't after that.

The day was typically beautiful, warm, and sunny, with a hefty breeze that animated the surroundings. At one point I fixated on the sight of laundry just hung out, dancing lazily in the August sun. Today, I felt free for a few hours of my youth.

Intake: 20 mg oxyco, smoked

Matt offers a good reminder to us all to enjoy those wonderful moments. Thinking weddings, birthdays, and Christmas would stand out most, I focused my much energy on those events. However, these were never my favorite moments; they were filled with hectic to-do lists, other people's unruly children, smarmy comments, and exhaustive itineraries. Moments that hold the most wishes for a time-machine-trip would be moments like Matt had here: watching fresh laundry in the breeze.

When I heard the learn'd astronomer,
When the proofs, the figures, were ranged in columns before me,
When I was shown the charts and diagrams, to add, divide, and
measure them,
When I sitting heard the astronomer where he lectured with much
applause in the lecture-room,
How soon unaccountable I became tired and sick,
Till rising and gliding out I wander'd off by myself,
In the mystical moist night-air, and from time to time,
Look'd up in perfect silence at the stars.

— *Walt Witman*

Despite his constant quest to find more narcotics, Matt reminds us that beneath it all, he hadn't lost his ability to tune into and appreciate the simple things that make life beautiful and meaningful. The thread of hope that runs through this book — both for addicts and their loved ones — is that no matter what appearances suggest, no matter how difficult circumstances become, there's still someone home; there's always a candle burning — and if that's the case, there's always hope.

— Matt's mom

August 3, Monday, 2009 (6.75)

Went back to Cindy's today and assisted her with washing the ceilings. On my way over I stopped at Bill's, saw Baldwin again. This time he was talking about buying some rocks—sorta surprised me because I thought he had been a "non-crackhead" for a few years. The day was once again classic. Started with some severe thunderstorms early this morning, but wore on into a beautiful and breezy August day. I took a ride with Cindy to Walmart, talked on the phone with Bill and also with Dick for a while. From Cindy's I went to work, and I worked with Joel tonight. I love working with that guy, such a great human character. Work went well, a little busy for a Monday, but things are back in order after EAA. I can see on the schedule that my hours are secure for the next few weeks anyways; that I really like. I'm getting excited to see Jenny next week and my mother later on in the month. August is looking up from here; we'll see how well it goes.

Intake: 10 mg. methadone, 30 mg oxyco oral

How was Matt was able to get methadone and oxycodone? I know from the papers and cards from his apartment that he went to a methadone clinic, but I am curious about how that works. He never told me that he was on methadone, which began as part of a 1970s government program to help heroin addicts, but has evolved into a way to get a heroin substitute at a clinic for approximately $300 a month. I have seen others on it, with their eyes rolling, checking out for 30 seconds and then coming back, but, Matt never did that.

— Matt's mom

August 4, Tuesday, 2009 (3/10)

Today was going pretty well; I once again bumped into Baldwin (happens a lot lately) and smoked up with him this morning before heading to Cindy's place. I just sat at Cindy's, didn't get to work at all. Lenny's sister stopped by and Cindy said doc was pissed about me failing to show up with any cash. That really sucked to hear while stoned!

Anyways, I cleared out (I always do) before going into work. Trish was working (that miserable bitch) and it was very slow, so I was off to the side just doing prep work. After about three hours I was pulled to the side—into the office in fact—by Elta. For the next 30 minutes I was "quizzed" about my entire life! From the medications I take to the people I associate with. I had to vigorously defend my little pitiful 7.50$/ hour job because I didn't "look myself" today, and some phantom workers (it's fucking Trish, that whore) don't "feel comfortable" closing with me. I think I did a damn good job defending myself in the face of this bullshit. At one point I offered my agent's (Probation Officer's) card to Elta and told her that if she had any concerns to call her up and discuss them with her. She refused the card!! I even offered to take a urine analysis for her, anytime, anywhere. She refused that (for the moment, anyways) too.

I can't believe this happened. I never go to work fucked up, EVER, and today I didn't even feel especially sick, even though it's day 1 and I had bad diarrhea all day—maybe I was a little pale, but I know it didn't affect my workmanship in the least. A lot of this I'm convinced has to do with Trish and her incredible bullshit. Fuck her. Now I have to dream up an intelligent way to twist the screws on her miserable ass.

What a bad day, but strangely, I don't feel it because I'm convinced I did a great job defending myself. I'm still really worried because I suppose I really am a "hardcore" user. But, I know that nothing I've actually done has indicated to anyone that this is the case. I'm careful, but I suppose this is a warning that I should be even more so. FUCK!

<u>Intake: ∅, day one—smoked</u>

I remember talking to Matthew about this issue — about how beneath him restaurant work was. I tried so hard to convince him that he could be a journalist; he could travel the world taking pictures and reporting back. So unafraid he was of foreign lands and strange cultures, and he loved politics. We talked about achieving dreams, getting away from small people, and living our potential. He chided me for not traveling more, as we had done when he was a kid; he lived with me in Italy, Mexico, Guatemala, and the Rockies. However, he hated all the moving and hated the food even more. All he ever wanted to do was come home.

— Matt's mom

August 5, Wednesday, 2009 (7/10)

I awoke this morning to a phone call from Joey telling me that there were easy 40s[6] around, with the right cash that is. I knew I was SOL in this instance because I won't have cash till tomorrow. I tried talking credit, but it was useless. Too bad.

I then walked over to Aunt Kelly's; haven't seen her in a few weeks. We smoked of course, and I told her that sick little saga

6. 40-mg pills

about work—she ended up letting me take 3 Darvocet, which was the only way I was even able to function today, thank goodness.

I retreated home, stoned and just feeling generally ugly, bad about everything. I got a call to come to work early for my evaluation, which frankly after yesterday I was dreading. To my utter surprise it went quite well!!!! I scored 2nd best on that written test, AND discovered that management had seen through Trish's little fucking game—I NOW HAVE CONTROL OF THE KITCHEN!!! I was told by Mark that I would be getting a lot more hours as well as a small raise to $8/hr. I can hardly believe I'm happy with that. I used to make 9 just for cashiering. Anyways, I was just so thrilled that Trish finally got put in her place. I was victorious and they saw through the BS and into the fact that I work harder for them than anyone else in that place, and now I have full-time hours to show for it. Little steps, little steps.

I didn't feel the best physically today, but the good news from work really made me forget my body, forget about the AS (abstinence syndrome). The Darvocet really helped the different systems in my body. I'm surprised they don't use this for treatment, no euphoric feeling, just ease. I didn't take enough to solve all my problems physically, but I got by today.

```
Intake: 300 mg propoxyphene oral, smoked
```

August 6, Thursday, 2009 (7/10)

Stayed up late and slept only a few hours in anticipation of my check and those easy 40s. Started the day washing ceilings at Cindy's place, met up with Kelly, who wanted me to help babysit Chad in Darboy for several hours. Lucky for me, Kelly gave me rides to get my check and then out to see Joey at his work so I could score said 40. I brought my whole kit bag with me, and the minute I got to Shelly's place I was in the bathroom shooting up. Felt so good, so familiar—wiped my sick away, but because I had smoked with Kelly on the way over I didn't enjoy my oxy high as much as I should have.

We were at Shelly's for way too long. I was getting tense at the end, wanted to go. I had Kelly drop me at Joey's when we got back into Osh, scored another 40 and went home, stoned. I shot that too and proceeded to have a VERY intoxicated conversation with Rose. It was tough; I was having a hard time keeping track of what I was saying. After that Jenny called and we concreted our plans for Wednesday.

I'm so excited about that, very excited. I wonder what it will be like to see this girl after 7 long years!! Wow, 7 years, unbelievable. If it wasn't for Facebook I would never have seen her again.

My day off from work was pretty good all around; smoked a lot and got high in style, exactly what I've been living for too many years. I really need to stop. This shit is so fucking expensive.

One more interesting thing: On our ride over I asked Kelly for a sip of her water, but she is so afraid of germs that she gave me the whole bottle. She then proceeded to tell me a story about some friend of hers taking a drink of someone else's water and then dying 3 days later from meningitis. I remember thinking that I would be happy to not only drink her water, but also to squirt it into my veins—which I did. Kelly thinks she is empowered, smart, independent, but she isn't; she lets corporate America scare her into isolation, believes everything she hears, and acts accordingly, like a sheep. God, how terrible to be afraid of fucking germs!!

Intake: 80 mg oxyco, IV, smoked all day

Kelly has always been so afraid of disease. She is quite an engaging individual, though she and Matt had a condone/condemn sort of relationship. Kelly was a regular user; in fact, I can't think of a time I saw her when she wasn't stoned on pot. But, she wouldn't eat bananas, stayed away from wheat, and took her fish oil daily.

The need to control things outside the addiction is a common theme with addicts — like Kelly with her germs. I wonder if all of us to some degree, and addicts to a higher degree, don't try to over-control those things in our lives that are metaphors for things that are out of control.

— Matt's mom

August 7, Friday, 2009 (6/10)

So today, with money in my pocket, I scored 2 more 40s, bringing my drug bill for this check to a whopping $160 total. That's out of a $408 check. In order to do it I had to clip 20 from my rent, roll over my little Payday loan, which I really just needed to pay off, and only allocate $24 to food for 2 weeks. I'm deeply troubled over my expenditures. I'm getting into a deeper hole with each passing month, and it's ALL over drugs; without drugs I would have enough money for everything I want, my license, car, food, anything—but because I'm into opiates I can't handle money at all, and it really sucks. I'm surprised I can ever pay my rent these days, let alone buy food at all.

Work went well, the whole kitchen worked in unison all night and things rolled smoothly. The whole "I wonder if Matt is a Junkie" thing has passed over, thankfully.

There was also a terrific lightning storm outside tonight, just beautiful, intense. It struck close to the house several times with a loud report that shook the bones, just great!

Intake: 80 mg. oxyco IV, 80 mg. Concerta oral

August 8, Saturday, 2009 (4.5/10)

Today was a fairly boring and average day. I went to *Cash in a Flash* and rolled both of my loans, all because I needed the extra money for dope. Kelly gave me a ride. We then went to the park, walked out to the point with Chad, smoked some MJ (just me anyways), and then I walked Nevada street home, a long ways in 85° heat!!

Work was alright; it went smoothly. April gave me a ride home and tried feeding me some shit about not being hooked up very well—bullshit; it's all part of the junkie's game. She's been just fine, probably better than me! Her loss when the Valiums come in.

Elly's car was broken into in the restaurant's parking lot—passenger window smashed, purse stolen—just like what happened to Ana about a month ago. I guess they have a serial burglar on their hands; kinda scary because this happened during daylight hours!!

Trish switched shifts with me, and now my plans with Jenny are a lock for Wednesday, great!

Intake: Ø day one, smoked

August 9, Sunday 2009 (7/10)

Today was a really wonderful day off—urgh! My nice pen won't work! [blue ink went to black here] It started with me walking to

Kelly's this morning, smoked and got lightly buzzed. From there I went to Joey's house to check the situation. Unfortunately for my self-control, I skimmed 40 more dollars from my rent and my only $20 from food just so I could get high. My drug bill this week stands at $220!! Now I will be paying $220 for rent next week, plus be way back in my loan payments. My next check is gone almost—out of about $400, $280 is gone just to rent and rolling my loan, plus it's morphine time,[7] so next week I can forget about food again. This is so sad. I'm thinking of taking a "drug vacation" in order to get that damn loan paid. Then maybe I can get out of this hole a little more, feel better about my situation for sure. September is the time. While I still have Vicodin coming in and hours, I should do it. In fact, after I get done with my journal tonight, I'm going to look at the calendar and formulate a master plan!

Anyways, I was hanging with Kelly and Chad [her grandson] was over. I feel bad for that kid. He's spoiled fucking rotten by Kelly, and it seems to me (just perception, I could be wrong) that Sharon [Kelly's daughter] lets him do whatever the fuck he wants to. His father seems to be quite the asshole, and Chad rebels against him probably because the two women (knowingly or unknowingly) fill his head with shit about this guy. I saw Chad tell his father: "You're not my daddy anymore," over which his dad got pretty pissed,

---

7. This may have been morphine off the street or Matt may have had a prescription for it.

slowly chased him down, and probably gave him a swat and a few choice words. I can see why Chad doesn't like him—watching this guy (Cody is his name?) play with Chad, I could see he was totally detached, just no desire whatsoever to spend 'my' time with this little brat, which he is. But, at the same time no one wants to change this kid for the better. Kelly lives vicariously through him and justifies the damage she does to him by saying, "I spend hardly any time with him. So what if he's spoiled a bit with me? That's what I have the right to do."

That's what my gramma said too, and although I love my grandmother with undying intensity, I do believe that perhaps the way she treated me had something to do with me becoming a drug user later in life. I had no discipline with her, and I expected quick rewards and gratification, just like I do now. I can see the same thing happening with Chad, just no firm direction, a really broken-up and convoluted family situation with people shipping him here and there when it's one grown-ups "turn" to "fulfill" whatever responsibility they have to this accidental human being.

Such is life in America these days. No one really cares about people in the way they should. They don't take pains to raise them to be balanced and principled adults. My mother tried so hard, and I think she succeeded with me on several levels, but it is my own fault that I throw it away on a daily basis with the drugs. I think Chad will inevitably become a drug addict, probably fail at academia, and then go looking for a factory job when he turns 18, by which time none will exist.

Kelly's whole family is really twisted. Sharon is fairly okay because she was raised by Cindy. I guess Kelly didn't raise any of her own children. She seems to avoid any real responsibility by living off of several (3) different men. Her life consists of jetting off to this place and that, Iowa, Madison, Rhinelander, Oshkosh, to make birthdays, parties, whatever. She doesn't work at all, but in each place she visits she has a male benefactor who puts up with her. Here in Oshkosh is Dave, a really nice guy, factory worker all his life—Kelly hardly sees him. When she is around they don't even sleep in the same room, but for some reason he pays all of her bills, buys her gas, MJ, pricey organic food, and all he gets? Well, she criticizes him and his lifestyle all the time, talks down about him in general, but his money and his home keep her there. She drives a nice newer car that Derick all but completely purchased for her. Derick is her "boyfriend" in Madison. She really never sees him— he is such a complete asshole, full of himself, millionaire—pretty worthless. I can't imagine any real woman putting up with him, but Kelly can—for the money of course. She also has a boyfriend all the way in Iowa, where she spends a majority of her time. I've never met this one, but it seems like maybe this is the guy she is truly romantic with, and I hear he is violent and crazy. Wow, great for her!

I'm writing a lot about Kelly, mostly because her personality and what she does makes me a little sick. The very worst part is that Kelly is one of the most self-righteous and hypocritical people I know. She is terribly judgmental, and has gotten quite fierce and heavy-handed with me on several occasions, which just pisses me right off. She hasn't for a while, so everything I am writing today is true feelings, not motivated by anything emotional, just simply observation and logic. I hang with Kell because she can be fun in a superficial type way, she always gets me high (one of my main motivations for even putting up with her at all), and I suppose in this way I am using her. Now I am the hypocrite! Not really, but a little. I strive to be better connected to her, but her mind is so twisted, her convictions and her opinions are so incredibly ignorant, a product I think of a simpler mind, and a deeply damaged persona.

As I mentioned in last Thursday's entry, she lives her life in fear of just about anything that kills, especially bacteria. She also eats organic food and takes tons of supplements completely out of fear. The decision-making part of her personality is quite easily swayed by 300-word newspaper articles and Michael Moore "documentaries" (he he, yeah right). She takes everything at face value, never ever bothering to fully investigate anything or even to think deeply for any span of time. These things bother me, but not enough to actually dislike her—I like all types of people; ignorance will not exclude anyone from my circle. I just don't like being judged by her because it's so insane coming from her. She should feel bad for bringing that damn Shawna into our lives. We found out later that Kell was having a lesbian relationship with her, but that whole situation just shows how incredibly clouded Kelly's mind is, how foolish and weak she is. I wonder how much longer we will have that contact? I really wonder if at some point her house of cards will tumble down. She has many good qualities—she is kind and giving, pretty also, especially for a woman of 50 years old, but in my mind she will not change, unless she finds Jesus, she is way too old to change at this point.

John [Matt's roommate] also got back from his trip. Went to Wisconsin Dells for four days to celebrate his 32nd birthday with his girlfriend. She ended up breaking up with him. He insists that he did nothing wrong, but then again he never sees when he does something wrong. He is always correct in his mind. In fact, a lot of the difficulties I have with him arise from him trying to apply his "correctness" to me, or situations I may be (even distantly) related to. He is a pretty selfish guy naturally. He sees none of his flaws, but he's been living by himself for several years with no real way to gain feedback on any of his actions. I certainly don't; not my place. I try my best to be friends with him, but his natural self-centeredness always sabotages any type of friendship we may have developed.

Not that his girlfriend is any better. I didn't know her too well, but she definitely exhibited a unique "fat girl" type of personality—loud and opinionated. She was nice to me, cordial anyways, but I didn't care for her. They had a pretty healthy physical relationship, which I was audio-witness to on many a late night! Gross!

Anyways, John is all broken up, says he's going to mope for "years" alone. He pouts like a damn child who hasn't gotten its way; this too is really sickening to me. I can feel now that he may be passively taking out his frustrations on me for the next few weeks. The way things look now, I am starting to think more about moving out, leaving this damn guy to his lonely, self-centered self.

God, deep down I just feel really badly for all the people I've written about tonight. If I were the praying type I suppose I would pray for them; maybe I will tonight. Pray that God lifts their afflictions from them, heals them, and brings them to the gates of heaven. I hope I can turn things around and one day be with those I love in Heaven above, deep inside it's what I really want—to be good in Jesus' eyes, to be whole and strive for the right things in this short life we all live.

Well, that's it! My longest entry yet! I really love this journal.

<u>Intake: 120 mg morphine IV, smoked</u>

As the journals progress, Matt does write some longer entries, but this entry really shows his progression from just trying to keep a record of his mood and drug use to his hope for everyone, including himself, to get better. He wanted to see things clearly enough to make a difference and stop making the same mistakes. This entry ties into his previous comments about hypocrisy. It's natural to point out your own flaws in others, yet Matt still had light inside and love for even those he despised. Was he forgiving because he also wanted to receive compassion and understanding? Was he looking at them the same way they looked at him, with judgment? Did he end his judgment the way he hoped the world would end judgment, with compassion? Reading this entry for the first time, I realized how none of us have a safe place to voice our honest feelings and hopes. What is inside each one of us needs a voice simply so we can see the forest blocked by the trees. You will see many trees blocking Matt's forest as you continue reading.

— Matt's Mom

August 10, Monday, 2009 (6.5/10)

Peaceful and beautiful day outside today. Got the vikes filled, now I only have 2 fills left. Thought I would've had 5, but they caught the mistake. I rode to Morton's Pharm with Baldwin, gave up 10 tabs just because I'm a nice guy! He didn't believe they were actually vikes, but I'm sure he does now! Spent the balance of the day before work just moping around, getting high, but only lightly. I can never get real messed up on those vikes. Traded 10 for a morphine, which helped a little.

Work was alright. Karl is a little asshole, but whatever, he'll self-destruct I'm sure, I hope anyways. Lisa was manager and she sucks, so that's how that goes.

Tomorrow I'll hang with Jenny! So excited about that! I so wonder how that will go.

I struck up a conversation with Becca on FB last night. It was interesting. We decided to hang out sometime soon. I feel slightly romantically inclined towards her; it would be wonderful to maybe get some action with her! Not to mention a real relationship.

Intake: 30 mg morphine IV, 10 mg hydroco oral

August 11, Tuesday, 2009 (6.5/10)

Today was pretty boring for the most part. I continued burning through my Vikes, got a pretty good hit early in the day from them, just wanted to kill time before I finally saw Jenny!

I've been avoiding John lately; he's just been more of an ass, for no reason. He's just getting meaner and meaner. Whatever, I just hope I can deal with it until I'm off paper[8] and out of this horrible

8. Being "on paper" means being tracked by law enforcement.

town. But, probably I will have to move because it seems to just get on my nerves lately.

Work went well and quickly. Trish didn't piss me off too much!!!

My whole next entry will be about Jenny!

Intake: 95 mg hydroco oral

August 12, Wednesday, 2009 (9.2/10)

Today was one of the best days I've had in years!! Jenny came from Green Bay to pick me up after work. Wow, how amazing it was to see this girl after seven years, to the month in fact!! The last I saw Jenny was Aug. 3, 2002. The first sight of her, wow, she looks spectacular! A little thin, but not unhealthy at all, glowing she was, absolutely beautiful and stunning just like she was before. She was so bubbly and happy too, it was so amazing to see her face, I never thought that I would again.

She took me to Green Bay and we immediately smoked some very good weed when we got to her place. We just talked and talked, about everything from people we knew, to places we had gone, to everything we'd done in 7 long years. IT FELT SO GOOD to talk with this soul, this beautiful human spirit. She showed me pictures. I showed her mine.

I can see that she is so happy now, so much in love with this Noah, a really nice guy.

I was just continually struck by this young lady's happiness, and also that she had worked so hard and had finally attained success! She told me (quite proud, great for her!) that she has $20,000 in the bank that she never touches. She may even buy a home! We ate breakfast with Becca. She was a little on the quiet side, but it was fun nonetheless. I was feeling great all day seeing these two ghosts from my past, and seeing that they were both doing so incredibly well.

I smoked with Jen all day. We drove to see some nature preserve, a waterfall which was dry, and Green Bay looked magnificent! The day was so perfect! It was spectacular.

I feel sad now after she dropped me off. I feel bad that here I am, doing so poorly while my comrades are so happy. I'm not jealous or envious. I just wish I was up there with them, happy also. I hope to keep up with Jenny now. I really hope I can!

Intake: 65 mg hydroco oral, smoked all day

August 13, Thursday, 2009 (5/10)

Today was a stereotypical day in almost every way possible, a day I would certainly forget about if it weren't for my trusty journal! I spent the day sitting at Aunt Cindy's with a big knot in one muscle in my back, didn't do much there, tried calling mom to no avail. Haven't spoken to her in several days, which sucks. Went to work at 4; it went well. I felt melancholic all day today. I figure it's just dealing with the flood of good memories from hanging w/ Jenny all day yesterday. I really miss home now. I'm really hating my existence in Oshkosh. Wish I had some friends or something to do. Poor, poor, pitiful me.

Today marks the one month anniversary of starting this journal. It seems that I made every day except one—pretty good. I'm happy about it. I love my journal now, and I make it a priority to write it every day before I go to sleep.

On the following page I will tabulate my drug intake for the month.

Drug Intake Record

Intake: 20 mg oxyco oral, 400 mg propox oral

Drug intake: July 13—Aug 13

oxyco oral: 275 mg _____ free

oxyco IV: 160 mg _____ $160.00

morphine IV: 600 mg _____ $300.00

hydroco oral: 850 mg _____ $65.00

Valium: 50 mg _____ $5.00

```
propox: 1000 mg _____free
# of days I smoked: 11 _____$20.00 (? maybe)
# of "sober" days in month: 3
methadone and Klonopin are negligible _____$10.00
```

So, here I can see my intake for the first time on a monthly basis. I have extrapolated the costs from memory and current prices for the stuff where I get it. For instance, I'm going to remember the $160 I spent on 40s because it stung. Now, I don't think that it's possible that I spent $560, but I believe it reasonable to assume that out-of-pocket for me was about $500 this month, out of around $850 total income—so, what I don't pay in rent goes into my blood-stream. That's so sad. The oral oxies are all from Cindy, 27 of them, quite a bit.

I NEED TO CUT THIS OUT!!

The voice in an addict's head is like a very small megaphone repeating lies: *Just this once* (once as in 10 years at a time?), *I deserve it as I have been good for so long* (so, being good means that you deserve to be miserable again?), *I will quit tomorrow* (didn't you say that yesterday?), *life without drugs is boring* (true, making all those connections is very entertaining), *I can't have fun without drugs* (true, handcuffs, getting AIDS, always broke, almost dying in deep nods, and all those quality friends... how does the tune go? memories...May be beautiful and yet, What's too painful to remember, We simply choose to forget), *no one will know* (the coroner will tell them), and everyone's favorite — *I would be miserable for days trying to get off them* (how many days of misery equals how many days of being in control of your life?)

I am rooting for everyone out there who can still read these words in hopes that you will gain some strength, knowledge, and hope for yourself and others.

— Matt's mom

August 14, Friday, 2009 (4/10)

What a day to be dope sick! A sunny August Friday with a full 7 hours of work! It was not a pleasant day for me today. I spent most of my morning chasing down my Valium, and the $15 I needed for them. Any normal day would be great to have Valiums because they are coveted by the junkies around me, traded easily for things I like better, but not today. Today my dealer was out. His old lady was crying, she was so fucking sick. His next-door neighbor was out also, but I turned him on in hopes of scoring a 10 methadone tomorrow morn. We'll see.

Work was shit. I took an 80 mg Concerta that I had lying around in hopes that it would push me through my shift. I haven't decided whether or not it helped any. I felt it, but I still felt pretty sick, strange too. I'm starting to hate work.

Anyways, tomorrow is another day. I have these Vals to help me sleep tonight, and tomorrow I have a few prospects. Damn, I just need to quit.

<u>Intake: Ø day one, 20 mg diazepam</u>

Matt's entries were prefaced in his first entry; he wanted to start a journal to record his life. However, I see another reason — his drug intake, spending habits, mood, and decisions. The decision he wrote here is not a sudden realization after years of drug use/abuse. He went to a rehabilitation center after spending time in a county jail for drug use. However, these decisions are written down, recorded for memory and reinforcement. His journals may have been an attempt to see the whole picture, a photo-documentary that gives perspective to his memory by including concrete doses and moods along with the cost and result of spending. His journals also served as his "trusty friend," that individual who listened without judgment, that individual whom Matt could not find in society.

— Matt's mom

August 15, Saturday, 2009 (5/10)

Today was average, as many of my days are. I ended up trading some Valiums for a few methadones. Thank God, got me straight for work. Now I'm out of Valium, but I have credit with my dealer for Tuesday next.

Stopped at Cindy's, had a great Biblical conversation with Lenny [Cindy's husband]. It was quite intense, very nice, we really connected for once in a great while. I really like Lenny, such a nice and good person he is. He just emanates it wherever he goes.

Work went so-so today. I look forward to that Concerta! I had to take 5 Valiums all told just to get through the night. What a terrible experience.

Talked with Rob on the phone for a bit; that was nice. Wow, he really has changed for the better—no drugs, no alcohol, doing quite well, bought a car. I'm happy for him. I hope to see him really soon!!!

Intake: 20 mg methadone, 45 mg diazepam oral

August 16, Sunday, 2009 (3/10)

Today started off really good and ended up in a real bad way. I got straight around noon when Joey hooked me with two Methadone tabs. That was nice. I sneaked in with Bill and ended up grabbing another one from him. What a nice guy.

I made the miss-step of telling Cindy that I had taken the metha-done Methadone to keep from getting physically sick on my day off. At first it was just myself and Cindy, and we had a good conversa-tion. Things were going pretty well, until Lenny got home and then, predictably, Cindy changed her tone and rhetoric. She became very heavy-handed, VERY judgmental. It really pissed me off, really badly. She is a total and complete hypocrite, as well as Kelly. They talk behind my back constantly, and well, I'm fucking through with it. I'm totally done with the hypocritical bullshit. Things are going to change here, right away. I won't stop hanging with them, but they will not walk on me anymore. No fucking way.

`Intake: 50 mg methadone oral`

I felt quite perplexed about these women's dealings, drugs and comments. Cindy was a devout Christian, and she confirmed to me that she would be happy to help Matt stay clean; she had been a cocaine addict years before, an alcoholic during the previous several years, and claimed to have beaten them both. She was the one for the job. I had faith in her ability, so reading this entry and comments Matt made to me the next summer really floored me.

I also had bi-weekly talks with her about Matt. The talks we had were mostly about how lazy Matt was, and how angry she was at Matt. She complained that he just hung around and didn't help her much; she wanted more help cleaning the house. She was also angry that he didn't seem to be making any headway on finances.

What kept her from telling me that Matt was taking Methadone? Why would she hold that back from me, knowing that he had been in treatment, was a risk to re-addict, and was my only son?

I did have my own problems at that point. I was married that year to one of Cindy's and Kelly's relatives. We had met at church 2 years before the marriage and had a very typical courting period — we didn't live together and just dated. He had been a terrible alcoholic, just miserable. However, he hadn't had a drink for over 7 years. A month after our marriage, he started going to lunch and having beer. Not being a big drinker myself, I could tell right away. Well, things went on from there. By August, 2009, he had dissolved — a complete puddle.

I tried to tell his relatives this, but, I guess I was the problem.

According to her I had to put the hammer down and control him. How can anyone be put in charge of another person? Not only was I not willing to try to control someone else, I knew that it was not possible and ultimately not healthy. Was this what she was doing with Matt?

This isn't about me, but why would these two women berate Matt, yet support his addiction? The one person who would have run down there and offered some help — me — was not even notified. Why would she tell me to control my husband and not even bother to tell me that my son needed controlling?

Not that I could have controlled Matt. He was happy to tell someone about his problem but angered when given 'the talk.' It is fruitless to condemn an addict for using. Nagging won't help.

How might this journal entry have gone differently?

Matt comes to Cindy's, and talks about being in withdrawal and getting methadone.

Cindy is understanding.

Good so far. No controlling; just two individuals communicating about personal issues.

Then she asks what he wants, asks how she and others can help, and offers to be there for him. They hug and promise to talk again the next day.

It's not so far-fetched, certainly not as much as the reality of what did happen.

Autonomy is important to an addict. This feeling of no control could be part of why they have turned to substance abuse. Taking that autonomy away will produce the same scenario you see in Matt's journal entry for this day — anger, retreat, walls.

These two women had an opportunity to talk candidly to Matt, to offer alternatives, to ask his permission to tell mom who might even be willing to help find the needed drugs if she understands the pain. That would have been such a welcome response.

I learned this lesson too late for Matt. I gave him "the talk" too many times. I believe he didn't tell me these things until the end due to a fear of losing control.

Matt had the following poem tattooed on his body.

INVICTUS

Out of the night that covers me,
Black as the pit from pole to pole,
I thank whatever gods may be
For my unconquerable soul.

In the fell clutch of circumstance
I have not winced nor cried aloud.
Under the bludgeonings of chance
My head is bloody, but unbowed

Beyond this place of wrath and tears
Looms but the Horror of the shade,
And yet the menace of the years
Finds, and shall find, me unafraid.

It matters not how strait the gate,
How charged with punishments the scroll.
I am the master of my fate:
I am the captain of my soul.

— William Ernest Henley, 1849–1903

August 17, Monday, 2009 (5/10)

Spent today helping Bob (the old junkie antique collector with Lyme's disease) clean out his bedroom. Wow, was that place ever a pit. I felt so bad for him because he lives in such squalor. Being a sick, old junkie will do that to you, on top of being a packrat.

I spent a lot of the day feeling angry about yesterday and the way Cindy got hypocritical with me regarding the whole drug issue. I must admit that I am quite the junkie, but they never see it, despite pretending to once in a while. I do nothing to indicate this, and even if I did she would still have no basis to preach to me about anything! She's addicted to Percocet like crazy, and she won't be off MJ for very much longer either, despite what Lenny feels like doing with church, God, etc. That shit just won't last long at all.

Work went well enough. I finally got on the same level as Ken. He really surprised me by being really mature tonight. I hope it lasts.

```
Intake: 5 mg methadone oral
```

August 18, Tuesday, 2009 (5.5/10)

Got some Chantix from Bill this morning and brought it to Cindy; she was delighted, I think. I kinda buried the hatchet with her, for now. I hope she sees that she is wrong, but it doesn't matter. I'm just going to leave things where they lie and hope she won't explode on me again!

Today is mom's birthday! I tried calling to wish her well, tell her just how much I love and miss her, but she was busy with so many guests and we couldn't talk long or candidly. Too bad. Maybe tomorrow I will catch her not busy.

Went to the food pantry for the first time in my life today. Got 26 pounds of different and wonderful stuff. Thanks to mom's suggestion! God helped me out today; thank You God for providing for me today, and thank You for the wonderful and kind-hearted people who make it happen.

Found out also that my morphine connection is gone. In its place is now methadone, which scares me because it's a much more powerful beast, harder to get off. On the plus side I won't have needle marks showing much anymore, and methadone lasts longer, too. We'll see how this turns out.

Hung out with April today, too.

Intake: 60 mg. morphine IV, 5 mg. methadone oral

August 19, Wednesday, 2009 (5.5/10)

Today was fairly boring and average. I had 5 methadone this morning, took 3 and just chilled until I went to work. Walked to Joey's and picked up some loose tobacco; that was interesting. Sat and talked with Kris and Bob for about an hour. I always find junkie culture interesting, more so than regular people's culture; the culture of money was never interesting to me. The culture of poverty is, however, deep and real.

Work was interesting—Mark, the boss of me in the kitchen, started my day by bitching about piddly shit (as always). He always ends his spiel by threatening my job. I took care of this by talking to Elta after work, something I rarely do. I even mustered up some tears to drive the point home! It worked quite well and I think I have Elta on my side now; my job is more secure after today!

Found out also that the 2 best workers in the kitchen are gay! Aretha and Jeff, both homosexuals!! I knew Jeff was, but I wasn't quite sure about Aretha. Now I know! I'm strangely okay with it; they are superb workers!

<u>Intake: 50 mg. methadone oral</u>

August 20, Thursday, 2009 (7/10)

Had the day off today. Had one goal, which was to just get absolutely ripped high. I did, in high style. I once again spent all my extra cash on dope, which wasn't much this week because last payday

I trimmed so many of my other bills. They were unavoidable this time around. I went broke really quickly this week. I've got Becca coming down, and now I need to sell my Vicodin just to have some cash to spend with her. I really hope I can!

Spent a lot of good time with April today. She was pill hunting with me while also cashing our pay checks. We bumped into one of her friends and got a bowl of really good weed. I got so stoned! Haven't been that stoned in a long time! Just riding around in the Riviera, no care in the world. I haven't even thought about probation lately. I probably should give Laura a call. I've been having some nightmares lately, about losing my room, about going to jail for five days, all kinds of stuff—I think the methadone is giving me these bad nightmares!

<u>Intake: 45 mg methadone oral, smoked</u>

<u>Paycheck: $390.00</u>

Before Matt died he told me of dreams he'd had. He told me of dreams he'd had while in jail; he spoke in these dreams to deceased loved ones. They spoke of what would happen to him, and these things happened as the dreams foretold. He did spend 5 days in jail, and then died several weeks later.

— Matt's mom

August 21, Friday 2009 (5.5/10)

Today was normal again, neither bad nor good. It was cold outside for August, a definite sign fall is on its way. I recently realized that my roommate John is severely depressed and that's why I think he is a super dickhead about everything. Just now his dog, Hunter, scratched on my door wanting into my room! That NEVER happens, even his damn dog, which he's owned for about a decade, doesn't want to be around him—the dog was actually happy when I got home today. This REALLY surprised me. The dog can feel his energy, and it's negative! I wonder if John will snap out of this or what will happen.

Work is going a lot better. I'm starting to get respect from the rest of the staff, as well as respect from above for my hard work. The only one who has yet to fall into line is Trish—Mark told me he spoke to her yesterday and told her that I was the boss now. We'll see what she does next.

I have yet to get the Percocet Cindy owes me. That'll be a trip! She's more of a hypocrite by the day!

Intake: 45 mg methadone oral

August 22, Saturday 2009 (3/10)

Wow, really bad day today. Since the beginning of summer my roommate/landlord John has just become more of an ass, more of a control freak, more of a hypocrite each day—it's to the point where I've just been outright avoiding this guy whenever possible. I've spent a lot of alone time in my room lately. Anyways, I've come to the point where I'm tired of being treated like shit for no reason by this guy. I get treated like I'm his guest instead of a paying resident of this house. He walks all over me, and I have just been letting it happen because I hate any confrontation, but everyone has their limits! Today I was accused of using his shaving cream, which I didn't, and I finally stood up for myself, just let him have the full brunt of my defense, and it caught him off-guard, and he got really pissed and told me I should find another place to live, at which point I retreated a little (I shouldn't have; I should've been ready). We proceeded to get into quite the argument/discussion about how things go around here. At some point I brought up the fact that this guy smokes in his room after outlawing smoking in the house, AND telling me that I couldn't even smoke in MY room. Now that caught him off guard, and he realized that he had been exposed as not only a hypocrite, but also as a bold-faced liar! He knew it too. He felt bad at being caught, not that he did it, just being caught. He is such an idiot, though. I saw the ashtray through the open door in his room. He tried accusing me again: "How did you know I was smoking in my room unless you were in there?"

I told him, but I should have said "Idiot" at the end. He's always accusing me of stupid shit. After realizing what the loss of $320 would mean to his bottom line he backed off ever so slightly, but the damage has been fucking done! I'm out of this fucker as soon as I can find a new situation! In fact, I would ideally like to find a place sometime in the next 8 days, move all of my stuff out secretly, and then come September 1 tell him to come up with a refund of my damn $320!!!

I have to do something. I won't be here past Oct 1 unless he comes up with a pretty damn slick apology and a commitment to treat me with some respect. Realistically though I should probably just get out despite what he may or may not do. He's always been a real negative asshole type guy. I'm tired of having to tip-toe around this place avoiding his horrible negative energy—it's tiring. I really have met few people as foolish, lazy, hypocritical, and mean-spirited as this guy is. He is just a real waste of a human being, a nobody who treats everyone around him with absolute contempt. I think I'm out of here!

```
Intake: 50 mg methadone oral
```

August 23, Sunday 2009 (7/10)

Today was a good day. Becca came down from Green Bay to spend a few hours here. That was a lot of fun. We talked a lot, but didn't really connect on a romantic level as I would've hoped. She is a beautiful girl, and I was hoping I might have been able to make some love with her. But, I didn't press anything—and nothing happened. I feel awkward anyways around women when it comes to initiating sex, always have. They usually have to press on me first, and those ones are usually the crazy whores anyways. Whatever. It'll happen for me some day!!

The other big story of the day is that I'm actively searching for a new room, and I like what I see as far as Craig's List goes—it looks like wherever I go that I will be saving money, and I think that if John isn't a dick about giving me September rent back that by this time next week, I may be penning this from a new location with a room-mate I may actually like!! John is just outrageous in his horrible-ness—selfish, hateful, and obtuse, a liar, and a hypocrite. I've tried so hard to be a good friend to him, but it just hasn't been any use. He is determined to be alone and hateful. I guess he just decides that he wants to continue to live this lonely existence, taking out his insecurities on me or anyone else around him, but no longer on me! I have had nothing but bad people experiences since I've been in Oshkosh; it seems that people are bent on being unhappy and unfriendly in this place. I can hardly stand it any longer!! I need not only to move out of this house but out of this town!

I've been hitting that damn methadone pretty hard lately. Fucked up my entire tolerance! Tonight I'm trying a cocktail of metha-done, Percocet, and Vicodin just to see if it works to overcome the methadone tolerance I already have. I would like methadone if it was the only thing I had access to, but if I try to get off on anything else then it's all fucked; that's why I don't like it. Plus, it's hard to come off of. I hear the AS (Abstinence Syndrome) is more severe with methadone. I guess I'll find out.

Intake: 25 mg hydroco, 60 mg oxyco,

<u>20 mg methadone oral</u>

If data suggested that drug therapy helped drug addicts, I would not hold a negative opinion of Methadone clinics, but I feel these programs are just a form government-sponsored addiction that rarely helps. Methadone is usually distributed by a government program designed to help addicts get free, but Matt and others believed it is very difficult to kick, more so than the addiction it was designed to replace. Methadone supposedly reduces withdrawal symptoms without causing the high associated with the opioids, but what percentage of addicts ever get free? Why does Matt use it along with opioids?

— Matt's mom

August 24, Monday 2009, (4/10)

Sad, lonely and depressed today. I don't quite know why. Perhaps it's my rooming situation coupled with the first hint that the seasons are changing. I hate the end of summer, not so much the begin-ning of fall, but just the end of the wonderful warmth and the wonderful warm sun on my face—just the knowledge that winter is fast approaching. I do hate winter, with a passion. I miss my mother, I miss the homestead, I NEED to get home for a visit, but I'm not sure if I can afford it with all of these damn bills I'm juggling—if I had a car, a license, it would be different, but I hold myself back with the drug trouble I'm in. I need to at least get it under-control financially, kill this loan at the Pay-Day loan place, just buy what I can each payday and just be done with it—get that down, my license back, and a car, and I would be set then. I need to do this quickly if I'm ever to make it out of this damn hole I'm in.

John has been a lot nicer lately, almost sensing that I have plans to move and leave him alone and in want of the funds I'll take with me. Maybe he's realized that he would have quite a problem in finding another roomie as poor as myself who's willing to deal with the shape of this house, the train noise, and his personality in general. I plan to line another place up, and then have a serious talk with him about my position in this household. Tell him I'm set and ready to get out. And, then see what he says, put the ball in his court so to speak.

Work was slow tonight. I'm getting tired of working there for what I make, so hard, head cook now, and I eat from the food pantry—such a damn shame. I have to look for better work, find it, and then have a bargaining chip with them, too!

I need to snap out of this lazy depression and get proactive about my life here pretty quick.

`Intake: 85 mg hydroco oral`

August 25, Tuesday 2009 (4.5/10)

Awoke today from a horrible nightmare, just terrible. I dreamed that I was in a house in Eagle River with my mother and my cousin Brian. My mother was yelling at me about my habit; she was trying to take my kit bag full of needles away from me, which I fought vigorously. I grabbed my kit bag and ran across a beautiful field to my grandmother's old house on Townline Road. I ran down to the lake and tried to hide my kit bag in the old boathouse there. My mother and Brian appeared, as if they had run after me, and attempted to take the kit bag. I don't know why this was so horrible, but it really was—put me in a depressed mood all morning long. I hated it.

Other things happened today, but nothing of consequence. This is all I care to write tonight.

`Intake: 30 mg hydroco, 130 mg oxyco oral`

Driving Matt out of Oshkosh and to his dream-achieved Madison apartment, I first heard of this dream. He told the dream in much more detail at that point. We both talked in-depth about dreams we had experienced, but this one was still upsetting to him a year later. Dreams, well certain ones, do speak to us, most certainly. This dream was haunting to him. Yes, it may have been induced by his earlier night's thoughts on home and the addiction he was battling. If one looks at the symbolism, the struggle, and the fear, one might better understand the mind of addiction.

I believe Matt's addiction was a response to his ability to completely feel the ills of life. I wonder if other addicts also feel this sense of fear and loss of control by the dark river, deep water, powerful current that carries us along. Are those who feel this in true reality actually more blessed?

Consider that in his dream, Matt's fear, his cousin who took him hunting/fishing/dirt-biking, and myself, who encouraged and coerced him to reconsider his path, were the two enemies he was hiding from. The two who threatened his addiction were the ones who chased him through the beautiful field.

— Matt's mom

August 26, Wednesday 2009 (4.75/10)

Today marks the end of my work week, kinda. I have the day off tomorrow, and then it's back to work for the weekend. I think I may have just enough narcotics to get one last good buzz tomorrow. That methadone really did fuck my tolerance up! After tomorrow I'll be dope sick, and I think that this will be "the big one" because I have no money, my prospects being dry anyways, and Cindy has started to guard her bottle a lot better. It's always zipped up or locked away now. So, that avenue is gone. I may just be sick for a whole week, or I could try to finally conquer this damn thing, do something with this life.

I looked at a new apartment today with this gay guy Kyle as a roomie. He seems nice, albeit VERY gay! I hope I get it, but I doubt that I will. They're checking C-cap (online criminal history) for this one, as always in this situation: I'm Fucked!

I've been keeping up with Paulina since December. She's doing well, and it makes me so sad that I can't be with her. That is the one thing I really regret in my life so far—messing that up with her. She was great for me, and I believe that if I had been straight when I went to visit her that I would still be with her today. If I was straight in general that is, kept straight anyways. She was writing to me tonight that she is about to embark on a month-long trip through Europe with her new love, spending most of her time writing about a desperate longing feeling ... I see everyone around me doing so well, going places, doing things I long to do, and then I see myself; it just drives me deeper into my hole of depression. Why won't I snap out of this? Am I really bound to my father's blood, my father's ways? I always thought I could be better than him, but so far it isn't shaping up. I've almost given up. I'm ALMOST suicidal. Things are just terrible lately.

`Intake: 60 mg hydroco, 20 mg oxyco oral`

*I'm way up, both in my per-day and length of use. I'm going to be getting really sick after tomorrow; I just know it, dread it.

Matt's biological father died at age 45 of alcoholism — well the report said 'heart attack' — but he was in a motel room alone, kicked out by his wife. He visited the emergency room regularly for various alcohol related system failures.

He did write Matt letters though — beautiful letters, full of imagery, voice, symbolism, and hope.

Matt didn't know his father very well; he only saw the man a handful of times in his life. I remember putting Matt on the plane to go meet him as an older child. He barely remembered him from his toddler meeting. The whole family welcomed Matt and stayed in touch ever after, even though he was only

12 at the time. An outgoing child, Matt stayed in touch with the whole clan, a very nice one at that.

One interesting aspect of this visit with his father concerned the addiction at its core; this man actually gave his son a cigarette "just so he could try one." Matt told me this years later when he was trying to understand why his dad would do that.

My deductions:

- Addicts want others to also be addicted for comfort; birds of a feather flock together.
- Addicts want others to feel comfortable. Drugs are enormously comforting to an addict in withdrawal. Comfort is why an obese mother buys ice cream for her obese children.
- Addicts cannot relate to anyone who has not also experienced the addictive substance, and in an effort to relate, Matt's dad was asking his son to be more like him.

After that, Matt did start smoking cigarettes — slowly, but the door had been opened. I wonder how much of a role nature plays in addiction. Matt certainly did not experience the nurture side of it.

— Matt's mom

$$\text{August 27, Thursday 2009 (3.5/10)}$$

Had the day off today, but it was still horrible. I felt terribly depressed all day long. Felt like crying most of the day also. I thought I had enough narcs to get off real good, but it didn't satisfy all day for some reason. I felt something strange, a twinge of AS[9] creeping in. It shouldn't start until tomorrow or Saturday. I think it's all in my head really; this depression is playing tricks on my damn mind.

Talked with Mom today. I'll be going home September 13th! Hope I can get clean by then, or stable on something, but prefer clean. It's going to be super hard. I start tomorrow, and I figure at the rate I've been going through the summer it will take me about 7 or 10 days to get completely off. That's 7 to 10 days of being just god-awful sick. I started taking the amitriptyline[10] today, for withdrawal as well as depression. Hope tomorrow is better.

Intake: 100 mg oxyco, 10 mg hydroco,

400 mg propoxyphene oral

Matt wanted to "get clean" but the result was "God-awful sick." Drug withdrawal is described as feeling like an incredible case of the flu along with an emotional breakdown. People

9. Abstinence Syndrome, a medical term for withdrawal.

10. Amitriptyline belongs to a group of medicines called tricyclic antidepressants. It alters the levels of chemicals in your brain to relieve the symptoms of depression.

experiencing withdrawal can have serious physical problems that require medical attention; people have died during withdrawal due to the body's reaction. Not only physical, withdrawal presents a daunting emotional change. Without a steady support system (friends, circumstances, counselors) the self-control necessary is so enormous that most people cannot resist the urge to escape the dual pain. Matt had none of the needed components, only hope.

— Matt's mom

August 28, Friday 2009 (4/10)

Today was another depressing, horrible day. I sat at Cindy's until 2:30 just feeling all … crying, and sad, and downright lethargic. Barely made it through work. April (luckily) spit me 2 of the Vikes I gave her the other day, which just took the edge off, made work just bearable. I don't quite have full AS, but tomorrow I should, and I have to work! Damn! April also smoked a bowl with me in the parking lot at work that helped a little. I really hope the amitriptyline is going to help. I'd like to kick WAY down, and get clean for a few days.

Intake: 10 mg hydroco oral, smoked (day.5)

August 29, Saturday 2009 (5/10)

Detox is going quite well; I'm really surprised that I'm not hurting more. Let's see; here is how I'm beating it today—100 mg amitriptyline and a Centrum vitamin at bedtime. I'm making sure to eat well all the time, and today I was able to score some Darvocet; boy does that ever help with the physical symptoms, but it surely doesn't ever get you high. I was also able to smoke with Kelly, and that helped with some thanks, too.

Today was a cold, dreary, shitty, and rainy day outside—felt like Fall. Tonight is the first night that I am sleeping with my windows closed, probably since May. Work was work; nothing spectacular happened. The amitriptyline is helping the depression I think, so I wasn't nearly as down today as the past few days. I'm looking forward to the week ahead now a little more.

Intake: Detox, day 2, 300 mg propox, smoked

August 30, 2009 Sunday (4.75/10)

I'm writing this half-drunk, decided to have a few Kessler's, just to feel a little better. Still horribly depressed. Really hope the amitriptyline kicks in sometime soon.

Hung out with Dave and Kelly today. Smoked a little. Helped Dave set up a tent; it was sunny out, but still a little bit on the cool side. I talked with Rob tonight; he has lost his job because of some bullshit. I felt so bad for him and his family that I ended up getting depressed myself.

Chatted with Rose and Kimmy on Facebook. They tried lifting my spirits, but I still feel down.

I'm on day 3 of my detox. I ate some more Darvocet today, so I hope I'll not hit bottom so hard.

I wish I could just be happy.

`Intake: DETOX, day 3, 200 mg propx oral, smoked`

August 31, Monday 2009 (5.75 /10)

I HAD NO OPIATES TODAY WHAT-SO-EVER!! I feel fine, a little lethargic, but nothing major, barely noticeable. I'm really surprised that I've made it [through] 4 whole days now of DETOX and I haven't gone nuts, or suffered all that much. It's been quite an easy detox. I think the vitamins and amiltrip have a big role in that. I hope that I continue to feel well, and I don't get surprised with detox later on.

Hung out with April for a good portion of the afternoon. We did a burn-cruise,[11] and after that we hung out at the dentist's office, a real nice way to spend the afternoon before work.

The depression seems to be lifting, for the moment anyways. Somebody cares enough to pray for me, I guess. I hope for continued sunny days!

Good bye summer 2009, another one wasted...

<u>Intake: Ø, Detox day 4, smoked</u>

11. Driving around and getting high

SEPTEMBER, 2009

SEPTEMBER 1, TUESDAY 2009 (4.5/10)

Today I had no drugs whatsoever!! I'm actually quite proud of myself for making it 5 whole days now—the amil finally kicked in, and my depression has all but vanished. I'm doing well.

Tonight was terrible at work. I just couldn't seem to please Elta with anything I did; she gave me the evil eye several times. Really sucked. I felt like I was going to get fired all night! I sure hope I can continue getting good hours after tonight.

The only bad part of the day was work. Everything else went fine. I'm feeling much better now. I know I'll be getting high on Thursday and for a few days after that, but I have made a commitment not to purchase drugs, unless prescribed to me. That should solve a lot of my problems I think.

<u>Intake: ø, detox day 4, smoked</u>

I am convinced that those who really honestly want to change cannot go on diets. Diets restrict the bad while never actually removing the need to be fed somewhat regularly.

— Matt's mom

September 2, Wednesday 2009 (5/10)

Today was a day full of walking. Man, I must have walked 4 miles or more today. First, down to the pharm to try to get my prescriptions filled, which didn't even work, so I ended up having another sober day—my sixth straight, which was nice to notice.

Work went well; it was slow. I was really glad for that because I didn't have a full crew. Work in general has been deteriorating though. I find that the owner is actually quit stingy, if not outright greedy. And my work is constantly scrutinized, so still no raise. I suppose I should find another job. Today I think I will fill out a few apps on my long walkabout, again.

Depression is gone, I'm happy to report. Amitriptyline really works well. Not only that but my cravings for opiates have gone down quite a bit, still there, but really diminished.

<u>Intake: Ø, day 6</u>

September 3, Thursday 2009 (7/10)

Great day today! I walked all over hell to get errands done. Went to Biolife[12] finally, got set up for a physical. Got paid, got my Vikes,

12. Biolife is a company/organization that buys blood. People who have passed the physical can sell their blood a couple times a month https://www.biolifeplasma.com/us/#/current-donor/compensation

and I GOT A NEW PLACE TO LIVE! I am really happy. I will be living with Pete, the prep cook from work. Damn, he is one cool dude, totally on my level, one of "my" people. I hung out with him today and we totally clicked! I am super-happy about this situation; it's going to be just great!

Intake: 65 mg hydoco oral, smoked, paid $397.00

September 4, Friday 2009 (6.5/10)

Interesting day today—April called and propositioned me to take a burn cruise. I agreed as long as she could get here and we could smoke before 1 pm (I always allot at least 3 hours to "air out" before work). Ended up that she didn't even get here until 1:15 or so. We didn't start smoking until 1:15, AND on our way from April's parents' house we were "caught" by April's boyfriend, Craig. She must have argued with him for 30 minutes! I thought I would be late for sure, but I made it to work just on time and still a tad bit stoned. Work went really quickly for some reason, which is great. Went well in general, too. Trish is working on Fridays now, but it doesn't bother me all too much anymore.

I feel a new energy lately, since I started the anti-depressant. I feel like a new phase in life is starting for me. I'm really happy, and for the first time in a long time I feel optimistic about the future.

I'm even starting to think about the Ukraine again. I would love to see that country and also see Irina again, maybe make some new friends, maybe fall in love again. It's my next big plan, to go there; has been now for a couple years. But, with all the problems I've had with drugs, I guess I was just never serious enough about it. I feel this beginning to change, slowly. I need to keep up with being mostly sober. This is the key, keeping my money. I haven't talked to my dealer in over 10 days, and I don't really miss him all that much. I'm happy that he's not getting my money anymore. Since I got paid I have spent my money on only good things: bought good food, bought some music for the first time in a long time, and on Tuesday I'm going to be paying off one chunk of my loan with Cash in a Flash, FINALLY! I'm going to be working hard to keep things going in the right direction.

<u>Intake: 105 mg hydoroco oral, smoked</u>

"Being mostly sober?" I am unsure if Matt's strategy was formed in consultation with his many physicians or not. However, someone with large and ongoing prescriptions for Vicodin (the registered name for hydrocodone) cannot really, ever be "sober." Typical, yet higher doses are 10 mg every 4 to 6 hours not to exceed 6 doses. Matt's intake shows more than 10 doses here. Yet, he feels optimistic because he is not using street drugs — cutting out at least 1 dealer.

— Matt's mom

SEPTEMBER 5, SATURDAY, 2009 (5/10)

Intake: 40 mg hydroco oral

SEPTEMBER 6, SUNDAY, 2009 (5/10)

An uneventful day today. John was in a good mood, finally got over the break-up, I think. First time he's been genuinely nice in a few months. I lounged around all day, eating Vikes and napping on and off—relaxing, nothing more substantial than that.

Intake: 65 mg hydroco oral[13]

SEPTEMBER 7, MONDAY, LABOR DAY, 2009 (4/10)

Failure today. I broke my promise to myself and called my dealer. Paid a high price for two 30s of morphine, and then bought a 40 of OC[14] later. I'm really disgusted with myself. That's $70 down the damn toilet, and a needle in my arm, again. Can't do it, just need to cut my ties with Joey; he will absolutely sabotage me and these efforts to improve and fix my life. I got really high, but what does

---

13. Vicodine© is hydrocodone, which explains the apparent discrepancy between the journal text and the intake.

14. Oxycodone (I assume)

that mean anymore? Nothing. It's all a waste!!!! The worst part is that tomorrow I feel like I'm going to be buying more, wasting my lead in the cash department. I took a break from my Amitriptyline and that has something to do with it. Tomorrow morning I'm off to Biolife. Hopefully, my shooting today doesn't sabotage that. Nope; change in plans. I've put too many holes in my arms to attempt Biolife. I'm just deeply disappointed in myself today—tomorrow I make my stand.

Intake: 50 mg hydroco oral,

60 mg morphine IV, 120 mg oxyco IV

The poison flow-chart of addiction is cyclical. I still blame myself for not knowing and reacting just as Matt was blaming himself for being weak. I had no idea he was struggling like this, and he had no way to tell me without feeling even more like a failure and maybe losing his autonomy. Unfortunately, all players in the cycle (parents, loved ones, professionals, friends, neighbors, and onlookers) cannot remove the one constant mathematical function that continues the reaction cycle — guilt + denial = failure. I could go into detail about how guilty I feel over my parenting style and my reaction/

non-reaction to Matt's addiction issues, but, how would my personal guilt not end with some type of denial, simply for my own survival? How could Matt's guilt not possibly end in some type of denial? We all wander through life and make mistakes, but we all naturally try to forget them, too. The problem with the addiction cycle is that the addict has daily reminders of their own failures.

We must all find reasons to continue our personal, great battles. Constantly examining the scene of each crime we experience will not allow us to continue to fight. This paradox is reality. Is my denial really just my way of surviving this paradox? I believe not. Short of putting Matt on full-time surveillance, storming his apartment, tying him up, and jetting him to Siberia, I was powerless to help. This is the reality for those caught in the cycle of addiction.

— Matt's mom

September 8, Tuesday, 2009

Today I betrayed myself yet again. I rushed off and bought yet another 40—a complete repeat of last month: 165 dollars down the fucking tube yet again. Something is different though. This time I have a genuine feeling of disgust, of failure and shame. This time I wasn't physically addicted; it was only my mind this time. I completely betrayed myself. Sick. I feel sick, and sad, and down. The OC didn't make me feel any better this time, it was terrible feeling. I got so angry at myself that I broke every one of my needles, threw them all away—the one bright spot in the day.

I've just realized, right this second, that the junkie thing just isn't working anymore, not at all. I am a ruined individual—I have no real friends, I don't have a real job despite being moderately intelligent, I haven't been to Ukraine or back in school, I feel like shit all of the time just trying to live with myself. *THIS STOPS NOW. THIS ENDS BEFORE MY REAL LIFE BEGINS.*

`Intake: (40 mg oxyco IV FUCK!)`

This is where the addiction equation needs different variables.

Removing Guilt + Removing Denial = Success

In order to remove the Guilt value, society would need to replace it with something. In order to remove the Denial value, the individual would need to experience a realization. However, the justice system, law enforcement, medical professionals, and society in general miss opportunities by inserting Guilt/Shame/Judgment into the formula. Is the other value free treatment programming?

Our society spends staggering amounts to stop drunk driving, eliminate tobacco, practice fire-drills, train police to protect us from active shooters, and build safe houses for domestic violence victims, yet we bar poor people from accessing high-quality drug treatment and put them in jail instead, make them pay probation, and give them a criminal record to ensure no one will hire them. With more people dying from drug overdoses each year, why would we consider them less important than victims of domestic violence? Can these victims divorce drugs the way a beaten spouse can divorce an abusive husband? Are they not both trapped? Can a family not call the fire department when their home is ablaze without proving that they did not act irresponsibly in allowing the fire to start? Don't ambulances arrive to save someone attempting suicide? Why make addicts feel guilty for needing emergency help, and then ask them to fill out a financial statement to see if they are wealthy enough to receive the service? Are those like Matt really so hard to love that we do not value their lives enough to offer them treatment?

— Matt's mom

September 9, Wednesday, 2009 (5/10)

Another day; another dollar. I'm broke now, after my wonderful little drug run of the last few days. Feel shitty about that still. Whatever; it's over now, and I have been shown quite severely what my mind will make me do to myself from time to time. Can't happen again.

Otherwise the day was average. I slept like 12 hours; drink + antidepressants will do that to a person. I started the amitriptyline again; depression was creeping in again today. I know this time at least the medication will help with that. I have enough to last the next 2 weeks at least. After that I'll be getting some more; just hope I can do a good long run without any narcs—get back on track.

I'll be home in 4 days' time. Can't wait.

<u>Intake: Ø thank God, day 1</u>

September 10, Thursday, 2009 (5/10)

<u>Intake: Ø day 2</u>

This was one year before the day I buried Matt. Odd that he did not enter anything except his intake.

— Matt's mom

September 11, Friday, 2009 (7/10)

Today started off kind of sour. I could really feel the depression start to come back, but once I got to work, everything was a lot better. I GOT A RAISE, I think to $8.50, which would be just great. Work was quite busy, one of the busier nights I've worked.

After work I went and spent time with my new roommates; we smoked and had a few drinks. It was really a lot of fun. We took a walk through the student neighborhoods. Wow! Friday night; there was madness in every direction. A lot of parties going on, for sure— never really experienced that scene before. It was really nice. I am really optimistic about this new situation.

Intake: Ø day 3, smoked

Matt was a low-life in many people's eyes, yet he never experienced college party culture. What a dichotomy — Matt, the drug addict who never experienced the party lifestyle that upwardly mobile America knew well. Matt could write a well-developed paragraph full of voice and depth while much of upwardly mobile America can't write a paragraph without copying it from the Internet. How can we continue to judge others with such broad descriptors as 'addict' while our culture believes going to college should include mass-drunkenness as an initiation rite for becoming fully American?

I had an encounter with someone who was going on about how parents don't do this and that … and the kids become drug addicts. Maybe instead of sending out all those flyers on social reform we should just send out mirrors. Maybe people would see themselves more clearly when they head for the medicine/ liquor/food cabinet while complaining about their $22/hour job. Judgment is so easy when we don't take the time to know the individuals and don't take a good look at ourselves, our blessings, and our own desire not to be judged.

— Matt's mom

September 12, Saturday, 2009 (5/10)

Intake: Ø day 4, Diazepam 30 mg[15]

September 13, Sunday, 2009 (7/10)

Today was a great day indeed!! My ride home ended up being with Kelly. I smoked with her and it just opened my eyes up to how

15. Diazepam is Valium. Quite possibly Matt was given this to treat anxiety; it is also given to treat drug withdrawal, oddly. It lessens the muscle spasms from coming off of opiates. Matt didn't think of Valium as part of his addiction because he didn't like it. He sold it to get what he craved: opiates. Hence intake is zero despite the fact that he took 4 Diazepam 30mg pills.

beautiful everything around me was. We listened to Morphine[16] and had a really pleasant ride. On August 9, I wrote a pretty scathing judgment about Kelly and her grandson and his father. I take a lot of that back now. I misjudged the situation totally. I didn't appreciate just how complex our relationships with each other can be.

It's great to see my mother and Dick again. I'm convinced he is having a battle with alcohol. This makes me really sad, to see my mother, the stone-willed, rock-solid woman I remember, having to deal with this guy. She always told me to marry well; she didn't and is so shattered by that fact. I still and always will love her, regardless of her losing a hold on this life at some point. I still respect and love her. It's just great to be home, an awesome feeling.

Intake: Ø day 5, diazepam 20 mg

I married this man I met at church. However, he ended up being a fake. I was devastated. Never being really took hard in my life, I got took. He was a non-drinker for the 2 years I knew him and for the months we dated. It was a lie. After a year with this mean drunk, I was a crumbled mess. Matt saw this

16. the group, not the drug

clearly though I tried to hide my dilemma. He may have seen me as "rock-solid," but what I should have done was be naked, be real, be me — human. I was always such a stupid symbol of the rock; I needed to show him more gravel. What the heck was I afraid of? I was just like him, a wonderful loser. Imagine if we were all taught from a young age how to communicate about feelings without shame. I should have been more open, but I was afraid, like Matt, of being judged.

But Matt was home then! He seemed so Matt, so calm. I had no idea of the storm raging. Instead, I was concerned with getting firewood — my constant beloved chore. Finding escape in work, I lost myself in the scream of the chain, the crash of the branches, the ping of the sticks hitting my aluminum trailer. Unfortunately, my voice echoed the scream of the chain telling him to buck-up.

But, somehow Matt relished his return to the homestead. Maybe this, the mundane, has value. He, for once, welcomed it all. He, like I, was lost in the repetitive mundaneness of survival. He was home!

Matt's mom

SEPTEMBER 14, MONDAY, 2009 (6.5/10)

Another good day today. I woke up to an empty house, so I decided I would help mom out by stacking some wood and splitting what was in back. It felt nice to be drug free and outside in my old home.

Dick got home late afternoon and we worked on my Caprice a little bit. I think we may be able to get that thing running well enough to sell, or possibly use in the future.

Dick and I also went out and got a big load of wood. For once I actually, really enjoyed it. Felt nice to be out in the woods.

Dick didn't drink today, thankfully. I feel so physically healthy. It's really nice not to be on the opiates. I wish, pray, and hope I can come to terms with and continue sobriety. I have so many dreams so many plans that I would like to accomplish.

SEPTEMBER 15 THRU 19, 2009 (7.5 OVERALL)

```
Intake: Tuesday 2009, 20 mg Valium
       Wednesday 30 mg Valium
  Thursday smoked and 40 mg Valium
            Saturday Ø
```

A great week at home, if not for it being absolutely crazy. I kept sober. I used Valium once or twice a day, and it helped keep me level.

Dick and Mom are now undoubtedly broken. I spent a lot of time with Dick drunk; it's horrible to see them in this shape. It makes me depressed. I can tell they are both miserable, and really want out—but don't quite know how to get out.

The kids seemed happy and well adjusted. The foster child, Marissa, is quite bright, thoughtful, and a polite child—she has a lot of potential.

I hated coming back from home today. I didn't take my TCA (antidepressant), so I was craving opiates like crazy! The first thing I did was walk to my dealer's place. He had nothing, but April sold me half an 80, which I actually snorted, along with smoking a bunch of weed. Oh, before April came over I went to Pat's (future roommate) and smoked a whole bunch of dope, with the upstairs' neighbors too. Even got a couple of 40 oz. High Life and drank that. The urge to get completely intoxicated was strong after seeing my mom the way she was. I don't know why, but I threw 10 full days of sober out the window the minute I got back to Oshkosh. Need to find a better way because this plan of mine just isn't working.

I totally fucked my Caprice up by trying to get it out of the forest. Too bad. I almost wanted to keep it, but instead I got $160 from Sprout. He gave me $140 up front, and the next time I come back home he'll give me the other $20 and catch me a buzz—great to look forward to.

Didn't get to see any of my friends. Mom was out of her mind on that one, too. Overall, I worked hard, and mostly hung out with Dick and the girls. I saw how bad things have gotten with the alcohol and Dick. I saw also that for the most part, they play it off pretty well. They're still upwardly mobile; they don't seem to have money issues at all.

Saw grandma. It was nice, but hard to see her losing her mind.

> I refused to let Matt go visit friends. Adamant about this being a 'home' trip and not a 'party' trip with a place to flop, I laid down the law. I was really Nazi about the whole trip being about visiting and not re-visiting, but I knew that a trip home meant a trip back into temptation. I was careful not to allow him an easy slide down into the depths. Little did I know he was already deep in the mud — probably because I was fighting my own battle with my new husband's mud. I had my hands full, yet I made sure to keep up "appearances."
>
> — Matt's mom

September 20/21, Sunday and Monday, 2009 (4/10)

I have been completely out of control these last few days with all of the drugs. I have spared no expense, just started shooting everything in sight from oxies to morphine to methadone.... I missed work for the first time ever today because I was "sick," actually just too high to make my shift. I really hit bottom hard this time.

Intake: morphine, OC, methadone, smoked

SEPTEMBER 22, TUESDAY, 2009

April is falling apart, too. She showed up at my place again just fucked up and out of her mind. I got pretty fucked up, too. I've been depressed and have just hit the ground so hard this time around—free fall.

Intake: oxyco IV, Suboxone, smoked

SEPTEMBER 23, WEDNESDAY, 2009 (5/10)

I have really been neglecting my journal entries lately. I've just been too Fucked up to make them lately. Things have just been out of control since I got back from up north, but they are starting to calm down a little bit now. Work is still going well, but I'm moving this week and it's a little stressful.

No intake recorded

SEPTEMBER 26, SATURDAY, 2009 (2.5/10)

Today was a bad, bad, bad day. I found out today that I would not be able to move to Franklin Street with the two young people I met. I am very bummed out. I spent the day with Kelly, smoked, and felt shitty. This is the worst news I've had in a long time. I feel terrible about it. I feel like I've done something to bring this along—I've been pretty bad with the drugs since returning to Oshkosh, so I'm depressed. I've started 100 mg. Amitriptyline with 10 mg. Lexapro just to see if anything helps.

Intake: ø day 3, alcohol

September 29, Tuesday, 2009 (5.5/10)

Today and yesterday you could really feel fall in full force; the dull flatness of autumn was readily perceivable in the light table.

I'll be staying at New Your Ave awhile longer I suppose, probably through the winter. Almost got out!!

Talked to Rose via Facebook. She is really sick, but she sounds absolutely glowing about where she is, happy to be in Poland and young. God, I get so jealous when I talk to her!! I need to get back that way someday soon.

Work is going well.

Intake: ø day 6, smoked

OCTOBER, 2009

OCTOBER 4, SUNDAY 2009, (5/10)

I have been bad about keeping up with my journal. I need to refocus and get back to my entries. I've been doing a lot of thinking lately; hasn't amounted to much in the way of action, but I will soon change that I hope.

The last few days have been okay. It's getting colder out, but I find myself almost looking forward to the rest of October. I used opiates on Thursday (payday, 40 mg OC IV) and for that I'm not happy. I had 8 whole days of sober and messed it up! Now I have 3, but it went by so quickly. Maybe that means I'm getting better? I've been smoking a lot more marijuana lately, and my drinking has increased a bit. I really just need to cut all of this out.

Rose is in Poland. She thinks she may just visit Pripyat and Chernobyl. Talk about jealous!

<u>Intake: Ø day 3, smoked</u>

OCTOBER 5, MONDAY, 2009, (5/10)

Another average day today. Work was busy, not only for a Monday, but also because we expected it would be slow for the PACKER

GAME OF THE CENTURY. Favre is playing against the Packers for the first time ever; it's not looking good for the Pack. The game is in progress right now.

I have a strange pain that is constant in my lower right abdomen. Don't know what it is, but I've been shitting nothing but water for the better part of the last 2 weeks. I hope it's not Crohns or [ulcerative colitis] or something worse. I first noticed the pain back in July but thought it was simply from taking too much APAP.[17] I will find out next week Wednesday when I see my doctor.

October is in full swing, but it was nice today, almost 60 degrees out. I already miss my 80 degree days!

<u>Intake: Ø day 4, NOTHING at all!</u>

OCTOBER 6, TUESDAY, 2009 (5/10)

A regular day today, again. The weather was really bad all day—super windy and full of rain. I walked to the food pantry and got me some FOOD!

Work is becoming more stressful because the staff was cut by one guy and we close earlier, so we are doing more work in less time; it's a challenge.

17. Tylenol is derived from N-acetyl-para-aminophenol (APAP). It is a formulation used so that hydrocodone or Vicodin will bind with the added pain reliever.

I felt "well" today; didn't use a thing. My mind, however, is still pulling at me, telling me that opiates are the best in life. It's terrible. I now have to bear my own mind.

Intake: Ø day five

October 7, Wednesday, 2009 (6/10)

Today was pretty cool. I did a burn cruise with April (always a good time). We took a drive out to Winneconne to see April's new pad, and it is absolutely gorgeous! Like a millionaire's palace! I'm really happy for her. I would consider her a good friend of mine.

I've been thinking a lot (still) about where I want to go with my life. Just starting something is tough. I figure my best option would be to find a second place of employment and just work my buns off, save all the money, and then move away to something better, my education, my life. I am glad that I can at least think in a positive way now—need out, need out.

Intake: Ø day six

October 11, Sunday, 2009 (5/10)

Had the day off today. Finally got ahold of Cindy and Lenny. Went over there and mowed the lawn, and helped Cindy clean the whole house. We all had a nice time. They are finally having a prospective buyer look at the house tomorrow. I would like to say that I hope they sell it, but I would be sad to see them go.

I finally accompanied them to their church tonight. They had a "faith healer" visiting from Atlanta. I believe in miracle healing, but this guy seemed to be more of an actor/salesman type. He put on quite a show, full of bravado, full of act and fire. He really rubbed me wrong. It seemed like a scam to my eyes and ears. I think I may go back to church with them, but we'll see.

Been good about drugs, laying down some real sober time. Contemplating bigger things now. Hope to reach the goal.

Intake: Ø Day 10

After hearing of this church visit, I was so disconcerted that Matt ran into this sort of anti-worship/worship of avarice and ignorance. We spoke at length about this encounter. I tried in vain to counter the whole experience. But, the fact was plain — Christianity delivered in our tradition, the hillbilly tradition, was being prostituted out.

I remember so clearly when I went down to Lansing, MI to aid in a conventional, church building project. This very conservative church did not allow me to sleep in the same house as the man I rode down with; we were not married. I went to help pour concrete and knew what to do. However, in the morning I was escorted through the kitchen to prepare snacks for the men. Then, to my horror, I was escorted to the skirt room. Kindly, I was told that this church believed that women didn't dress like men, and as I was wearing pants — I needed to pick out a skirt. The room was like the biggest walk-in closet I have ever seen. I smiled, declined, and asked if they would still like my charity work. The woman was a bit struck by my candor. "So what?" I thought. Her mouth fell open only for a second and then her perma-smile came back. She led me out and decided to serve donuts herself. I worked the day pulling and mixing mud.

An interesting addendum to this experience was the reason for pouring this massive slab. The church was building on a section in order to produce more Bibles. It seemed that the Bible production business was quite lucrative. The owner of the business was very warm — a really affective person — so, we spoke at length. He explained that he only sold King James versions as he made a better profit. He complained about his wife who was around 500 pounds and couldn't even walk anymore; he remarked about his sons' new, expensive vehicles; and to top it off, he asked me if he could visit me (wink wink).

I am not sure what to make of all this: Matt's need to connect with God, his experience in seeking, my experiences with avarice, and the true existence of God. My son needed to see Jesus but was given Satan by those who claimed to know the love and power of submitting to a Higher Power. Institutions that claim to hold a singular and rigid Truth are dubious in my opinion. The good and evil with which Matt struggled was here and tangible, so he was understandably repulsed. Unfortunate that again he was seeking a relationship with a power higher than himself, one that could guide him to success, and was shown only another type of addiction (giving over one's whole life for the short-lived, fake feeling of joy. I regret not helping Matt find those real people who knew and showed the mercy, charity, and peace of allowing God to be that higher power.

— Matt's mom

October 12, Monday, 2009 (5/10)

First time I've seen snow all year. Broke my streak today. April also decided to treat me like garbage over a deal we were doing. That's really too bad.

Intake: Valium, 20 mg. methadone oral

October 13, Tuesday, 2009 (5/10)

Today was quite odd in so many ways. April finally did it, finally fucked everything up. She missed work, and Andrea and I found her in the parking lot, basically nodding her head out. I thought she had ODd; she was that fucked up. Craig was called and showed up with her parents. She was just acting absolutely wild, pissed at me because I took her keys and gave them to John. I guess her boyfriend broke up with her. Good for him as April really needs some help. I think she is a sociopath and maybe nothing will ever work for her, except prison again. Crazy night. I brought this Jake guy over and he split some heroin with me, first time I've done that in quite a while. Bad thing. These people are bad news for me.

Intake: Valium, 20 mg. methadone, heroin IV

October 14, Wednesday, 2009

Page 100 of journal! Weird, but this is the 100th post too.

Today at work I had a conference with John and Elta for about an hour, all about April and what happened last night. I had to out her, had no other choice. I told them all about April and the heroin she had and all the lies. We called my PO and I told her the whole story as well. That was tough, breaking the code of silence, but it was absolutely necessary. April is a danger to herself and everyone around her. She would end up dead if someone didn't intervene. She will be in a world of shit now. I feel like I sold her out! But, I felt a force inside that pushed me towards it, inexplicable. I just hope I don't get caught up in all of this and go down with her, too.

April called me today trying to convince me that she could fix everything by telling some more lies. This time she wants to tell everyone she's pregnant—just sick. I don't think I'll be seeing April much anymore; we're not going to be friends, I don't think.

<u>Intake: heroin 1 shot IV</u>

Page 100 and a tenfold change, Matt seemed to be rethinking, maybe practicing how to reject this drug-culture reality. Breaking "the code," he realized, was the only way to save her life, and maybe his. However, the reaction he expected was frightening. Why would he be so frightened? Why would calling his probation officer looking for help be risky? Matt felt it "was absolutely necessary" due to "a force inside me that pushed towards it." What force was that? Was this his higher power? Was this his belief in humanity to reward honesty and brokenness? See if you notice any changes in Matt's circumstances caused by those charged with, paid for, or capable of delivering a safety net in following journal entries.

— Matt's mom

Instructions on back cover of first spiral notebook

Instructions for myself when I actually get to this end page!

Plan—continue journaling until Jan. 13, 2010, at which time I will collect the 6 months of entries from July 13 to January 13 and edit them, type them up, make a 6 month copy, laminate it, and also memorialize these words electronically so as to ensure their survival in multiple ways. Do this every sixth month for the rest of my life so I can leave an appropriate record for the next generations of my family and friends, as well as for history at large!

May God help me in this endeavor!

This is the end of journal 1. Is this enough to help generations to come? Will he change history? I hope his efforts will make a difference for other moms and their children. I also hope this brings some form of redemption for Matt.

— Matt's mom

Journal 2

Today ends a crazy week. I used opiates all week, but I managed to only spend about $70 all told out of this last paycheck. I paid off a chunk of my loan at Cash-in-a-Flash, and just generally spent my money on bills this week. I'm quite happy and proud of myself—I exercised some real control over this damn habit, and plan to keep going in this direction taking little steps that lead to bigger things. First, I gotta get that damn pay-day loan paid off. Then I'm getting my license assessment and getting my damn license back. After that I'm buying myself off probation, and then getting a car. After I've achieved all that I'll be moving with Rose to Madison and hopefully get the balls to finish my education. And I almost forgot my trip to Ukraine; that's in the works still. I've let so much time slip away; it's unbelievable to me.

I have been doing an awesome job at the restaurant lately, and I am now the top guy in the kitchen, and I'm going even higher than that. I've found a new energy since breaking my addiction and depression at the end of August. I'm still using but every week I bring it a little more under control. The anti-depressants really help the whole situation—need to stay up on those for sure.

I don't know what's up with April; I hope every day that I don't suffer some type of retaliation from her, but if she finds out about me answering questions, I'll be getting some retaliation I'm sure. I hope the best for her, and for myself; I need to get completely clear, too.

Intake: 30 mg morphine EV, 50 mg hydroco oral,

7th straight day of using *BAD!

Two worlds in direct conflict and with guarded rules both spurned Matt's actions. The paradox of addiction is reinforced by those within the separated cultures because Matt faced judgment and shame by his peers. The retaliation he speaks of threatens all addicts: lose a job/apartment/relationship, left without connections, sold-out to police. This shame and fear defeats the addict's efforts to move into recovery — and to encourage others to do so when it is clear they have crossed some intuitive "safety line."

Matt claims to "bring it a little more under control" yet ends saying he used for 7 straight days. Is he writing to convince himself, hide his shame, or something else? He hopes for himself and others, yet who is hoping for him?

— Matt's mom

OCTOBER 19, MONDAY, 2009 (5/10)

Warm day outside today. I guess we get our "Indian summer" in one dose on one day—too bad. I bet it'll be cold again tomorrow or in a few days; it's all downhill from here.

An average day other than that. I'm starting another "off" period for opiates. This will most likely last for about 10–12 days, unless Joey throws me something tomorrow (He owes me big, but he's been a scumbag lately. I hold out little hope that he'll ever set me up *sans cash*). I'm looking to take a nice long run without the shit; I find that it's really good for me, for my mind to be away from that shit. I'm working towards the ultimate goal of being completely off someday soon—it's been an epic battle, back and forth. I need to win; I need to come out ahead on this one, for the first time in a long time I think that I can do it; my confidence builds with every multi-day run that I complete.

Someday soon, God willing, someday soon ....

<u>Intake Ø day 1</u>

OCTOBER 20, TUESDAY, 2009 (4/10)

I think I'm finally coming down with a cold. I've missed it the last 2 years, so I figure I'm overdue.

Loneliness is starting to get to me a little. I wonder when I'll bump into love again. No use, sleep, work, a few friends, whatever drugs I can get my hands on. Another day rolls by, inconsequential, nothing gained, and a little more youth lost every day.

John has been really nice, for how long no one can tell. Fed me a good burger tonight; what a guy!

Small steps, small steps …

<u>Intake Ø day 2, smoked</u>

October 21, Wednesday, 2009 (5/10)

Today was busy for a Wednesday at work. I finally convinced them to put a third man on Wednesday night. I'm really starting to get burned out with the routine. It's been quite the struggle at that place lately, so much for 2 people to get accomplished. Other than that, I'm happy there. I don't dread going to work anymore; I get along well with the people there; it beats the shit out of Subway, so I always remember that at least.

Something quite strange happened today. Leah, a girl I was friends with back in my Subway days, called me at 1:30 in the morning. That in itself isn't outrageously strange, but when she started asking me if I knew where to get any cocaine it became strange. I haven't spoken to or seen this girl in months, probably 3 months, so it caught me really off guard. Of course, I told her I didn't know where to get anything (I really don't; I don't mess with coke; it's really no fun). Anyways, I saw today that she had called me on my caller ID while I was at work. I called her back to discover that she thought she had OD'd on coke. She had been smoking it, and she thought she had had a tad too much. I told her to find some Valium and if she couldn't that she should go to the E.R. Damn, I've been departing from drugs lately. I notice, it seems a lot more, how messed up that whole world is, just sickening to me more and more. Perhaps that's a good thing.

Intake: Ø day 3, a little alcohol

OCTOBER 22, THURSDAY, 2009 (5.5/10)

I broke my streak of sober today, scrambled up $20 from Don and bought 45mg of morphine. Too bad; it was an awful waste of money, as is always the case.

Work was short, 3 hours, and of course Trish was being worthless as always. I finally brought my case before Elta, and she totally agreed with me. I think the problem will be handled in short order. If not, I think Trish will be in danger of losing her job; at least I hope she loses it. She is just about as worthless as a cook as anything else.

I notice that my teeth are beginning to cavity and decay all over the place. I need to see a dentist for some very serious work soon if I hope to keep them past age 30. I really wish I had taken better care of them. I'm beginning to become quite self-conscious about them. I think they have kept me out of the love game to some extent. I regret wasting and not taking better care of them. I sure do now, but I think it may be too late to do anything about them.

Intake: 45 mg morphine IV SHIT! NO !

Day 1 tomorrow Please …

OCTOBER 23RD, FRIDAY, 2009 (5/10)

Today was average. I worked, and at work Trish was finally pulled into the office by Rita and given a "talking to." It lasted a really long time, past close, over an hour. I don't know why. Who would have anything to talk about for an over an hour in that place?

Went out with Pat and his girlfriend for a drink after work. It was so-so as is always the case when I drink.

The big story right now to me is that John fucked up his computer good. I can't access the Internet! Bastard! It's just because he has a low IQ and can't understand the basics of something so complicated as a computer!

Idiot. I feel naked without my Facebook!

<u>Intake: Ø day 1</u>

OCTOBER 24, SATURDAY, 2009 (5/10)

Another workweek has ended. I wasn't able to capture my 10-hour Saturday shift like I wanted. As such I will only have a 70-hour paycheck, which will be my best yet, but which is pretty damn sad considering the money that I used to bring in. Need to work a little harder, I guess.

Was going to hang out with Pat again tonight, but he was worn out from last night still. I have the Internet back, so that's a nice bonus.

I hope my day off tomorrow isn't so boring as is usually the case. I know Thursday will be a good day off (getting high, getting paid). Can't wait till Thursday.

<u>Intake: Ø day 2</u>

OCTOBER 25, SUNDAY, 2009 (5/10)

Day off today. Got with Pat and helped him clean out one of the properties that he oversees. It was a depressing affair, cleaning out the possessions of those tenants. The place was an awful mess. We spent 2 hours just getting stuff in piles in the middle of the floor. After we got done, Pat fed me and we had a few drinks, not really an "ideal" way to spend a day off, but something to do rather than sitting home alone.

<u>Intake: Ø day 3</u>

October 26, Monday, 2009

Went up to Cindy's today, visited with her and Lenny for a while—helped Cindy go shopping at Aldi's and Pick 'n' Save. Her bottle was out, but I took nothing—good for me.

Work was slow. I worked with Jason—once again a great guy.

I took an extra 50 mg of amitriptyline last night. It didn't help me sleep any more soundly, and I felt so dazed today, just way out of it. Lucky for me this disappeared by the beginning of work.

Once again I feel like I may be getting sick. Maybe it's just my mind. I hope I awaken and I feel fine, but who knows. I may have the feared "swine flu!" I figure I'm strong and healthy enough to get over most any bug. We'll just see.

<u>Intake: Ø day 4</u>

OCTOBER 27, TUESDAY, 2009 (5/10)

I think I definitely am getting sick with something, but the onset must be slow because all I have is a little cough and a small sense of discomfort in my upper trachea. I was coughing only a little today. I hope I'm not worse tomorrow. If so, I'm sure there is a way I can up $36 for my Vicodin refill. We'll see.

Work was moderately steady today. I had Andrea with me, so we rocked out. Rita said she had to talk to me about something, sounded negative, but she never got around to it. I guess if I make my shift tomorrow we'll find out.

I have begun to notice that my life is moving along at a predictable and steady pace lately. As nice as that is, I also notice something else quite troubling: I am not as creative or outgoing as I once was, almost as if I am in a funk. I seem to have lost the ability to assert myself to other people. Previously, in life, this was a hallmark ability that I possessed—gone now almost completely, I'm sad to report. I need to regain this if I am to ever succeed in the way that I want to.

Intake: Ø day 5

OCTOBER 28, WEDNESDAY, 2009 (5/10)

Today was all right. I got paid ($455), my biggest check ever from the restaurant. Sad part is that it's already gone to food and bills! I bought my Vikes out, $36, and that's the extent of the money I'll be spending on drugs for the next 2 weeks—good for me.

I got pretty fucked up today—smoked with Pat and ate some Vikes. Later Andrea came over and we got really ripped. Ate some more Vikes, went shopping for food, an average day.

Even though I was getting high and spending time with friends, I noticed that I had the most depressed feeling. I thought this was strange. I think that very slowly, my mind and subconscious is turning against this lifestyle I've been living. I need to move on to greater things. I must make a complete change.

It's important, I think, not to become content with my progress and instead continue to strive for more, more, more. I've been seeing light at the end of the tunnel lately, even though I sometimes wonder if I possess the strength to reach it. One day, God willing, one fine day …

Intake: 60 m hydroco oral, smoked A LOT, 2 beers

OCTOBER 30, FRIDAY 2009 (7+/10)

A great day today. Irina called me from the Ukraine. Any day she calls me is a good day. We spoke for over an hour, just catching up. She has a new boyfriend now, someone she thinks she is in love with. She is going on a business trip to Dubai! Amazing. I miss her so much, and I feel great to know that she likes me enough to keep up with me. I MUST gain a second job and buy a damn ticket to see her soon! She told me on the phone that she would be more than willing to help Rose out upon her arrival in Kyiu. Great!

Work was busy. Trish (that miserable Bitch) left after only an hour because she was "sick." Sounds offhand like some bullshit to me, but I really should just put all of that out of my mind, think neutral and nothing about her. Andrea is a trooper. She was off the side of the kitchen throwing up into a can at one point, and she never even thought of asking to go home. Some people know how to work; some people just don't get it.

Traded Andrea some Vikes for a few bowls—the stuff is amazing, one of the best I've ever smoked. One hit really does it.

I once again have the thought in my head of pulling completely out of trouble, get that second job and go to the Ukraine!

Intake: 2(50 mg hydroco oral, smoked great weed)

*Today also marks the 4-year anniversary of me beginning my journey into IV drug use.

October 31, Saturday, Halloween, 2009 (4.75/10)

I was in a sour mood all night at work; didn't really say anything to anybody all night long. People were dressed up, and everyone had plans to go out and party somewhere. I came home, smoked a bowl and listened to music by myself—went to bed early. Hell of a night. I could have gone out and done something with Pat. I hadn't the motivation to do so.

I take these breaks every two weeks or so, breaks from my anti-depressants. I really notice the depression creep back in, especially if I'm smoking weed. I go off of it because if I partied my Vicodin with my TCA, I wouldn't be able to wake up in the mornings! I've thankfully been able to reserve myself to just my Vikes this week and only $36 cost—half of last paycheck's total.

I'm just itching to go to Ukraine and do something worth bragging about. I have a plan and now I am moving more steadily towards it. I need to be proud of who I am once again, need to be worthy once again of a woman's love.

Intake: 3 (50 mg hydroco oral, smoked)

NOVEMBER, 2009

NOVEMBER 1, SUNDAY, 2009 (5/10)

Went to church today with Jason from work. It was actually quite nice. Went out to eat chicken after that; just had a grand old time.

Got home from that quite sleepy, took a nap, and then walked over to Pat's place, smoked some weed with him; just took it easy.

I can feel something inside now. Every day I believe I get a little more uncomfortable with my situation; every day I get a little more comfortable with change. The change I need to make in order to be happy again, it's coming; it's coming soon.

Intake: 4 (55 mg hydroco oral), smoked

*Today marks the 2 year anniversary of the last time I spoke to Paulina.

Paulina is a girl from Poland who Matt loved deeply. Matt remembered dates in an inexplicable way. He remembered the day grandpa first let him shoot the rifle, the day on the calendar that he lost his virginity, the day that someone died, left, or first said hello. He marked the calendar of his life with important memories. He marked his days. He valued them highly, and each individual who marked his life was marked forever on the day of the arrival/departure in his mind forever, not written but remembered.

I should be more like that. I forgot my own birthday several times, but Matt never did. I still have the chopsticks and the Last Supper plate he bought for me to mark those days. I guess we should all learn to mark our days.

— Matt's Mom

November 2, Monday, 2009 (5/10)

I've had enough. I've had enough drugs. I've had enough heart-break. I've had enough of playing the loser. I want out; I want out now! Tomorrow I'm hitting the pavement hard to look for a second job. When I find that job, I'll work my ass off until I get enough money to go back to Europe. If I haven't gone to Ukraine, back to Poland to see Paulina again by Nov. 2nd next year, I'm going to end my life; I really will. If I can't make something this simple happen by then, I'll do the un-thinkable. Better to DIE than to go on living like this, never achieving anything, always just being satisfied with survival. No more.

I'm real emotional tonight because I have just seen some pictures of Paulina from her trip to Italy. I find it impossible to believe that 3 years later I still find fire in my soul for this girl. I wish it was gone. I wish there were some way to extinguish this feeling, but no—it creeps up into the very depths of my soul; it is extended there. Why? Why? Why? What exactly does the future hold now with this? BE GONE!

I hereby RESOLVE to have traveled to Europe by this time next year.

<u>Intake: Ø day 1</u>

NOVEMBER 3, TUESDAY, 2009 (5/10)

I have made a suicide pact with you my trusty journal, and I intend to keep it. I intend to keep my pact with you: End of Life, or travel— I do not want to die, so I will travel!

Today I put in 3 applications; I am serious about his. I have told my roommate, too, that I am serious about getting a second job in the next month.

No more Drugs. I need to get on a plane and get gone!

<u>Intake: Ø day 2! Drunk!</u>

NOVEMBER 4, WEDNESDAY, 2009 (5/10)

Today was pretty domestic I would say. I went to the food pantry today, got some good food. God bless the help. Hopefully, one day soon I won't need it any longer.

Work was okay too. I picked up a sixth shift, working tomorrow for Trish, who is ill with the flu. Good for me. It seems that a lot of people are sick with this. Whatever is going around, it's taking a lot of people down.

I'm still committed to finding that second job. I need to stay committed to this, too. I just can't live like this any longer—I really would rather die than continue living in this way—never realizing my dreams, just surviving, no more—death or dreams.

Intake: Ø, Day 3

*Tomorrow is the 2-week day separating me from my last IV use. Keep it up. I'll keep this up.

November 5, Thursday, 2009 (5.5/10)

Worked today 6 hours for Trish. It went quite well, busy, which is nice to have. I am now the only one proficient on the grill. I can flame 6 pans at once, no one else in the crew can do this, so I hold a little extra value in this aspect. I do enjoy doing it though, at one point I noticed that John, Abbey, and Elta were all looking at me with some kind of awe for moving so damn quickly on the grill; it is quite a feat.

After work I walked over to Pat's place. I smoked a bowl with him, watched a great show: "It's Always Sunny in Philadelphia," and then

I walked home. It was quite a pleasant walk, my mind buzzing in a thousand different directions. A lot of my thoughts rolled back inevitably to Paulina, still, so long after that has died. It still lives. I wonder what it all means, why it persists so.

I suppose I will indeed see her again, if only for a couple hours on some random day during my trip back. I need this to happen, just to get back there, to achieve this goal; it will be a terrific, a dress rehearsal for things to come.

Intake: Ø day 4, smoked

NOVEMBER 6, FRIDAY, 2009 (5.3/10)

Work went well. It was busy, but I did a hell of a job. They see how valuable I am, and it feels really good!

Went out to D-Pub with Pat, almost got in a fight with this old guy; that was a close call! One day I won't even drink, and then I can do what I want without having to worry about drunk run-ins with random people!

One day soon
No more dope
On wings of power
I'll realize my life is begun

One beautiful day

I'll kick everything

I'll know love

I'll atone for all that's done

One day soon

One day soon

<u>Intake: Ø day 5, drank till drunk</u>

November 7, Saturday, 2009 (5/10)

Well, a slow night at work, but things are alright being a little slow once in a while. I am dreaming a lot again about my next trip, Ukraine, my God it WILL be something to behold when I get there. I just keep dreaming about it, and I need to get a second job going on so I can make it happen. I am developing a will, and so there can be nothing except absolute success. I have done it before; I will surely do it once again.

Our Lord, He is coming back into my life. I'll be going to church tomorrow again with Jason, and tonight on my walk home I felt something, something made me stop, it was when I was thinking about God when this happened to me … I'm finally coming to submission, and it is a powerful thing.

I pray He takes from me those things that will lead me into sin, that He leads me to where He wants me to go. I pray mostly for patience.

<u>Intake: Ø day 6, God bless it</u>

November 8, Sunday, 2009 (5ish/10)

Went again with Jason to church this week. It was really nice, "International Sunday." They had booths set up, and ALL KINDS of very good homemade food! I got really filled up! I think I'll make this a habit. It's good for me. I really think so!

I got home and got very bored. The second half of my day was ruined by absolute boredom. I need to find a Sunday afternoon hobby!

*8-year anniversary of losing my virginity to Jenny.

<u>Intake: Ø day 7</u>

November 9, Monday, 2009 (5/10)

Today was interesting. I called Laura, my P.O., and asked her if I could get off probation. She said YES, but that I would have to pay $750.00 before I could do it, so it was bitter indeed. I have composed a letter to Judge Nielsen in Vilas County asking him to change it to community service, so hopefully that will take care of $330 of that total. I crunched some numbers, and I feel that I can, with proper discipline, devote $200 per month to my fees, which puts me off sometime in March without community service, or late January with community service. This is my first goal. Second goal is getting that $200 I need for my assessment. Third goal is getting to UKRAINE.

Move towards it. Get it started. It will happen!

Go Get 'em Matt!

<u>Intake: Ø day 8</u>

November 10, Tuesday, 2009 (6/10)

[Matt starts using a red pen at this point to denote drug days and black to denote sober days.]

Only made it a mere 8 days. Today I broke my streak and borrowed $40 in order to get my Vikes filled. Shame. Even though I give myself these days of looking forward to getting high, it isn't something that's advancing my goals of overseas travel—unless I can sell them, which isn't something I'm doing at the moment

I need to get a little better each and every day.

<u>Intake 55 mg hydroco oral, smoked</u>

NOVEMBER 11, WEDNESDAY, 2009 (5ish/10)

Today was an attack on sobriety from all sides and angles. I had a standing refill on my Valium at Morton's, which I filled. I also went to see the good doctor Basilliere. Unexpectedly he filled my cup overflowing with narcotics—100 Vicodin, with 3 refills that commence every 16th day, another 30 Valiums that commence once monthly for next 4 months—this will help in one way though—I took them to Walmart and all they cost me was $36 for 100 Vikes and 30 Valiums, not bad. I'll be getting a lot more pills AND they cost less.

Andy Nesbit, one of the guys I was locked up with, called me out of the blue today—after robbing me for over $200 total and disappearing 6 months ago. I happen to think that he's a good guy deep down, minus the drugs. I told him we should get a beer sometime soon. We might, but he is not really responsible and dependable. He's doing the whole "methadone" program. Don't know how he gets rides to Green Bay and back every morning, being unemployed and all. Methadone clinics are expensive! Let alone the driving. I wonder what he'll look like when I finally see him.

<u>Intake: 70 mg hydro oral, diazepam</u>

November 12, Thursday, 2009 (6.5/10)

Got paid today: $425.00. Finally started a checking account at the credit union. I can close that damn useless one at Associated now. I also ran to Walmart and bought up my 100 Vikes/30 val combo— the stars have aligned and I have a ton of shit for once in a very long time—170 and 60. This is not good, I spent too much money on it: about $86, too much out of one paycheck for dope. Plus, it's too much shit for me to be doing anyways. I'm on the way out, not In. I want Ira and Paula and Lukasz to see me again.

The good news is that tomorrow I'm off to pay my bills. I have decided to kick $100 to Cash in a Flash, and then pay $50 towards my supervision fees. Next week I'll probably only have enough for about 50 or 60 in fees. We'll see. Bottom line is that it's going to be a hell of a time, but I will succeed, of that I'm sure. Next on my list is my tick to Ukraine!

I got so high today. Three Valiums and about 13 Vikes, plus an IV/oral 30 mg dose of morphine, which I traded for—not the best 30 mg hit, but it was something.

No more! STOP! STOP!

<u>Intake: 2 (65 mg hydroco, 30 mg Valium oral)</u>

NOVEMBER 13, FRIDAY, 2009 (6.5/10)

Had a crazy drug-fueled party tonight with all my friends, the ones I had met randomly a few months back. Found out they are all coke-heads, not that they were doing coke, but they had that intensity to them. They were (most of them) pretty young, late teens and early 20's—I MARVELED at their stories of trouble. Some of them had been in so much trouble and are all so damn young!

I got so high, on Vikes, Vals, and weed. I really went 2 steps back tonight from trying to stay sober. Stayed up all night—just got fucked up.

This is not helping me get to Ukraine.

Intake: 3(A LOT, 70 mg hydroco, 40 mg Valium, smoked)

NOVEMBER 14, SATURDAY, 2009 (6/10)

Today started off okay, I slept until 3:30 pm, and had to run to work in order to get there on time. Trish pulled shit again with me when I wanted to leave early (that whore). I'll make her life miserable now!

Had a repeat party with those guys, did a bunch more drugs. Need to stop this. Every time I think I'm getting good, the Devil throws something my way to tempt and mess me up.

Intake: 45 mg hydroco, 30 morphine IV, 15 mg Valium

November 15, Sunday, 2009

Fuzzy from Valium/morphine/hydro

November 16, Monday, 2009 (2/10)

I was burglarized tonight while I was at work. The thieves made away with 11 Valium and a nice bowl of pot. I feel violated. John got super pissed, threatened to kick me out but backed off. I'm locking the doors now.

   I think that scumbag Joey did it.

<u>Intake: Valium 10 mg, smoked a lot!</u>

Gotta be done with drugs.

November 17, Tuesday, 2009

Still felt really bad about the robbery. Hung out with Cindy. She mercifully gave me 3 perks. I grabbed another 3. I almost forgot how clear oxycodone makes your mind and soul feel. I miss it so. I need to stay away from that shit, it's too good.

   I now, almost conclusively, know that Joey Davis was the one who robbed me of my pills. This guy who just a few months ago was that pill king, who fronted out and ran tabs, is now robbing me by walking into my home and stealing my shit. I think that I'll set him up. I'll contact the NEG unit and go undercover, set him up really good, get him a set of bars to think over his numerous crimes. We'll see.

Intake: 60 mg oxyco oral, smoked kinda

NOVEMBER 19, WEDNESDAY, 2009 (5.5/10)

Thought I would have a sober day today, but Walgreens filled me early on my Vikes, so runs yet another "high" day. Ate 10 of those fuckers before I started my journal entry.

I woke up so depressed today, like my life will never be going anywhere, ever. Like I won't find love, or light, or peace while I'm on this earth. Like I'll be a junkie, an active one at that, forever. God, I just want to travel again. I want to know love, and peace. I want to be happy again, I just want what I used to have.

Tomorrow I'll be going back up north, home, with Jenny!

Intake: 50 mg hydroco, smoked

—not helping me get to Ukraine—

NOVEMBER 20, FRIDAY, 2009 (9.5/10)

Exciting journey today. I'm dressed quite finely at the moment, sitting in Menards, waiting for Jenny to get off work so we can drive up north, back home! I got a ride from Jason, always a wonderful man, here to Green Bay. Saw a Korean War veteran in the store here, thanked him for being one hell of a warrior. I should do that more often.

I'm really excited to be going home. I think I'll wander around Crandon tonight, seeing who I can visit. I've thought about visiting Mr. Ferk, who I would like to see again—as well as Pat, and Kim. Just spending time with Jenny is funny enough! Not to mention getting to see Deb and Jerry again—after 7 long years.

I got 70 Vikes last night, 26 of which are already gone! Going to be handing the rest out to Kelly, Pat, and whoever else I meet along the way. Not to mention stayed pretty high myself! Took the long car ride up to Crandon, where Pat is the head chef; he picked up our meal! Went next to Jenny's parents' home. Wow, what a place to be! After so many years! Seeing that Jerry and Deb was amazing. Had a drink with them. Pat took me to his place, and we really partied down, drank, took some Vikes, had a great time overall.

Amazing to be home!

Intake: 90 mg hydroco, smoked

NOVEMBER 21, SATURDAY, 2009 (6.5/10)

Woke up today at Pat's house. He ended up giving me a ride up home. Got there are around noon. Mom was out hunting for opening day, so it was just Dick at first. We went over to Long Lake, saw Kelly, smoked a bit, headed home.

-The rest of the evening I spent just talking one-on-one with mom. We must've talked for 3 or 4 hours. We both drank, but mom drank a lot more than me. I didn't even get drunk. I would suppose that for two of those hours I was in tears, just talking to mom about how upset I was that she was drinking, that things were falling apart in her family. My mother really opened up to me, I think for the first time intentionally. It was so hard for me to sit there with her, to see that she had fallen so low. At one point we went to the cemetery in the dark to see my Aunt Carol's headstone which was just put in. It was really sad. I reminisced with mom about the people we knew and missed who were in that damn graveyard. The whole night was just one sad scene for me, thinking about the past, unable to come to terms with the present or future.

I have no control. All I can do is pray.

Intake: 90 mg hydroco, smoked

November 22, Sunday, 2009 (3.5/10)

Jen came up with her mom today and gave me a ride back to Crandon. We had brunch at La Feta again, saw Pat one last time, and then we headed back to the valley. I was just so down, felt terrible about what I had seen with the family. The ride back was overcast skies with peaks of sunshine here and there, just sad.

Stayed Jenny and Noah, helped to cheer me up quite a bit, smoked a bunch, played some cards, it was nice.

Too down, need to get into myself and be happy!

Intake: Ø day 1, smoked a lot

November 23, Monday, 2009 (4/10)

Noah gave me a ride back to Oshkosh today. Got back around 1:00 PM, depressed as hell. I still had to go to work. Work was busy. I felt like emotional shit the whole time, as is the case every time I return to Oshkosh from back home. Takes me some time to get back into my groove, to forget about things at home and get into my little reality again. Such is life.

Another day.

Intake: Ø date 2, smoked

November 28, Saturday, 2009 (4/10)

Wow, I really let my journal slip! Rob came down this last Tuesday night and stayed until Thursday afternoon. It was one long party!

We smoked and ate Vikes and Ads[18] like they were going out of style. The whole thing was a lot of fun, but it was twinged with a little bit of sadness, on both our parts, for our position in life, our issues, our hard times now and ahead.

Thursday was Thanksgiving, really boring. Had it at Charles and Janie's place. I found when I arrived I didn't want to be there very much, but I needed to make my appearance anyways.

Haven't had any drugs since Thursday. Don't plan to have any until December 11. It shouldn't be too hard, but boring. I've had a bit of withdrawal today, but nothing too severe. It's good for me after all!

Intake: Ø day 2

November 29, Sunday, 2009 (4.5/10)

Had the day off from work today. It started out okay. Pat and Alicia took me to a downtown diner for breakfast. That was a nice experience; gave me something to do for a few hours anyways. I retired to my home around 2:00 PM and just played around on the computer. Bought a 48 oz, just tried to relax and take it easy. Later on I got in touch with Andrea, and she scored a bag for Pat, which I got a tiny piece of.

18. Adderall

I've noticed lately that smoking MJ has made me quite a paranoid wreck. The stuff I got today I smoked with Andrea, and after she left I ended up getting super depressed, paranoid and I have a curious "critical" voice inside that tells me all manner of bad and critical things, about myself, my personality, etc.. Despite this I continue to smoke MJ at every chance. It is a very pleasurable experience most times, but the way I feel when I smoke alone bugs me.

In general I have a permeating feeling of being completely trapped. Money wise I don't make a whole lot; that keeps me back. As well, I've been waging a battle within my own mind that keeps me held back. I feel captive within this time and this place. Hopeless at times.

<u>Intake: Ø day 3, smoked</u>

November 30, Monday, 2009 (5/10)

Today was normal and average in every way. I didn't do much, cleaned a house, moped around a bit, saw Don for a bit, worked my Monday shift with Jason, best shift of the week I think.

The only other observation that I can attach to this day is that while I felt the month of October move slowly, the month of November slid by so quickly that it was scary! I now almost hate the pace at which time slips by with me—the unmoving rock jutting up in this swift river of time. I partied way too much this month, but that won't be happening this December; I won't have money nor opportunity. My scripts are 16 days apart now, horrible for my terrible habit, which is great actually.

We'll see what December brings, another year almost over. In fact it's the end of the decade again. I remember New Year's Eve 1999 like it was yesterday. I'm getting old!

Intake: Ø day 4

Entering school in Colorado, Matthew enjoyed puppies, sunshine, and the outdoors. He is pictured here in our Durango backyard with Mia.

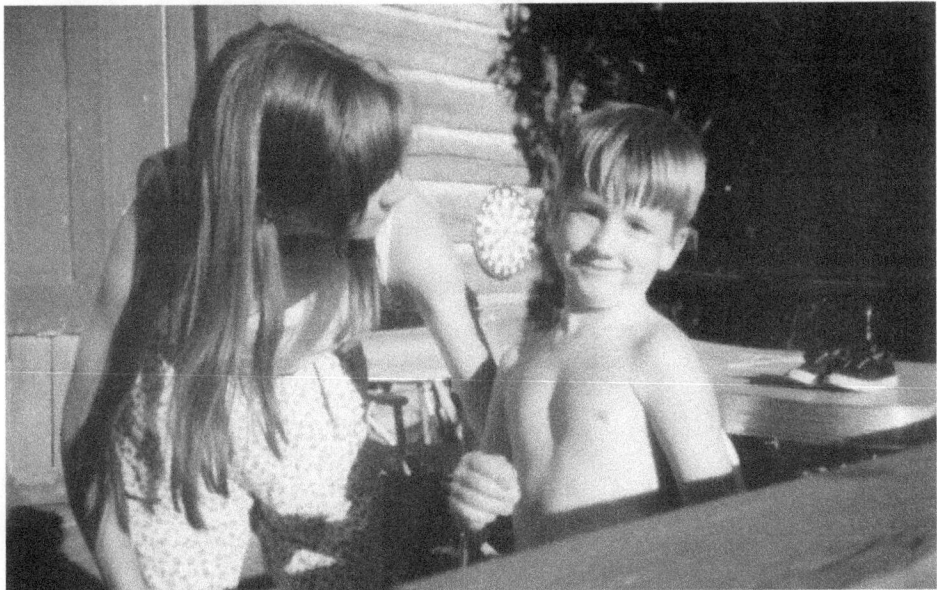

We moved to a rural cabin in Colorado where Matthew spent most of his time playing outside in nature. He is pictured here on the deck with me.

When Matt was 7, he and I (left) spent the winter on the beach in Mexico so I could finish my Spanish and teaching degree by polishing up my fluency.

After I graduated, we moved to Cedar Edge, Colorado where we continued a rural, outdoor lifestyle. Here Matt is age 9 with dog, Mia.

After Matt's sister was born, we all moved to be closer to family. Here Matt is in our Wisconsin home at Christmas. He always loved music, so that year he got his wish and began learning to play the guitar.

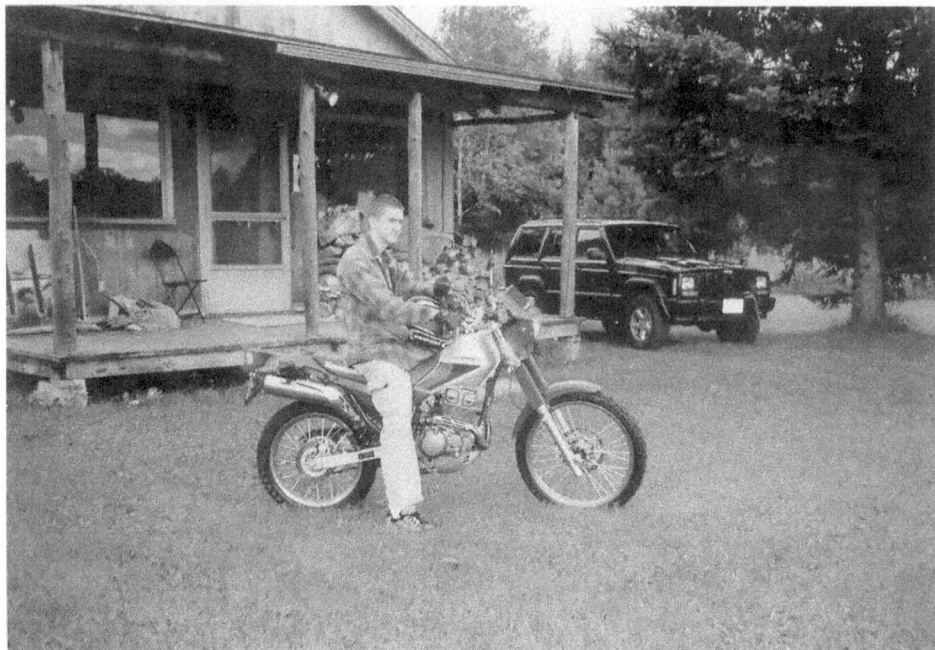

Age 15: He got this Super Sherpa dirt bike for his birthday. Here he was riding around Grandpa Chet's cabin, close to our home. Seemed we had quite a wholesome life — leisure time together, green fields and forests, home-cooked meals, and country docs. (His toenail infection happened around the same time.)

Matthew (right) and his cousin Brian in our backyard: Matt and Brian loved to hunt together and spent many days bonding in the outdoors. This is the largest buck Matt shot.

Pictured here with his little sister, Matthew was such a loving and warm brother and son.

After high school Matt moved into an apartment in Eagle River, Wisconsin, a small tourist town not far from home. This was his invincible period; he descended into drug use with little fear.

The time came for professional family photos. After all the group ones, Matt asked if I would let him pose by himself. I remember clearly how he showed up late to the shoot and then lied to leave early for clandestine purposes. This photo really did capture his reality.

For his birthday, I took Matt on a trip back to Colorado. Here we are taking a break from driving. As demonstrated with his body language, Matt was avoiding a big issue during this trip — he was high on pills the whole time. We even spent 12 hours at an emergency room so he could get "mediation" for his rotten tooth.

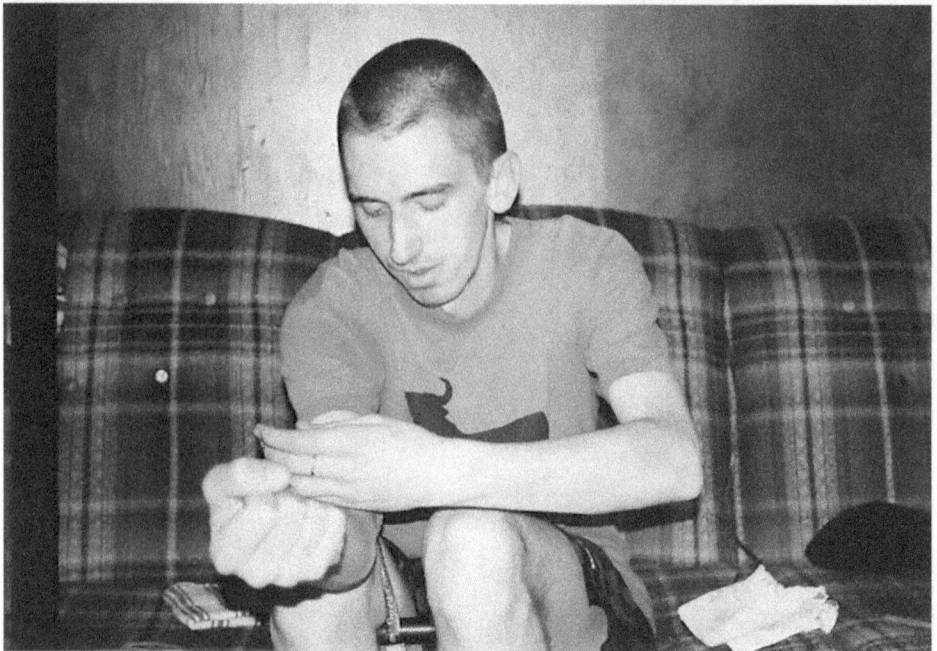

Although he was smug and self-assured during his invincible period, he also tried desperately to record the ugly truth. At his request, Rose took this photo of him shooting up cooked Oxycodone in his Eagle River apartment.

Age 23 and just out of jail, Matthew was spending the summer at home. He was happy and stable, but had no direction and no car/job/license/freedom. Standing on the shore of Lake Superior, he had a peace and sense of hope he had lost years earlier. If I could go back to any point in time, it would be this moment. The time before this was hard-won steps to wisdom and the time after was spiraling stairs of despair.

Matthew age 22: He was staying at home for the week, as he often did when he was "trying to lay low," although he did have an apartment. The professional camera used for this shot is a reminder of things not adding up at this point. It was a very expensive device, and he was trying to sell it to me for $500. I snapped this photo while playing with it, and the look on his brow tells its own story.

Outside his Oshkosh house, Rose and Matt pose for a picture during her stop. Matthew was 24, and the ravages of drug use are apparent. However, the joy of seeing Rose, talking about the move out of Oshkosh, and renewed hope are, too. Although his body was decaying, his heart was transcendent.

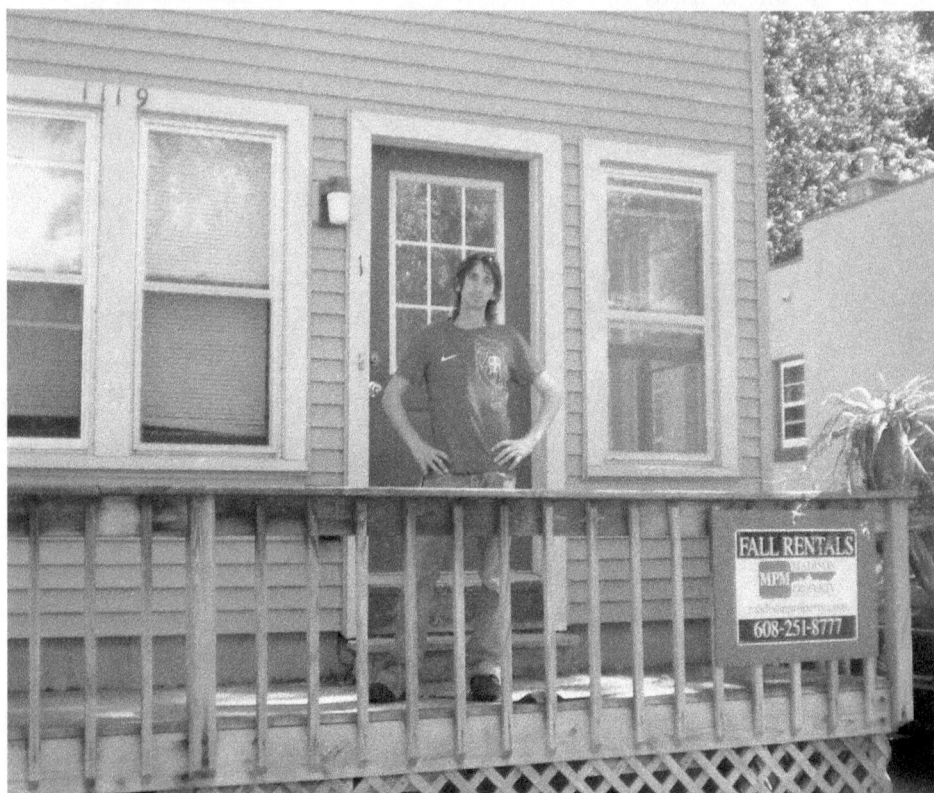

This is the last time I saw Matthew alive. We had just driven to Madison to move his belongings into his new apartment. As I drove away, he was watching me from the front porch, so I stopped to take a quick photo. His look was so forlorn; I believe he somehow knew he would never see me again in this world.

Not far from his new apartment in Madison, Matthew spent his last days alive with Rose taking photos and planning for a week full of visiting lecturers and coffee shop hopping during their free-hours. Unfortunately, he had run out of days.

This is the treasure chest where I keep my most precious possession. It is set close to my dad (Grandpa Chet) and mom, next to my sister (Aunt Carol), and in front of my grandma and grandpa.

March 26th, Friday 2010 (Sia)

11 hours today. 4.5 mcD's, 6.5 pizza hut.

Lost. Very lost.

I look old and spent for 25, where did my youth go?

Depressed.
Dispondent.
Disapointed
Discouraged
Discontent

Help. Where is love? All I ever wanted in life was Love.

Intake: (∅ day 1, smoked)

If he could only have expressed this page to those around him, and if only we could allow people to freely express their bondage, we would not have to bury so much treasure in the ground and in our souls.

Mom
Jane
Funk
August 18, 1963

Son
Matthew
Edwards
March 19, 1985
September 2, 2010

Matt 5:4 Blessed are they who mourn, for they shall be comforted

This is the last present I bought for Matthew. Seeing as I couldn't buy him any more Christmas or birthday presents, I went all out. Somehow I hope it weeps and seeps all the love he needed.

DECEMBER, 2009

DECEMBER 1, TUESDAY, 2009 (5/10)

Another average day. Don gave me a ride to Cash in a Flash to pay my [debt] (just rolled it), and then I went to work. Went to St. Vinnie's today, got my food for the month. God Bless charity like that; wouldn't survive without it.

I've been reading the Bible nightly lately. I originally thought that it may have been my grandma Edwards' copy, but just tonight, while flipping through it I found a handwritten note:

"I command you Satan in the Name of the Lord, pick up your weapons and flee for God has given me authority to walk all over thee."

It doesn't seem to me that grandma Edwards would write such a thing, plus it looks like Mark's writing style (at least what I can remember of that style). I think now that this must have been his Bible, or grandma gave it to him and they both have stuff in there. It's a really strange feeling finding this type of stuff, knowing that this may have been his Bible....

I found the note in Jeremiah chapter 7.

<u>Intake: Ø day 5</u>

Praise be to God!

DECEMBER 2, WEDNESDAY, 2009 (5/10)

My young buddy Jimbo came by today and caught me a buzz. I once again became a paranoid, self-aware wreck. I feel really bad for this Jimbo guy. He gave me the most depressing chronology of his life. He has truly had it rough, through his whole life it seems. Has some obvious learning disabilities, which he explained, as well as a lot of family issues. He reminds me of Greg Barker from my time in jail—really nice, but not quite all there.

It's really a shame that I'm having these problems smoking weed. I think that it's just because it's winter and I have a rough mindset lately. It used to be so pleasurable to smoke, and now not so much, at least when I am alone.

<u>Intake: Ø smoked, day 6</u>

DECEMBER 3, THURSDAY, 2009 (5.5/10)

Spent the day at Cindy's; it's NDS today. Helped her clean and do things around the house. She was quite talkative, and it seemed that she was really happy to have me over. The day was good, peaceful. It was actually snowing outside for most of the day, without any accumulation. Winter is here indeed.

Asked Cindy for two perks, and she helped me out today. Broke my streak, but it's back at it tomorrow again, and unless something pops out of the blue, I won't be high again until next Thursday or Friday, probably Friday the way my refills look.

Intake: 20 mg oxyco.

December 7, Monday, 2009 (5/10)

Another Monday goes down just like the rest. Slow at work, don't have much going on besides that.

We had our first "measurable" snow of the season this day, about 3 inches. It's going to be a real bastard shoveling walks and driveways if a snow blower won't work.

Things have been peaceful and quiet for me lately. I have struck some type of equilibrium between myself and the world around me. This is nice, but I lack drive. I feel anxious all the time, I notice. Can't seem to get over it, but I'm working on it.

Intake: Ø day 4

December 8, Tuesday, 2009

Intake: Ø day 5

DECEMBER 9, WEDNESDAY, 2009 (3/10)

"BLIZZARD of 2009"

Woke up to about 14 inches of snow on the ground! Blowing and drifting in the high blizzard WINDS. Helped John earlier shoveling and blowing. It's quite a job! Big driveway and sidewalks.

Found out today that my grandmother Edwards was contacted by a scam artist who was trying to scam her out of $2300! And my cousins actually think that I may have done it!!! I haven't spoken to grandma Edwards for about three years at this point! It really shook me up how my cousins were acting towards me on Facebook, as well as making me very afraid that my computer may have been hacked, and that people are spying [on] my information. Now I have to prove or persuade my family that I had nothing to do with this whole thing!

Went to Cindy's because work got canceled. [The blizzard] closed the whole restaurant down! I am pissed because I lost 5 hours because of this shit. I ended up playing some games with Lenny, and then crashing at their place. Swiped 3 perks easily.

<u>Intake: 30 mg oxyco oral</u>

Matt was so hurt by his father's family after this scam surfaced. He called me and desperately asked for advice. All I could say was "Call them, defend yourself, and hang in there." In later conversations we decided that the truth would have to come from someone besides Matt, and it did. Months later, the media reported on these scammers; his grandmother was apologetic. However, Matt never quite recovered. Even his own family would believe anything negative where he was concerned. And Matt admitted to being a thief in the last line of this journal entry. Guilty of one crime; guilty of all? It's easy to believe that an addict would scam their own grandmother — and some would — but the assumption that all addicts are unprincipled criminals contradicts the importance of maintaining relationships with addicts while they struggle with their problems.

— Matt's mom

December 10, Thursday, 2009 (6.75/10)

Awoke at Cindy's. Was able to grab 5 more perks without any problems. Had a really good conversation with her. Aaron D. came to town today to make a trade, Vikes for weed. He hooked me up with $30.00 and a 16th of really good nugget. I also got my Valiums filled along with those Vikes. So I paid for my script and got weed with only 20 pills. This is a great way to offset my overall expenditures for my medicine, as well as not having to pay for smoke, too.

Got paid today. Was able to take care of all my bills, but also pay something to DOC on my back fees, pay 1 loan off, 1 loan down, as well as reimbursing John on alcohol and Don for his loan, and I also have extra for some much needed grocery shopping.

After the pharmacy and bank I went to Appleton with Aaron, smoked with him, my first blunt,[19] too, no less—a good trip. Got dropped off at Pat's and smoked some more with him before walking home in the bitter cold. I got quite intoxicated on several different substances today, and I have a good collection of dope to last me the next few days. A good day-off overall.

```
Intake: 2(25 mg hydroco, 50 mg oxyco oral,
          20 mg Valium or all…,…
        Smoked really great weed)


          Pay: $421.00
```

December 11, Friday, 2009 (7/10)

Today was a great day! Slept great, no nightmares (I've been having horrible nightmares for almost two weeks straight). I'm starting to

19. Blunt: street term for a cigarette that is hollowed out and refilled with marijuana to avoid detection.

really like Valium plus smoking weed because I can actually enjoy it without negative effects. I think that Valium in weed is really a swell combination. I didn't even take any Valium tonight! Didn't feel the need to!

Stevie said she is coming to visit on Sunday. I don't quite know for sure, but I think she has a thing for me. We'll see if she wants to spend the night. If not, well it's going to be nice to see her just as friends, also. I wonder if she looks the same?

A lot of substances today.

Intake: 3(20 mg diazepam, 50 mg hydroco, smoked x 2)

DECEMBER 12, SATURDAY, 2009 (6/10)

Today was another nice day. Andrea smoked with me and took me to Cash in a Flash to pay my note. I was *sooo* fucked up on that trip! Ha! Came home and became catatonic for a bit. Those Valiums, wow, they just make everything a lot better as far is being high is concerned—not only that, but I feel far more confident at work, speaking with people, getting stuff done.

Work went really well too.

Intake: 4(35 mg diazepam, 30 mg hydroco, smoked)

DECEMBER 19, SATURDAY, 2009

I've had a major setback in my fight against drugs. This last week has been a blur of pills, needles, and pipes. I saw Stevie, she spent the night and we got high—must have been last Sunday. Since then I've just been smashed.

<u>Intake: Ø day 2, smoked</u>

This entry was written sloppy, like when Matt was doped up, but it says day 2.

— Matt's mom

DECEMBER 20, SUNDAY, 2009

STONED AND DRUNK.

FREE FALL, SUICIDAL

AND DEPRESSED.

NEED TO MOVE FORWARD

Get out

Want out

Need

Need

<u>[sic]Intaroke: Ø day 3</u>

Smoked and drunk

December 21, Monday, 2009 (5/10)

Boring day, except that I made my way to Cindy's because I was so depressed. She took pity on me and gave me 5 perks, which changed and brightened my day.

I'm coming to discover how deeply addicted to opiates I am, no matter how many sober days I put together I always end up falling apart and moving backwards. I need to approach it from a better direction I think. Somehow I really need out.

The winter is so very cold. I cannot wait until it ends.

<u>Intake: 50 mg oxyco oral</u>

December 22, Tuesday, 2009 (5.5/10)

Today, shot down on a raise at work. I asked for a raise a week ago, and today I was told "No; economy is bad. Obama will kill us with healthcare taxes." Bullshit! They have more than enough money to pay me $9/ hour like they should for running that damn kitchen.

John has been in a good mood lately, but I have been "hiding" from him nonetheless. Don't really know why I have been avoiding him, but I do, and it isn't very healthy.

And Christmas will be depressing this year. I'm thinking about the end of the decade, and I've damned near wasted the whole thing!

Intake: Ø day 1

December 23, Wednesday, 2009 (6/10)

Found my red pen!! Great for journal entries that find me using opiates. I hope to use it not as much in the coming months and years.

Cindy gave me quite a scare today. I was supposed to go to do her floors for her today; when I called Lenny answered and told me he was rushing Cindy to the hospital because he thought she was having a stroke. I got super worried, but it turned out later that she merely had a bad reaction to a new medication she was given for headaches, Topamax, or something like that.

The other day Cindy told me that April had been arrested and would be in jail for a while. From what I've gathered she got all fucked up (opiates) and missed a corner, took her car into the ditch. It seems she wasn't injured too badly, but police arrived and she was arrested. She most likely has new charges as well as facing a revocation and going back to prison for some more of her sentence.

It's really a damn shame; she is too beautiful to be such a horrible junkie. She already has done two years in prison, and she is facing a lot more time. I bet that she will be sitting in county for a long time, and if they don't send her back to prison, she will most likely be transferred to a very secure in-patient treatment for more than a few months. Sad, sad tale. I've rarely met anyone with this bad of a habit as she has. It's just such a severe drug problem, incredible.

I hope that my fate is never the same. I run the same risks for fucking around with dope like I do, but right now my habit barely compares with anything "problematic," at least not socially, not yet anyways. I wish I had never tasted opiates, that I could simply put down the needle forever, but it's proving to be so very hard; still I fight, still a struggle, one day I will win!

I got my Vikes filled today, probably the last refill I'll get on those until my doctor comes back from Florida, and I don't know when that will be. I have a very powerful lust for opiates lately, more than is normal for the past few months. I was (and still am) furiously trying to find something that I can inject; that's what I'm looking for tonight and all day tomorrow. I have the cash. It's only a matter of time now until someone connects with some "shotgun shells," as I like to call them. Still don't know what I'm doing for Christmas. It's either with Cindy and her family or alone with my pills. I'd almost rather be fucked up alone, we'll see.

```
Intake: 1(95 mg hydroco, smoked)
```

December 24, Thursday, 2009 (6.3/10) Christmas Eve

A challenging and mixed day that ended much better than it began. Firstly, the damn weather is just obscenely terrible. Terrible. First sleet, then snow, and now DRIVING RAIN! Just like a spring mixed winter storm, not a deep December day. Mere hours into an official winter type of storm.

My mother woke me up with a phone call at 9:00 AM. I had gotten to sleep late, sometime around 4:00 AM, so I was sorry to have lost the extra hour of sleep. Mom sounded fine, brimming with her old energy, happy sounding—but also very stressed between work, Dick, the kids, the animals … the alcohol, the fights, which I hope have ended, God willing.

The talk with Dick bothered me quite a bit. He is very depressed. They have him on damn Zoloft and Xanax, both brain disabling drugs—he tells me he wasn't depressed before taking those drugs, but now, roughly 6 months later, he is SO depressed he can hardly bring himself to do anything. He even mentioned suicide to me in a fairly serious manner. He has been thinking about it. His cardiologist has him on it, not even a psych doctor! There has been no one monitoring his descent into depression and therefore madness. I stressed very much that he's got to get into a good doctor ASAP. I told mom also. Cindy is just as worried as I am and promised to speak FRANKLY and in private with Dick at the family Christmas party on Saturday.

I went to work thinking I would be doing 3 easy and slow hours working with Pat—instead we got hit and in EPIC fashion, just the two of us. Nick, the third guy that was supposed to be working, CALLED IN early in the morning. I was cursing that douche bag's name all day long, openly calling for his termination, and I think I'll be able to tell him to his face just how I feel when I see him on Saturday. We had people that could have easily worked that shift given prior notice, but no, this guy just shrugs off all responsibility, leaving Pat and I for hours to dance in the flames; Nita could hardly help, she was busy up front I guess. I got SO stressed because Pat doesn't know the dinner menu, so he struggles with speed on tickets. Things were coming out so slow, and cold at times. Jeez!

I ate 10 Vicodin at roughly 10:00 AM. That shit made me so sick, I was throwing up here at the house and at Cindy's place. I walked to her place to get 1 of my Valium back from her, which did ease my stomach. Stopped at Joey's place to check the situation, bought a bag of shwag weed, which isn't so bad. I ended up scoring a 40 mg oxy from Joe, easy drug deal, and now I feel quite great, having only paid $20 for the OC 40 mg.

```
Intake: 2(40 mg oxyco IV, 50 mg hydroco,
        10 mg Valium, smoked)
```

December 25, Friday, 2009 (5/10)

Went to Cindy's and Lenny's place this morning, spent about 2 hours there and then I came home. John was gone. I really did nothing—I sat on the couch for a good 10 hours or so, eating Vicodin and smoking weed, just watching TV. No family, no friends, nothing this year.

I'm getting lonelier by the day. More depressed from riding this dark rollercoaster of drugs in solitude. I'm really angry at work now because I didn't receive my raise. Now I'm getting bitter and almost hateful about the entire situation. I did not work today— but lately I've been either alone or at work, a terrible combination considering that I'm not working toward anything in particular at the moment. It feels like this will go on forever.

Intake: 3(90 mg hydroco, smoked)

December 26, Saturday, 2009 (4/10)

Burned 80 more dollars today on fucking Oxycontin. Sound familiar by now? A habit that will not break. I rely on my opiates now too much for all my mental and emotional escape.

I worked today. It was slow, but one thing did happen—I had Andrea lying to me about some bullshit. I guess she doesn't want to burn me any more smokes—interesting considering I give her all types of Vikes just so she will hook me up with smokes at work. It seems to me that she has been doing nothing except using me. I keep waiting for some type of return. She does officially owe me, for all type and manner of things I have given her in the past, but she refuses to ever front out anything of her own. I've grown tired of this. I think that I will hang out less with her, if not completely quit hanging out with her because of her two-faced nature.

Broken and alone now. I do not want to continue like this, but I haven't any escape.

Intake: 4(85 mg hydroco, 80 mg oxyco IV)

December 27, Sunday, 2009 (4.5/10)

Rob stopped by today... out of the blue on his way back from Christmas and Watertown with his grandparents. It was nice to see him, but also a little melancholic as is the case lately when I see old friends.

I have begun again to sink into a hopeless feeling of depression. Perhaps it is the holidays, but I feel very sad lately. Maybe it is because I halted the amitriptyline last week and only began to take it again a few days ago.

It's mostly a feeling of hopelessness when I think about the future. I hope I can get out of this hole.

Took my last Vikes today. No refills left and I think the doc is gone till spring.

Intake: 50 mg hydroco , smoked

December 28, Monday, 2009 (4ish/10)

Had a bad day at work today. Elta was shooting me dirty looks and everything. Very busy, *forte* busy, just outrageous amount of business for a Monday night. Let's hope it's nothing more, I do not need this.

The rest of the day on both sides was alright. Don't know whether it was the TCA's or vitamins. A little depressed still, but this is beginning to break. Looks like a pretty long run ahead without scripts. Probably 2 or 3 months, we'll see. I would like to focus on paying back bills and not on drugs, but it's hard with or without scripts. I should do fine, it's almost 2010 after all, a lot of work to do to get normal and successful, upright and mobile.

Intake: Ø Day 1, smoked

December 29, Tuesday, 2009 (5.5/10)

Got pulled into the office and talked to for like a good 30 minutes a day. Absurd, "wants to see more leadership" nonsense. Just out of touch. Took all remarks under advisement as to change my actions so as to keep my fucking job. $8.00 per hour buys hours upon hours of a man's soul, his youth.

Bought a bag for New Year's. Knocked aside loan payment, late charges will ensue. Shit.

Marked withdrawal today, stomach, cramps, everything. Took some vitamins, should improve from tomorrow on.

Intake: Ø day 2, smoked

December 30, Wednesday, 2009 (3/10)

Got very sick today, some type of stomach flu early this morning, fever, muscle aches, etc. Stayed indoors all day, depressing, just laid around smoking dope and resting. Missed a shift at work for only the second time, so feverish.

Intake: Ø day 3, smoked all day

December 31, Thursday, 2009 (3.5/10)

Woke up today feeling well enough, still a little sore but fever was gone, still felt a little exhausted but better.

Stayed inside house for second day in a row. This somehow compounded the effects of cold in winter on a man's mind. I was deeply depressed most of the day, this house seeming more like a prison at the moment.

I have been ruminating, of course, about the year 2009. To me, offhand, I would say it was a "bad" year, the later 6 months more difficult than the first 6. We lost Carol in late May; this seems to be the defining point of the year —Dave's alone, Carol is gone, and to me this feels like a real tragedy. Last year at this time I was still with Cindy and Lenny. Now I'm free. I have a slightly better job than I did last year, but I feel like I make less. I'm on some sort of a slight uphill pace that I wish to build on in 2010.

<u>Intake: Ø day 4, smoked</u>

JANUARY, 2010

Woke up, felt almost completely better from my little flu, although today I felt very depressed and suffered from what I like to call "emotional friction." It was a spiritual tension, almost like I had [experienced] back in jail. I went to Cindy's early afternoon; her family was having a New Year's get together. I ate well, and was generally content, except for the emotional friction and moderate depression.

It's January again, already I mean! I hate winter, hate the cold, and get generally more depressed as winter winds on. I come out of it around spring, jump right back to life. Looking forward to that is sometimes what keeps me going on the really bad days.

I'm in a sobriety jungle. My check this week won't be much, already gone in fact, and I'm dead out of refills. We'll see where this leads. It usually leads to periods of stable moods and other good things.

These are indeed dark days, and I'm very down.

Intake: Ø day 5, smoked

I remember this day, too. It started out as a typical New Year's Day: ham, scalloped potatoes, and pie. It ended with a 911 call.

Dick was being typical: jokey followed by sharply critical, but I still pulled off dinner and spent time helping the girls (ages 11 and 12) rearrange their rooms. After they went to bed, I sat in the kitchen doing dishes and trying to visit with Dick. I remember so clearly how the conversation took a sudden turn.

"So, how long are you going to keep all your money to yourself? As my wife, you have to support me (like the Bible says), and my heart is too weak to work."

"Why don't you get a job at the local grocery store? You could at least get some sort of income. I'm not putting you back on my checking — no way — done with that whole noise."

"Are you kidding! Are you going to pay for gas?" He went on and on about how beneath him a minimum wage job was, how he tried so hard to find something in construction, and how he couldn't keep up with a crew due to his health, all while puffing cigarettes and drinking whiskey.

"Dick, I work. I am not about to give you what I earn. I already pay all the bills, including food. All you do with money is go to the bar."

"You are such a selfish bitch! I deserve to get paid for all I do around here, and big fucking deal if I drink. I drink because I can't live with a bitch like you. You couldn't live without me, anyway. Who filled the porch with wood, huh?"

"The girls did." [Silence] "I can't afford to pay for a main-tenance man. What I need help with is cooking and cleaning. How about you mop the floors once in a while?"

"You expect me to do woman's work?" At this point he went off on how I was a ball snatcher, was taking advantage of his cabinet making, and was generally just a stupid cunt.

I couldn't take it anymore and flatly told him that I was going to file for a divorce if he didn't get a job. The room sat silent. I finished washing the dishes and noticed the fire needed stoking, so I walked to the back door, just behind where he was sitting watching TV and smoking.

Walking into 30° below zero weather with only wool socks on, I stepped onto the back porch with one foot and left one for holding the screen door open. I felt a shove and the door closed. Dick said, "This is my house; you get out."

My instincts kicked in and I pushed with all my strength against the door. We struggled for several minutes until I was able to get my fingers through the crack to the interior door. With raging anger I threw my shoulder into the door and Dick went flying. He hit the floor after first hitting the edge of the kitchen table. He began screaming that this was his house and I needed to get out.

I was back in at this point but Dick would not give up. He came at me again. This time I was ready and balled up my little fist and struck him right on the side of the cheek, making his glasses fly. We struggled for a minute. He searched around for his glasses on the floor and then, grabbing his whiskey and cigarettes, he retreated to the living room.

I sat fuming at the kitchen table. I began to rant. "This is *my* house. I built it! I paid for it! Your piddly little additions over the last 2 years were all funded by me, and you couldn't even begin to pay half the expenses if I paid you $25 an hour for what you'd done. You're a bully, a drunk, and a user. I don't care if divorce is a sin; I can't take this anymore! You were actually willing to kick me out of my own house in this weather?! You are one sick asshole!"

"You can't hit me and get away with it! You abused me, and I know the law. I'm calling the police!" At which point he did. He actually called 911 and reported that I punched him. What a joke!

They arrived, interviewed me, looked at him for bruises, of which there were none, and told him he had to leave the house. This is standard protocol for domestic violence calls, I guess.

He was asked to either find a place to stay or go to the station, as he was obviously drunk and I wasn't, and he was obviously fine, and I showed signs of a struggle. Stupid me. I told the cops he could stay in the shop and I would keep my doors locked. I should have just let him suffer.

I was so busy trying to battle this situation that my radar was off. My son sat several hours away in deep darkness and depression. If I had only known that the same officer who replied to this 911 call would come to my house again in September bearing a little slip of paper with Matthew's name and the coroner's number.

Regretfully,

— Matt's mom

January 2, Saturday, 2010 (5/10)

Wow, it's really a new year, already, again, etc. Work was quite busy— gallery walk or some such. Ran the dishwashers out of pans twice, no three times—at one point sending Kevin to wash me some damn pans. I'm really fast, but it's next to impossible to run a crew of people and cook a Saturday night FORTE grill ..., 5000 fajitas ran me out of everything I had. Ha ha ha!

Got a card in the mail today from my mom; it was a Christmas card that Aunt Luanne sent in absentia for grandma, who isn't doing well. I can't help but think that this might be the last $50 or card I ever get from her. I have $44.00 left (having purchased one pack of smokes), and I wish I didn't feel so compelled to spend it on dope—but the dope is absolutely mesmerizing; it [overpowers] even 1000 Christmas cards. I hate it.

Really need to focus on getting something to probation this and next month. Need off; need out.

Intake: Ø day 6, smoked

JANUARY 3, SUNDAY, 2010 (4/10)

Sat around today except for a quick trip to Citgo for a coffee this morning (it was bitterly cold outside). Bored as hell all day long.

Depression seems to be lifting, except I still retain the normal dreary winter spirit. Other than that I feel normal. I wonder sometimes if my depression was due to the holiday season this time around, or is it so obviously drugs? Am I that shut down to think that anything else could possibly be the matter?!

Going to try getting high tomorrow. I have some prospects.

Intake: Ø day 7, smoked

JANUARY 4, MONDAY, 2010 (5.5/10)

I hate the way I waste fucking money. Today I paid $40 for 60 mg of cold-water morphine, overpriced bullshit—it's all overpriced, worthless—I would be better off just throwing the money down the gutter.

I'd be healthy and strong. I feel absolutely terrible when I buy dope, just sad and ashamed of myself. I really need to quit spending money like this. Even if I can't quit, I need to quit dropping cash on this stupid game. Although this whole "I need to quit" talk is a predominant theme throughout my journal, I haven't put control down like I used to, haven't made as much progress at all. My goals need to be a realized. I cannot afford to waste a second more.

Goals for January:

1. Put at least $60 to[ward] probation, try for $100.
2. Spend no more than $40 on outside dope for rest of month.
3. Work as many hours down as possible; never say "No" to more hours.
4. Ten applications to new job prospects; land at least an interview.
5. A good date would be nice

IN fact, I have just made plans with Brandy W to do some type of date this week. She graduated from Crandon High, and is 2 years younger than me. She knows my mother, of course, from school. Said some nice things about my mom on Facebook tonight. I had to confess to her when she first added me on Facebook that I couldn't recall ever really meeting her. She said the same thing! Ha! So, I think she may have a "thing" for me. I hope it pans out for once.

I've been spurned sexually 4 times this year! Really makes one feel like a big ugly monster. Women just don't dig a poor, junkie pedestrian who doesn't own a car or drive. My personality has changed, too. There's something either inside or outside that drives women away from me, and it makes me feel really bad, lost self-esteem. I can hardly approach a woman to engage in anything romantic. It just kills me. Valium helps with this, but that too is a fine line: if I take too much, I may get out of line and make an ass out of myself. I'll have some Valium when I meet Brandy; I'll take just enough to ensure that I am loose without being too loose. It will be a lot of fun. She sounds very lonely, as I am. It should be a good chance to score—the last time I had sex was in April or May of 2007! Almost 3 years without sex, and it really just stinks.

Follow your January goals Matt. Do it to it.

Intake: 1(60 mg morphine IV, smoked)

January 5, Tuesday, 2010 (5.5/10)

I dreamed that I was everywhere last night, one of my best and strangest dreams ever. First, I was camping or something on a school field trip with Rob, but we were in Colorado, back home. This part of the dream is very vague, but it ended with me returning home to Eagle River, to my grandma's old home on Townline Rd.

I had my cousin Brian's old black Silverado, which I loved. It was my birthday and he was giving the truck to me! Alta was there, cooking in the basement, as was the rest of my family. I next walked to Twelve Pines. Upon entering the door I saw that both Paulina and Jenny were bartending. I just about fell over when I saw Paulina, but she paid me little attention. She had short blond hair. Nita was working the kitchen at Twelve Pines. I next went outside with Paula, but I couldn't get her to talk to me. At one point both Paula and Jenny were riding together on a mini crotch-rocket[20]. I had followed Paula through the bar, but by the time we reached the other exit she transfigured into a young boy. When I patted this youngster on the back, he screamed not to touch him.

Next I tried walking back into Twelve Pines, but it had transfigured into a mile-long dining table with many guests. The setting was now cave-like and red, and had a big sign that said "HELL." I could see a place set for me, but I turned and ran. The last words I heard were: "YOU NEVER SPURN THE SPOON AT HELL'S DINER." I could recognize everyone at the table, but I ran out.

Next I was in a large library with many stories and many tiers— staffed by very old women. The sign leading to it said "HEAVEN." I remember feeling that this was where I belonged, so I walked on. I appeared again at grandma's house. Brian was out front with

20. A fast motorcycle

the black Silverado, discussing with Luanne why he was giving me this truck.

He took me next for a ride on highway 70 towards home. I was initially driving; traffic was heavy because it was 4th of July weekend. We were going highway speeds, but every time we hit even a small bump the truck would bounce all over until Brian took control and drove. The dream ended with Brian and me driving on the freeway towards Wausau.

Now I'm home from work, and parts of the dream are still with me, especially the scene in Twelve Pines with Jen and Paula. I have very rarely had dreams that are as clear as this one. I know what caused it, too. Lately I have been taking that TCA right along with whatever other drugs I happen upon. Last night the mixture of 60 mg plus 80ish mg of amitriptyline took me to a new level. I wonder if this is repeatable. I fear, however, that I could end up having a really bad trip, a nightmare of some sort. The TCA by itself has given me nightmares, sometimes for days on end. I was pushed into a position of not taking it, and not sleeping or taking it, falling asleep and finding myself trapped in another nightmare. Nightmares aside, I really need my sleep, so I always take my big red pill. I feel that it evens me out, perhaps by dulling the emotions, but I'm not quite sure.

Went to the food pantry today, God bless the help. Lenny gave me the ride. Cindy is in the throes of withdrawal. She is trying to get off of it (the Percocet) in the hopes that she may alleviate her chronic headaches or find out if the oxyco is making them happen at least. She looked pretty dope sick when I was over, admitting to me all the symptoms characteristic of AS. I gave her some insight into what she was going to go through, offering as much support as possible. I wonder if she can do it. She has been on those perks for a good 9 months solid, 40 to 60 mg per day—that's quite a habit to break.[21]

Cindy also told me about Kelly, that she is getting pretty pissed at her because she has been such a "bitch" (Cindy's words). She was supposed to come down and visit, maybe keep Cindy company, but she never called Cindy back! Kell missed both Thanksgiving and Christmas. Cindy told me she thinks Kell is on drugs, meaning something other than just the usual MJ, which is a constant with Kell. I wondered too, but I haven't even spoken to her in almost 2 months, haven't spent any real time with her since the end of September. I haven't the foggiest idea what's up in her world. I do not think she would get into anything else, but I do not know her very well. I'm sure we'll find out one day.

Intake: Ø day 1

---

21. "Food pantry"– a free grocery bank for those who financially qualify/.

January 6, Wednesday, 2010 (5/10)

Came into work 30 minutes early and talked to Elta today about food quality. Apparently, we're burning food off the grill. New method; problem solved, I think (and hope). Karl was in today, useless, stoned off his ass. He got pulled in by Elta and apparently he lied right to her face about still being on paper. Little scumbag, not for lying so much as just being useless…. I'm going to have to rectify the situation.

Another cold January day. Spring, I want spring!

Intake: Ø day 2

January 7, Thursday, 2010 (6.5/10)

Today was a really good day. Had the day off, payday, and I spent time with good friends. First, I went to Pat's place, hung out, had a quick smoke—then it was off to the Flats to pick up another dismal check that was only worth $269 today. (Almost forgot to mention that the weather was terrible today—four inches of snow that was blowing with heavy gusts. Had to wear my good Columbia snow boots, but walking was in 28° F weather, so not "bitter cold.") -Andrea and Danny gave me a ride to Cash in a Flash and Walmart to pick up my prescriptions. Fun drive. Andrea was pissing me off not too long ago, but I think she noticed this and started treating me like a friend again. From there it was back to Pat's and then up to Cindy's place. Spent some time with her. She seems to be doing a lot better. She gave me 3 perks, not sure if she meant to give me that. I only asked for 2, and when I checked the bottle to get her some it didn't look like she had a lot to share. Maybe it was because I gave her 3 Valiums?

Anyways, after that I went to Joey's. Bought/traded for 10 x 5 mg oxy IR's. They shoot well enough I guess. Tomorrow I'll buy a real 20 OC.

Came home and smoked and snorted with Pat, Alicia, and Andrea. Got baked and took more vals and oxys.

A good day of drug bliss.

```
Intake: oxyco 25 mg IV, oxyco 37.5 mg oral,
Valium 20 mg snort , smoked 2 times.
```

January 8, Friday, 2010 (3/10)

Today was a horrible day. Started out well enough, being able to score a bunch of oxy IR 5 mg, shootable no less. I'm also powering through the Valium, which I can tell is destabilizing my personality quite a bit.

Work has become absolutely unmanageable. I can't seem to do anything right these few days. Elta is all over me for stupid shit, I'm getting bitter, and I can't seem to maintain anything in my mind, which would probably be the case regardless of my Valium intake—I'm just so angry, and anger keeps me from thinking straight.

I need to find another job ASAP. Today I'm going to McDonald's and Pizza Hut to fill out apps. McDonald's sounds promising for sure!

Intake: 40 mg oxyco IV, 30 mg Valium oral

January 9, Saturday, 2010 (3.5/10)

Intake: 50 mg oxyco IV, Valium

January 10, Sunday, 2010 (3.5/10)

A mixed day today. I put in two applications for McDonald's and also for Pizza Hut, so made progress on those goals, but also chased drugs yesterday and today. Took out more loans to pay for drugs yesterday, bad! I'm in a hole, another damn freefall from which there is no escape. Very depressed today. I have no self-control.

I want an end to the emotional suffering: death seems to be an option, as it seems less possible to climb out of this hole that I am in. My determination seems wrecked, my will broken. Just no way out at all it seems for my own mind, self-destructive traits. No money, dreams seem to die more every day as I move on and on into the abyss. Bright spots swallowed up into darkness.

Change, I need change.

Get off probation. Get off probation.

```
Intake: 50 mg Valium, 5 mg oxyco IV
```

January 13, Wednesday, 2010 (8.5/10)

Got a call early this morning from Mr. Matthew D. He finally came to see me! After not seeing him for almost 4 years, it was an incredible thrill. He took me to IHOP for breakfast and then took me to Appleton to his beautiful house. Man, it was amazing to see him, and to see how well he was doing. He deserves everything he has. He worked so hard for all of it. Jenny, his wife, was looking wonderful, as well. Matt really has it all. They're trying for a kid now. Man how much time flies by.

I was moved to tears when he offered me money. I didn't accept of course, but it was such a kind gesture. We plan to hang out again next week. We also spoke on the phone with Janessa G. We may travel to Madison to visit her one of these days.

Seeing Matt gave me a feeling of empowerment, a feeling that I could overcome my drug use and be right up there with him. If I keep up with him, it may be the kind of friendship that I can build on to get myself out.

I'm so glad we're reconnected.

Intake: Ø day 1

Relationships are critically important to those trapped in addictions. Matt was not one to refuse money, but this was different. This was someone who saw his desperate need, which would cause anyone fighting for life to react with tears. How could Matt explain that he did not want the money at all, but wanted his friend's support and respect instead? His best friend from high school (also named Matt) could see the decline and showed his honest concern; he could not see how his friendship and aid would give his old friend hope and acceptance. Addicts do have principles; these are based on a couple of things in my opinion — survival and relationships. When those they meet offer a true relationship, different survival instincts kick in that trump the need for food or a fix.

— Matt's mom

January 14, Thursday, 2010 (5.5/10)

I think I may be coming down with something again. I slept for 13 hours, naturally, no less, and awoke with phlegm in my nostrils and throat. Strange rash by my injecting site. Hope I didn't give myself anything.

Things at work are strange. We have a big meeting coming up the first week of February. Sounds really important. Hope nothing bad happens. I think work is going well for me personally, but I never can tell what they are thinking about me for real. I hope I can find another job here soon, but my record keeps holding me back.

Need to keep on the good path. Get out. Get out.

<u>Intake: Ø day 2</u>

January 15, Friday, 2010 (5/10)

Normal day; nothing gained, nothing lost. January is half over, thankfully. No drugs, thankfully.

Got an email from mom today. Sounds like things are going really crazy back home. Dick is sinking into alcoholism, and I know mom is drinking, too, but I believe (from what little knowledge I have) that Dick is a lot worse than my mother. I think the kids are suffering because of this shit. I can't do anything but sit by and watch. I don't know what's going to happen next. I'm quite scared.

I'm also in the process of coming to terms with cutting my ties with Paulina completely. It should happen sometime within the next week. It's part of my plan for putting the past away. Is this the correct move? I wonder.

Intake: Ø day 3

I remember this point in my life clearly — deeply depressed, deeply ashamed. Before meeting Dick I drank only occasionally and only with friends, but at this point I poured a drink as soon as supper dishes were done, or I went to the local tavern to escape my puddle of a husband. I had never seen anything like it before. By the time I arrived home from work he would already be drunk, angry, and violent. The kids learned to hide in their rooms, and I just tried to play with the 5 new puppies in the kennel room. However, there was no escape. In order to continue taunting me, Dick would even crawl into the kennel room with the puppies and curl up right in all their feces. If I tried to move him, he would strike out. If I left him there, he would eventually pass out, but the room was easily visible from the main house, and the sight of dog shit on his face and body made me retch.

Strange that I turned to alcohol myself, but I felt dazed and as if I were sleep walking through a nightmare. Before my closest sister died in May of the previous year, I spent at least six months crying myself to sleep, so her death compounded my ability to deal with my new and consistently drunk husband. I didn't know how to escape this reality. I didn't want to cry anymore. I didn't want to be there. I didn't care about myself anymore. Nothing I did helped, so I became apathetic, not caring about much of anything. And so the cycle began of loss of control followed by loss of loved one followed by loss of self. I didn't think it could get any worse. Little did I know the worst was yet to come.

— Matt's mom

JANUARY 16, SATURDAY, 2010 (5/10)

Another day, and that's all—just another day. I worked 6 hours, and that totals me out at just over 35 for the week, a good week, and that's terrible. I should be working twice that, getting up and out of this damnable hole.

I wonder sometimes (most times) if this is worth anything, life in general. I haven't made the most of mine, whereas I see so many of my generation making a great time out of it. But what exactly is a "great time" actually is hard to explain. I suppose I could be happy as a peach right now, despite my financial and social situation, if I just had the right mindset, but I know that I'M NOT DOING WHAT I SHOULD BE DOING. Am I really paralyzed? No. I have the power to do it; I just need to do it.

I wonder what dreams I will have tonight?

Intake: Ø day 4, a moderate drink

JANUARY 17, SUNDAY, 2010 (5.5/10)

Went to church with Cindy tonight. She gave me a single perk, nice.

Intake: 10 mg oxyco oral

THE PREACHER

(FROM MATTHEW'S FACEBOOK PAGE, DATE UNKNOWN)

Seven or eight years ago I was still a teen, and as such I was still living under the rule of my mother, who at that time was a deeply religious woman and had aspirations for me to follow the faith as well. To this aim I was sent to a Pentecostal church camp in a rural area of Portage County for two weeks (I know; sounds pretty lame). This camp was nice enough, not very flashy due to the fact that its budget was funded mostly by the offering plate. We had activities, fair grub, and a lot of prayer. So far this scene shapes up to be one easily forgotten behind many other memories of much higher impact and influence, except for something I saw that changed my life and the way I saw the world around me.

There was a fair spectrum of personalities there, but very few characters, and I mean characters only in the sense that you may see them in some fiction film or book perhaps. The one person I would identify as a real character was one of the preachers, who was from a congregation in Racine. The man's name escapes me, but he sticks out in my mind because of the fact that he was blind and not just legally blind—this man had zero vision in both of his eyes. Despite this (or perhaps in some small way because of it) he was somewhat of an overall leader at this Pentecostal camp.

One evening we were rushed out early from our six o'clock prayer service. At the time no one knew what was going on; it appeared to me that there was a young woman who had come to altar who was having some sort of a seizure. The group retreated across the football field to the main block of dorms about 150 yards away from the temple. As we stood outside we began to hear these terrible screams escaping the temple–horrible, shrill screams. The one thing that was remarkable about the screams was not the tone or person-ality of them so much as the volume–it was tremendous, bellowing even. I don't think then, or even today, that 5 people could have achieved such a volume. It was stunning, and it was probably the most terrifying thing I had heard up to that point in my life.

I wanted to investigate; the others did not for obvious reasons. I am skeptical of such things, and I was overwhelmed with curios-ity. I made my way across the grass and back to the temple; I went inside. The first thing I saw were perhaps 5 or 6 adults holding this girl down. This girl was not having a seizure, but what was it then? The blind preacher stood over her and the men holding her down. He was praying, quite loudly, but his words were drowned out, enveloped, by the still, shrill screams coming from the girl. At this point it didn't even seem that they were coming from her at all, but instead from all around, the center focused at her center. I was struck with the visuals of this thing unfolding before me. I was one of only perhaps 3 bystanders in the temple; one of the others informed me that the girl was possessed, and they were in the process of cleansing her of her demonic affliction. It made sense where nothing else did; it was the only answer to what I was seeing in front of my eyes.

The scene unfolded for about 30 minutes. During this time I saw feats of human strength from this girl who astounded me. She was able to un-seat and almost lift 3 men at once, with one arm, and she was maybe 130 pounds herself. I can't explain it.

When everything was over she walked past me and out of the temple, completely clear-eyed, completely collected, and her energy was different. I don't want to explain anymore for the fear of sounding like a fool—just realize that she had completely changed.

That blind preacher was the one symbol of that whole event, the whole duration of the camp even. I've thought back on this instance infrequently over the last 8 years. It proved something to me that I cannot deny to this day. I don't speak from a position of faith. On the contrary I have drifted far away from my faith, and have come to embrace other ways of living, but still, in all that I have seen and done in those 8 years nothing has unseated logically what I saw on that day.

Today I was riding the bus through the university and a blind man got on at one of the stops. I recognized him immediately as the preacher from that day. I had not seen nor heard anything about anyone else in the church for all those years. It was a real surprise.

I thought about approaching him, but I did not. I simply sat back and studied him, remembered him, and marveled at the way fate re-introduces people into our lives at times for which we cannot appreciate for their value until years later.

I wonder why I saw him today, I wonder why I saw him here, and I wonder why fate didn't bring me around to say a few words to him as we both rode on that bus to wherever life was taking us next.

January 18, Monday, 2010 (4/10)

Waking up depressed lately, trying to blame it on the winter blues.

Worked training a new guy; he seems nice. Let's hope I don't lose hours to him.

Intake: Ø day 1

January 19, Tuesday, 2010 (7.5/10)

Today started out really badly. I was feeling really down and so depressed, but a few things happened late in the day that made the date really exciting.

First, I noticed my last paycheck was short because it was at an hourly rate that was 75¢ lower than it should have been. I walked away from work with $40, a big plus considering it's 2 days until payday.

Next, I got a call while at work from Pizza Hut, where I had put an application in this last week. I'm almost sure it's for a job interview! It's what I've been waiting for. I'm really just excited about what this could mean. If I can get this job, and keep my job at Tortilla Flats, I could do anything! Ukraine, Poland become visible again to me. The end of my state supervision, my license back, a car, EVERYTHING IN THE NEXT 11 MONTHS.

I'm downright excited!

<u>Intake: Ø day 2</u>

Also, it seems Scott Brown won Ted Kennedy's senate seat tonight. Remarkable. Democrats are no longer "bulletproof." Exciting; it's all over AM radio.

JANUARY 20, WEDNESDAY, 2010

<u>Intake: Ø day 3, smoked</u>

JANUARY 21, THURSDAY, 2010

Smoked all day. Hung out with Pat. Got paid $421 today.

<u>Intake: Ø day 4, smoked</u>

JANUARY 22, FRIDAY, 2010

Got a second job today working at Pizza Hut. Great, really excited.
I start next Thursday.

Intake: 40 mg oxyco IV

JANUARY 23, SATURDAY, 2010

Intake: Ø day 1

JANUARY 24, SUNDAY, 2010 (5.5/10)

Things have taken a warm glow since I got that job at Pizza Hut.
Can't wait to start this upcoming Thursday.

Helped Pat with the cleanup of the upper unit at Jackson Street
apartment that I was at a few months back. Having nothing better
to do today, I brought a 12 pack over there with me. There is this
guy living in the lower unit now, obviously has some very severe
mental impairments. We invited him in for a beer. He brought out
the weed, so we just smoked and drank. I felt really queasy towards
my fifth or sixth BEAST. I hit the restroom and more or less lay on
the floor for a solid 20 minutes or so. During this time the guy drank

the last of the beers I had in the case, AND everyone's open drinks that were just lying around. Bogus. Came home and after that and just lay around. Seeing if the clinic refilled my Vikes for tomorrow morning. My mind is craving opiates badly lately. If I have to go pick those up I might as well buy a new red pen. I'll be needing it, unfortunately.

Intake: Ø day 2, smoked

January 25, Monday, 2010 (6/10)

Got a call this morning from McDonald's. Looks like they want to give me a job. Let's hope it bounces off my schedule. Let's hope it's morning work because that's what I want from them. Let Tortilla Flats or Pizza Hut be my second job. Let the money flow like the blood of my enemies, unquenched.

Today is also notable for being the slowest day I have ever worked at the Flats. It was very slow; never before have I seen this. Lonnie (the cool dishwasher who always brings an extra smoke for me) told me that last Thursday was legendarily slow. I think that jumping ship is a very good idea right about now. We'll see. I'm keeping every option very much open, to gain the most traction from what I do choose to do. Ukraine. I can almost see it.

Intake: Ø day 3

JANUARY 26, TUESDAY, 2010 (6.5/10)

Today was really swell. I woke up early (7 AM is early for me at this point) and got ready for my McDonald's interview. To my surprise the manager doing the interview was a girl about my age. She seemed smitten by me, but it could just be my imagination too; it usually is! Anyways, I got the job! My third nailed interview, second I mean, third job anyways. Happy happy joy joy!

I start [work at] McD's tomorrow with my orientation, and Thursday will be my first 12 hour plus day in almost 4 years. I'm back on track in a big way. Ukraine here I come!

Got my Vikes filled today too—I've been painted as a drug addict by the nurses there, but the doc's still on my side; have to see him come February 11, a different guy; I'm not concerned, I don't think I will get cut off, but if I do so what? All the better. I'll need to learn to live without it if I am to be a good English teacher in Ukraine.

Intake: 95 mg hydroco oral

JANUARY 27, WEDNESDAY, 2010 (6.5/10)

I'm standing on the precipice, I'm standing still before I start the 1000 mile walk that is my journey out of social darkness, my journey back to Europe, back to the very heart of my dreams.

It is made tomorrow. I work all 3 jobs tomorrow; McDonald's at 6AM until 1PM, Pizza Hut from 1:15 to around 4PM, and Tortilla Flats from 5 to 10. It will be a break-in for what I'm up against. I will cry my heart out when I see Irina and Ukraine. It is the mantelpiece that represents my total recovery.

Spent day with Pat and Alicia. Drank a few beers after my orientation at McDonald's. Maybe the last time I'll be able to do that for a while if I get in too deep with my hours.

Intake: 50 mg hydroco oral, smoked

[Written on spiral notebook divider page]

To Find: (my priorities) 1/28/2010
1.   LOVE: Would love to love a woman. End lonely. Best in life.
2.   Peace: Through education and a decent career. Peace in life means hard work, as far as my knowledge of the situation goes at age 24.
3.   Love.

January 28, Thursday, 2010 (6/10)

My first long day since 2006 today! Took a very cold and windy walk to work at 5:40 AM in the dark, and then 12 hours at the new 2 jobs plus the Flats.

A new strange energy I feel.

Need to realize that I go to Ukraine in search of love. From love comes peace.

Keep going Matt! Keep going!

Intake: 50 mg hydroco oral, smoked

JANUARY 29, FRIDAY, 2010 (7.3/10)

Great day today! Started my day by waking up at 4 AM for the longest "on the clock" day that I've had since 2006. Today I worked an incredible 14.5 hours; that's what I actually got paid for! Started work it 5 AM at McDonald's. My second day, my coworkers tell me I'm picking up quite quickly! Great. I feel like I am, too. I like McDonald's so far. The people I work with are nice, varied, and the days go by quickly. It's because it is so fast paced there. You are just always moving.

Tortilla Flats is also going better. Trish is digging her own grave! Just last week Nita suggested to me that she may fire Trish for all the bullshit she's been perpetuating lately.

After work I saw Sam (dealer Sam). She looked pretty good to me physically, petite frame, lightweight. She's single, and looks pretty good, but she's way into oxys, which means I know all about the sad story behind those pretty eyes. I don't care anymore; tomorrow night I mean to have her over and try my best to score. I'm desperate for the plain touch of a woman, just anything. Talking to Rose I notice how much I long for certain sweet tones in a woman's voice, one that would be my woman's voice touching my soul, bringing out the best of my personality.

Traded 20 of those nearly useless Vikes for 40 mg oxy, and shot that—best thing in the world, those shots.

Intake: 40 mg oxy IV, smoked, 60 mg hydroco oral

January 30, Saturday, 2010 (5.5/10)

Music is emotional states articulated.

Another decent day. Having this new work has brought me a sense of confidence that I have lacked the last 3 years or so. I am once against consumed by my dreams, which will now come true this year as long as I can keep working, keep moving and making this money. This week's paycheck will be the end of Cash in a Flash I think; after that it will be rent for the month, and then March will be the end of probation, April will see my license back, and after that all my money will go towards Ukraine. I'm thinking that I will be going in August, make the start of semester, and become an

English teacher there—I'm looking at staying an entire year—this is the new plan.

Keep moving; this will be the start of a very great period in my life if I can just keep up this pace.

Intake: 40 mg hydroco oral, smoked

JANUARY 31, SUNDAY, 2010 (5/10)

What is death, symbolically? Broken down to its base constituents, death is the past.

Day off today. I dread days off in a way, seem born and depressing. No one was home when I called. I took my last 8 Vikes, drank a few Highlifes, and smoked dope.

January is mercifully over in about 2 hours. The dreaded month is gone! It really dragged on, slower than December, very slow. The last hard 28 days starts tomorrow: February, then it's done.

Intake: 40 mg hydroco oral, smoked

FEBRUARY, 2010

Spent 12 hours and 45 minutes on the clock today, great for me.

I see I finally have got Fabrizio on Facebook! Talk about a blast from the past! It's going to be amazing to talk with him, see what he's been up to all these years.

```
Intake: Ø day 1, smoked
```

Fabrizio — truly a blast from my past, too. I never really explained to Matthew why I broke up with this longtime boyfriend. Until reading this I never really wanted to admit it myself, but I was attracted to addicts.

Fabrizio was a chef in a north woods kitchen where I worked. He escaped Italy and a heroin addiction by immigrating to the United States. I was a young mother going to college. Preparing to study overseas, I was swayed by our romance, and he talked me into going to Italy instead of Spain. Some may say I was attracted to his foreign accent, but now I realize I was attracted to addiction. What else could it be?

Though I only drank lightly and socially, never used drugs, and was only a witness to illicit anything, Matthew's father,

Mark, was a prescription pill addict turned alcoholic. We married to give Matthew a name, which was the custom for unwed mothers. We divorced the following year due to his alcoholism. Young and adequately pretty, I could have easily accepted advances from other than Matthew's father or his successor. Yet I was drawn to Mark, Fabrizio, and in the end, Dick. What was it about these men? Who can truly understand the human mind and its choice making schematic? Somehow I was wired for codependence. Do I have a dreaded disease? Was Fabri also diseased? Maybe I don't have the necessary immunity to fight this type of infection?

Fabrizio and I never married due to his addictive tendencies: other women and drugs. However, we remained together for almost 7 years as I hoped he would settle down and become dependable. Our breakup was final for me due to one too many bobby pins found in his sheets (it smelled of Channel #5, which I don't wear), too many issues with money, and too many concerns about my future with someone who couldn't step foot into Italy or a big city without looking for a heroin connection. But, Fab still came by to visit Matthew, to take him hunting and mountain climbing, and to let the boy know he loved him though his mom had moved on.

I never told Matt about the heroin issue. Fabrizio came to visit me at school in Italy. Matt was at pre-school and needed picking up. After their late return, I hurried to prepare Matt for dinner, and I found a syringe in his little backpack. Both of Fab's parents were witness to my finding, yet they oddly refused to believe what they saw. They denied that it was in my hand as I looked at the group standing on the terrace. Fabrizio even admitted he was late because he was "finding old friends." They were ashamed to the point of absolute denial.

I guess I denied Matt had a serious problem just like them. Even though I clicked my tongue at them for such insanity, I was just as insane in later years. Like them, I thought that any evidence of past issues was just ghosts — not real, not able to do anything except haunt the present during hours of darkness. However, addiction is not shameful. It is all too common, all too cliché. It's not the ghostly footsteps we imagine down the hall; it's the family photo, the family tree, the royal hemophilia gene that passes generation to generation even though we try to stop the bleeding and continue to forge alliances and find a cure for our good names. It is a reality in every family, every last one.

Addiction discussion belongs at dinner tables and not in secret file cabinets. We can't shave it off our legs, color it with dye, touch it up with Photoshop, or dignify it by calling it a disease. It's not a disease. We are not born defective just because we are sensitive to emotional or mental pain and find a quick relief that removes us from the task of healing. It's what each of us will experience under the right conditions and with the right ingredients. It's not even an epidemic, as the media calls it — a medical term used for the spread of something people can catch or contract. People don't catch drugs or alcohol. It's more like a market trend, a sales explosion, a capitalist response. It's just people exchanging goods for services. Bad people just take advantage of the weakest.

People are emotional creatures and as such crumble under emotional pressure. People bleed when they get cut; but some bleed and bleed due to a stronger heart pumping through a wound that refuses to close. Fabrizio lost his brother to an accident, which caused many emotional wounds in the family. Who is to say if he had the dreaded "gene" or not? Matthew's father suffered when his own father numbed the stress of losing his fortune by turning to alcohol, and Mark became a pill addict as a teen. My own father broke his spine and got addicted to codeine due to the continual pain. I didn't become an addict, but I obviously am attracted to them. My sister married an addict. My cousin married an addict. My other cousin's son is an addict. How many addicts are in your family? Are these all just mentally defective individuals?

Look at your family tree and start admitting the reality: We are *all* susceptible to addiction, and those who are more emotionally sensitive even more so. We need to stop hiding it and start addressing the issues: pain and access to temporary relief.

We have way too much pain in this world and way too much chemical relief. We can't throw pills at people, and we can't say they are malformed/diseased; they are just people. They need to heal, and chemicals that only dull the senses stop that process.

Fabri healed, married, and is doing very well. When I spoke to him after Matthew died, he reminded me of his childhood experiences — the intense trauma a family experiences from losing a loved one unexpectedly — and warned me of the gathering storm. He was so correct.

— Matt's mom

February 2, Tuesday, 2010 (5/10)

Laid back day, 1 job, Flats for almost 7 hours on a Tuesday! It was the day of our meeting, which took FOREVER. At first they really put me on point, asking me to cook grill shit and then attempting to point out how it was all wrong. Very demeaning, but I got them back by cooking most of the stuff perfectly. I could see what they were talking about ahead of the game, really kept my job well today.

Tomorrow is another easy day. Thursday and Friday will be tough. Those are double down days, big money days. First day of work at Pizza Hut is Thursday, excited to start that gig, excited to finally be making some money.

<u>Intake: Ø day 2</u>

FEBRUARY 3, WEDNESDAY, 2010 (5/10)

<u>Intake: Ø day 3</u>

FEBRUARY 4, THURSDAY, 2010 (6/10)

A great day today. Worked morning at McD's. They seem to really like me, and I like the job, too.

Thought I would see my first shift at Pizza Hut today too, but it was just the basics, some computer work, getting familiar with the system computers. Got off early, chased down some oxies, about $100 worth, generics for once—terrible waste once again, as is always the case. 1) eliminate drug spending; it will help my trip to Ukraine.

Got Valium filled. Into the cave then for next few days.

Payday, Flats: $364

<u>Intake: 80 mg oxyco oral, 20 mg Valium</u>

FEBRUARY 5, FRIDAY, 2010 (6/10)

Worked at McD's this morning, another good shift. I get along well with my coworkers and mgmt. This will be a great job.

Had an epic battle with Trish (that miserable bitch). I just decided I was through taking her shit and I finally got shitty with her. Nita pulled us into the office and talked to us about it.

That bitch kept trying to go point for point with me about it, but of course I always end up winning those types of arguments. Basically, Nita told us to get along or our hours would both be cut. I just smiled because anything I lose at the Flats I can pick up at Pizza Hut anyways, but if Trish lost hours she would be doomed because she doesn't make much anyways. I'm happy about that turn of events.

Partied after work again, too.

Too many expensive drugs

I need to put this money elsewhere.

Intake: 40 mg oxyco snort, 20 mg Valium

FEBRUARY 6, SATURDAY, 2010 (6/10)

Too many drugs. I spent all my money on drugs this week—MJ, oxy 20s, Valium, beer. I have just gone crazy this week on drugs, tonight especially. Valium removes all inhibitions. Still, not a good thing. I had Kevin over tonight for the first time. I'm trying to mentor him from the standpoint of coolness. We shared drugs, hung out, and it was good. I gave him advice about the 'evils of drugs'—where it's going to lead him and just how sad it is.

Intake: 30 mg oxyco snort, 30 mg val snort, smoked

February 7, Sunday, 2010 (6/10)

Slept like a dog from all the drugs last night—too many. Went crazy with drugs again today. Leah came over and I gave her the first shot of morphine she had ever had. I wonder why I do this? A lot of it has to do with the Valium and loss of inhibitions. I spend every extra cent on drugs these last three days; only paid $173 worth of bills. Backslide city.

First day at Hut today, Super Bowl Sunday, and it was too busy to train me!

70+ hours ahead working this week.

Intake: 40 mg oxyco snort, 60 mg morphine I VE, 50 mg
Valium, smoked

BAD!

February 8, Monday, 2010 (4.59/10)

Paulina's 25th birthday.

Worked about 10.5 hours today. Getting used to it. Another long one tomorrow.

Intake: re-cook morphine AM 4 mg? 40 mg Valium, smoked

February 11, Thursday, 2010 (6/10)

It's been a very mad last 10 days or so. Have been working steady at both the Flats and McDonald's, very crazy schedule. Broke down Tuesday night, couldn't go to the Flats, called same McDonald's Wednesday morning; just needed rest. Intake has been pretty bad, insane too, way too much. I had good weed, a bottle Valiums and oxys and morphine coming my way to satisfy, but I spent way too much on the whole deal. My sick way of celebrating all the extra work I've got on my hands. Just called the pharm/clinic and they have a 100 bottle of Vicodin just waiting for me at Walmart with 5 refills.

Started this journal around noon today, since then it has been a drug storm of all kinds of substances. I demonstrated proper IV technique on myself, as well as seeing Joey.

Drugs, Drugs, Drugs

Intake: 20 mg methadone oral, 35 mg hydroco oral, 4
5 mg morphine IV, vodka cranberry, 24oz Highlife,
smoked a bowl of very good weed

Aaron brought the weed.
I picked up my Vikes.
Kevin provided the morphine.
Joey with the methadone
of course
I had the alcohol

February 13, Saturday, 2010 (3.75/10)

Took it easy last night after work, slept in this morning. My biggest mistake of the day was eating those 10 Vicodin. Made me sick as shit when I awoke from a short nap.

Ended up being nauseous as hell, threw up a couple times during my shift. Trish saw one episode, but those management fuckers thought it was a put-on because I had been trying to get today off for a week because I could have gotten a ride home with Jenny for the weekend. Had to drag my sick ass around for 4 hours before finally being sent home. I was told by Lizzie right before I left that Nita and Elta didn't believe that I was sick! How offensive! Fuck that place!

Drug use is OOC[22] at the moment. Need to reign that shit in.

22. Out of control

Intake: 50 mg hydroco oral, smoked

FEBRUARY 14, SUNDAY, 2010 (5.75/10)

All day off today. Hung out with Pat and Alicia today, rested. I'm waking up earlier more naturally now; this is good.

6 to 2 tomorrow at McD's, 4 to 9 Flats. I've cleared out the Vikes, no cash, smoking the last bowl of weed now—I may be physically addicted by now. The next 4 days could be very hard, but needs to happen. Healthy is the way to go with this whole plan.

Off the amil. Strange and vague suicidal feelings. Nothing dangerous, but very curious little feelings. Antidepressants can be hard to come off. I just don't want to take it anymore, but will probably be forced to restart tomorrow night.

–The week is a meat grinder

–Day one is tomorrow

–By day 5 I will be a sausage creature

Intake: 60 mg hydroco oral,
20 my methadone oral, smoked

FEBRUARY 15, MONDAY, 2010 (5/10)

Twelve and a half hours on the clock today. Tomorrow only 9, but it's more than 8! Will talk with Pizza Hut about starting on Thursday.

Trying to convince Rose to visit on Sunday. No drugs today; first day in a long time. Smoked the hash rez in my pipe, brushed my teeth, off to bed!

<u>Intake: Ø day 1, smoked</u>

February 16, Tuesday, 2010 (5/10)

Spent 9 hours on the clock today, tomorrow is another 13er; gotta get to bed.

The pace is sickening, getting used to it anyways, making money that needs to be made.

<u>Intake: Ø day 2</u>

February 17, Wednesday, 2010 (5.5/10)

Spent 12.5 hours on the clock today. Woke up really early this morning, 3:10 AM (a little early for what I went in for, 5 AM). Slowly getting better at McD's, but I am still so slow for them. One guy gave me the nickname "Pokey" as in "Gumby and Pokey" to describe my speed at this current point. I laughed it off, nothing serious, just playing I guess, not going to interrupt any money making at the place, nor my drive or courage to keep pulling the fuck out of these shifts, one day at a time, all the way to the goal of Ukraine.

<u>Intake: Ø day 3</u>

FEBRUARY 18, THURSDAY, 2010 (5.75/10)

Good day overall. Five morning hours at McD's, then an afternoon spent drinking, smoking, resting, talking with friends on the phone. Some vague bullshit getting paid 40 minutes late, nothing more.

<u>Intake: Ø day 4, smoked</u>

FEBRUARY 19, FRIDAY, 2010

Work 3 hours at Maggie's farm (McDonald's) this morning. 7 hours still ahead at the Flats this being my midafternoon wall.

Walked downtown and bought a few CDs after my first shift. It's nice out today, low thirties, sunny, saw the first motorcycle of the year today, [a] real die-hard all bundled up and riding a Honda.

Fifth day without opiates—the social and spiritual tension are almost unbearable. No real physical symptoms all of AS minus the intestinal revolt the last 2 days—probably has as much to do with the beer I drank last night as much as anything else. Drug market is dry as a bone in just about every direction; people all over are telling me a about a real disruption in the market. Good thing I don't bank off drugs and am not supporting a daily habit anymore. That's moving in the right direction. Just worked the wires again here and scat out of luck! Well, at least I have a certain thing to look forward to next Thursday or Friday. That is a very long time out from this vantage point. I guessed certainty requires patience sometimes.

6 hours later, no luck, Flats went well.

<u>Intake: Ø day 5, smoked[23]</u>

FEBRUARY 20, SATURDAY, 2010 (5/10)

Didn't want to do anything today, but forced myself to clean room, [do] laundry, and then grab my check from McDonald's (then my bank wasn't even open to cash!). That was a long walk for nothing!

Warm outside, but snowy. Work was just painfully slow last night; tonight should be the same, but no knowing with that place. Tried sleeping in; woke up at 6:15 AM for the day after only 7 hours of sleep. Not tonight, no sir, tonight it's Beast, Bud, and more amitriptyline; going to try sleeping until noon tomorrow, just to catch up, get rested and cool for another big week.

23. When an addict is on opiates, marijuana and alcohol don't even qualify as "intake."

Six hours later: Notice at Flats that I lost 5 hours on next week's schedule. Sucks; got to rectify the situation with Nita next week, hopefully.

Intake: Ø day 6, smoked

FEBRUARY 21, SUNDAY, 2010 (5/10)

Q: Why are you working 6.5 days a week?
A: To support my Sunday afternoon habit.

To whatever demon controls that tentacle of my personality. [Reflective delay]

Day off today, seems like Matt D. might come on down for a visit. Haven't seen him in almost 2 months. We'll find something worthwhile to do for sure.

Bored otherwise; wasn't able to sleep past 7 AM, despite extra amyls and beer and smoke.

"On my first day back, my first day back in town, the clouds above were hummin' our song, hummin', hummin' our song."

Morphine: "The Saddest Song"

Maybe I should give Rose a call? I'm pretty bored here waiting for Matt to call. John has the downstairs monopolized. Computer is off limits until further notice—antivirus work, etc.

… 7 hours later. Matt D did stop by. Hung out at his cool home for a few hours. Fun time, but [I] notice feelings of powerful dissatisfaction with current situation in life, kind of depression.

Work starts in 7.5 hours.

<u>Intake: dry spell day seven, smoked</u>

February 22, Monday, 2010 (5.75/10)

Twelve and a half hours on clock today. Got home at 9 and drank a 6-pack, talked to Rose for about 2 hours. Good day, went quickly despite my reluctance to get back in the work week. Start Pizza Hut tomorrow at 10 AM, good for me, money machine, wonderful.

Ukraine

<u>Dry spell continues, Intake: Ø day 8</u>

February 23, Tuesday, 2010

Started the 3rd job today—Pizza Hut. It seems like it will be easy enough to learn but tossed together it will seem a little harder to do. I am determined to do this.

I am turned upside down with hours, turned sideways because it seems like I will explode from not having enough time to myself.

Get through, get to Ukraine, Matt. Do it! You'll (hopefully) thank yourself later!

Intake: no time for opiates, day 9

February 24, Wednesday, 2010 (4 to 6/10)

Blur. Everything is a cloudy, tired blur of clocks, burgers, faces, pizzas, tacos, mops, early morning walks in windy, freezing weather. I'm tired, dog tired, and I'm drinking my second beer trying to score a few oxies … (A few minutes later) … looks like it's a "sure" thing. My oxies are "in transit" so to speak, 2 x 20s, one tonight; one for the morning.

Fuck, so many interesting things I could write about.

Look at the cans, bottles

Tall, shiny, perfectly straight

Rising like the shimmering skyscrapers they represent

Perfection, the human race calls out: "perfection"

Perfection in piece, visually impressive

Underneath, the sin it contains

The imperfection implied, never expressed

Realized online consumption

Consumption in red, blue, green

Death realized in life.

```
Intake: Ø day 10 or 20 mg oxyco IV,
     not sure at 10:48 PM
```

1:27 AM—called into McD's. Shit! Can't turn my mind off for sleep.

FEBRUARY 25, THURSDAY, 2010 (6.3/10)

Busy day. Went to Appleton with Aaron, hung out with Pat earlier in the morning. Before that he gave me a ride to Walmart pharmacy early in the morning to pick up el Vicodin.

Called in for 6AM to 1 PM shift at McDonald's today. Shit. Just been way tired, exhausted and an insomniac to boot. Went to Pizza Hut for third shift because it was just my second day and I couldn't make an impression like that without the risk of being fired!

Spent some time on pill hunt with Joey. Scored a lid of arm candy. Joey also told me some old junkie stories that were interesting.

Talked to mom and Dick as well. I know mom had been drinking a little, not sloshed, but Dick was pretty drunk. He was excited to talk to me, but it was depressing because he intimated to me that he knew he was dying, that his health is getting worse, and that he had all but given up the struggle. No wonder he is depressed and drinking all the time. I would [,too] if I thought that I was dying! Urgh! I miss them so much; I must get to see them sometime soon.

Intakes: 1(40 mg hydroco oral,

60 mg morphine oral, 37 mg oxyco IV, smoked)

Have you ever become lost in a game — maybe as a child? I can remember playing house with my sister Carol and walking away still thinking I was the mommy figure, ordering my sister around and having trouble relinquishing my character. The games we adults play are similar but more purposeful. Matt played this game with his doctors, and he was darned good at it. Only within his journal could he safely slip out of character. I played this game with the neighbors: "Look how normal and respectable we are." After my divorce and Matt's death, my costume fell on the dressing room floor leaving me naked and looking in the mirror for maybe the first time.

Dick was playing this game. He was marketing the character he wanted to be. He wasn't dying or even sick. The year before he had had several stints put in his heart and then received an enthusiastic pat on the back to do whatever he wanted. Problem: he lost his want; he lost his ego. He lost his former character as cabinet-maker and Christian musician. Inside he felt inadequate and so turned to drinking and breaking mirrors. I tried hugging and listening to him, but he didn't want my approval or my ear. I was only an object, a non-human, a woman. I couldn't give him back his ego; he needed to feel like a man again. My presence made him feel emasculated, and he hated me for that. He wanted a male audience to applaud, and was giving Matt his best trailer. Dick was talking to Matt but was working to convince himself and perfect his scripted lines.

— Matt's mom

February 26, Friday, 2010 (3.5-6 mixed/10)

Nutso day today. Worked all 3 jobs for abbreviated periods; Pizza Hut is impressed with my work and gave me a guarantee of 32 hours per week starting if I would give them open availability, so to Tortilla Flats I went and told them that in 2 weeks I would no longer be working weekends, which I feel may change into just a pure quit seeing as they almost cut my hours in half with no explanation or notice—what a horde of worthless bitches they are. I can't believe they play me like this—not so much the cut, but the no notice part.

Partied with Pat and Alicia after work. Took a ride to Appleton with them and Joey to see Aaron, who stood us up because he had passed out after a party.

A lot of drugs the last few days, no good, haze. Broke again.

Intake: 120 mg oxyco IV, 40 mg hydroco oral, smoked

February 27, Saturday, 2010 (4/10)

Slept most of the day today, just dog tired and super doped up. Rest, so needed today, tomorrow morn will probably be the same way too.

Flats was über-busy last night and tonight. It was enough to make me very hateful and angry at the whole situation, thought about quitting, probably will here soon, just hate the thought of leaving like that though, after doing so much hard work for them. It finally comes to this, eh?

Sleep, rest, alone time await me for tomorrow!

Intake: 40 mg oxyco IV, 30 mg morphine snort, smoked

February 28, Sunday, 2010

Intake: 80 mg hydroco oral, smoked

MARCH, 2010

MARCH 1, MONDAY, 2010 (4/10)

Draggin! Today marks one year that I have been in this bed in this corner of NY Ave. Unbelievable! This town gets more terrible by the day. I feel like more of a loser every day, just horrible, suicidal—very much so! I get more comfortable with the thought of suicide every day! It seems like I should be getting out of this with the best direction and prospects that I've had since being in Oshkosh.

9-ish hours on the clock today.

Intake: 40 mg hydroco oral, smoked

MARCH 2, TUESDAY, 2010 (5/10)

Worked the dreaded 7 to 3 at McD's with the evening off from the Flats. Rested. It went way too quick, as is always the case. Meat grinder: I'm in the middle of another big-hour week. Shit is starting to wear on me for sure. Need to see the benefit here soon through disciplined spending.

Intake: Ø day 1, smoked

March 3, Wednesday, 2010 (5/10)

Worked 12.5 hours today.

Intake: Ø day 2

March 4, Thursday, 2010 (5.5/10)

Worked 9 hours today, tired, early morn again tomorrow, last day of the week waking up early. Tired!

Intake: Ø day 3, smoked

March 5, Friday, 2010 (5.5/10)

So ends another stretch of the long hour week. My goal on Sunday night was to work all of my hours at McD's and all my other hours, which was easier this week because I only had 18 hours at the Flats, 36 at McD's, of which I missed only 2 hours because of being sick on Monday and being sent home. A little over 50 hours this week altogether. Tomorrow is my last shift at the Flats and then I'm done there. After a year I won't be working there anymore—strange, but I think that I'll miss it, the skill it took to cook really good food there, the good times (which seem few).

The weather has finally turned warmer. The forecast is calling for low to mid 40s for the entire week ahead. I'm happy about that; my mood seems cheery when it gets warm out.

Just working, still wasting money, trying to get the plan, get on the path I should be on.

Intake: Ø day 4, smoked

At this point, Matt stopped using the red pen to denote drug use days. Did he give up a bit? Maybe it just didn't matter or was a detail that he now found too depressing.

— Matt's mom

MARCH 6, SATURDAY, 2010 (6/10)

Pain. What is the nature of emotional and spiritual pain? I suffer much lately, horrible feelings of remorse, loneliness, regret and longing—the longing is the worst, it is the sharpest knife.

I have another brief respite from my schedule. This morning off and all day tomorrow. Tonight is my last night at the Flats, fitting that it's also "Gallery Walk" and should be intensely busy for the 5 hours I'm there.

Looking forward to seeing AIR live in Chicago on March 24, going with Pat, should be an amazing adventure.

...(8 hours later)

My last night at the Flats went alright. Kind of a sad affair. I could tell those who liked me truly will miss and respect me, but those other fakers just kinda silently turned their nose up at me because I was never part of their "clique" so to speak. Looking back at the last year I spent at the Flats, it was wrought with all kinds of bullshit, from being pulled into the office at various times for B.S. reasons, to working my ass off, leading that kitchen and still never being able to make 40 hours or $9/hour out of it. Elta is pretty stingy; perhaps she has a touch of greed. All I can say is that those people never truly liked me despite all the great things I did at that place—they just didn't like me personally, and perhaps this is one reason for my depressed mood and lack of self-esteem, all social input being of no gainful consequence.

The kitchen will be in a horrible state of free-fall for a while. I've left, and what they are left with is just a group of disorganized, sometimes incompetent people who have no real leader or common direction. I do not know how they will survive it. They will, but I can't see what path they will take. At the end of the day they need a bona fide kitchen leader, something like what I was doing for most of my time there, but they have no real clear intention on what they will have to pay for this. I'm going to keep up with the news from there, see just how bad or good the whole thing is going.

I was motivated by OxyContin (betrayal of self once again) to clean the hell out of my room. I have to say that it is cleaner than it has ever been, looks quite respectable for once. Everything has a place, no clutter, no dust or pet hair, clean folded clothes—great, I really like it and hope that it will stay as such.

Trying to do small things to boost my self-esteem, to perhaps get out of this horrible hole that's in my mind and spirit, to gain access to the good parts of my personality again. Spending $80 on OxyContin is not a positive action helping me in ANY endeavor.

Intake: 80 mg oxyco IV smoked

Can't Find a Single Friend Here

(Taken from Matt's Facebook page)

I haven't ranted for a while, but I just feel the need to describe something. This is to anyone who cares enough to read the things that I write. It's about the place I live … or perhaps it's about me; I can't quite figure it out.

I've been in Oshkosh since November 2008, and I've just realized that I don't really have a single friend here, at least no one who lives up to my definition of a friend. You know, someone who you can talk candidly with about anything, someone who values your person, recognizes your soul and the features of your entire personality and appreciates this enough to actually let you inside their head—their triumphs and struggles. Someone who's going to be able to tell you the hard truth about the things that you ACTUALLY do and the way you act; I mean real feedback. My most basic definition, I guess, is just someone who corresponds with you honestly and lets you in when you let them in.

I have the chance, of course, to bump into individuals out there, whether it be at work, through acquaintance, or through random means. A lot of people I've felt could really turn out to be friends of mine just haven't really come around to that point after spending time with me. Back home, it was really quite easy to make these personal connections; once you had met someone it was fairly easy to pull them to your level, or to be accepted into theirs. People wanted others around them who would be true, good for a laugh, some company, or a drink—God, just anything. But here it's quite different. Here it seems that people are locked into this death battle for some type of relative status over those around them. They compete fiercely with each other in everyday circumstances. They have a very set idea of what they believe, of who they are and their image. You really can't shake this "better than you in some damn way" kind of thinking. Maybe it's just because I won't compete with them, or that I really can't. I don't have status at all, not much money, no car, not really upwardly mobile at this point. When I was a successful person, not too long ago, I rubbed elbows with all kinds of people—from rich to abjectly poor, from students to addicts to lawyers and even homeless. Whoever you were, I was happy to be in your level of view. I really wanted to see what you saw from your point under the sun. Your lack of money or status or mobility didn't bother me. Just to be around you was enough. I felt a great sense of warmth getting to know different people in my few years on the earth.

I found deeper people, too. Not so here. I can't seem to find anyone that feels the least bit like discussing anything beyond the reaches of their own paradigm. No one wants to be bothered with deeper meanings, symbolism in life, or a greater, grander picture. As for the people I have met so far here, it's like this all boils down to your position within this system, and where you can get to in it. If you happen to vary from the upward swing, or don't care about the money or the status then the interest level drops right off.

So far I have been really biting into the culture down here, but you know that I'm not really sure. I wonder about myself sometimes like maybe it is all in my head—or worse yet, that it isn't them at all but that instead it's me! This could be so true considering that I've been walking around completely blind having no real friends to give me input or feedback—my image through their filters. Regardless of the cause of the situation, I feel quite helpless and more than a tad bit depressed about the whole thing. I get really scared sometimes and start thinking that all of my countrymen have gone absolutely mad, all of the U.S. completely gripped by this infinite power struggle for status or riches, their minds blinded to real meaning and beauty in life. But then the question arises: Am I so self-assured to feel that I know the meaning any better than them? God, what a position to be in.

So yeah, I'm pretty lonely, and I'm confused because I always thought I was pretty personable and likable—deserving of real friends. But, I lack some sort of characteristic to draw people to me, or perhaps they HAVE all gone mad?

I hate this place. I came here quite optimistic, but I find that as the days go by I feel less and less like even trying. I feel a lot more like keeping my mouth shut and just doing things by myself. I feel like getting out of here for sure. I just hope that this doesn't end up killing me before I end up making it out. Things have been happening lately otherwise that give me reason to seriously doubt myself on a lot of different issues … to trust myself less.

We come back always to the truth that God knows what's going on, that He's leading you down and around some trail to bring you to some destination. Trusting in the future or outcome is tough. If I look back on this in 20 years and recognize it as the penance that it is, then what? I guess I will have learned something quite profound. Until then we leave the mind to suffer.

Matt and I talked about this topic a lot. And, he was right — he had tons of friends everywhere else but Oshkosh. Everywhere he went he made friends, before. He worked in several little tourist towns in Wisconsin, in some small cities, and around home. He made the strangest, most eclectic group of friends I have ever seen: store managers, business owners, chefs, foreigners from just about everywhere, people from rehab, doctors, old ladies (how the old ladies loved him), and just about anyone you can imagine.

Well, he did make it out of Oshkosh, for a total of about three weeks. He died just after moving to Madison. And only two people from Oshkosh came to his funeral (they were related), but EIGHT people he had just met came from Madison and even spoke at his funeral! The place was absolutely packed. And, talk about the flowers! Flowers were arriving from everywhere, and so many. We almost didn't have anywhere to put them. Matt had friends — just not in Oshkosh. He really did feel very, very alone.

— Matt's mom.

March 7, Sunday, 2010 (4/10)

Sat around all day—wasted yet more money on drugs, fucking useless shit. I feel so down and depressed when this happens, just worthless as a human being without anything to offer myself or my future. The hemorrhage of cash has to stop. It must, or I will continue to be nowhere next year this time. I NEED to get off paper ASAP, and then get my buns to UKRAINE, and then back to Colorado.

The only thing holding me back is the dope....

I feel more useless every day.

Intake: 40 mg oxyco oral, 55 mg Valium, smoked

March 8, Monday, 2010 (Valium cave) (3/10)

Started on Valium again last night. Made me suicidally depressed all day long, but I have learned to detach from the emotion in order to study it. It still leans on me, though; it hurts like mad. I would like to pull myself out of it somehow so I could enjoy Valium a little bit more. It does have many possible aspects as well, but the depression negates its overall effectiveness.

Intake: 30 mg diazepam, 40 mg oxy IV, smoked

March 9, Tuesday, 2010 (Valium cave) (3/10)

Took a lot of Valium today. Felt shitty and depressed the whole day, but relaxed later on.

<u>Intake: 60 mg diazepam, smoked</u>

Valium is creating amnesia.

MARCH 10, WEDNESDAY, 2010 (VALIUM CAVE) (3/10)

Called into my only 8-hour shift today just in order to get high. Low point. Things seem to crash once I get into Valium. So ashamed of myself it's unbelievable. I can't fucking believe I'm doing this again; need to quit. I spent all but $100 of $600 on drugs this last time around. So ashamed. Need to quit that shit; have to quit that shit. Hopeless feelings of deep desperation almost overpower me now. I have my Vicodin today; should help level me out.

High levels of Valium are making me amnesic.

<u>Intake: 40 mg diazepam, 85 hydroco oral</u>

MARCH 11, THURSDAY, 2010 "THE MARCH TO SUICIDE"(2/10)

Profound, unrelenting depression. Faked sick to go home from my shift today at McD's. Got home, met Aaron D, sold him some pills, went grocery shopping with the proceeds.

Diazepam makes me want to kill myself. So depressed I can hardly work! Plus, Valium makes everything go by like a blur. The last 4 days "POOF"—gone like a flash. Too much drugs. So very ashamed at myself to be working so much and then losing all that large sum to nothing but WEAKNESS and STUPIDITY.

I miss Rose

I need Rose.

Rose.

Intake: 40 mg hydroco oral,

30 mg val oral?, smoked

MARCH 12, FRIDAY, 2010 (7/10)

Rob is coming down out of the blue today. I'm trading away most of that devil damn Valium for some methadone, selling the Vicodin (most of it hopefully), giving the rest away, just anything to get it away from me.

Called into work again today, tricked Pizza Hut into thinking I didn't have shift hours, going to be doing the rest of my drugs, and then pulling more crazy hours next week. Tired of the drugs. This week's target will be to spend my meager earnings on probation fees. I need to step in that direction.

Rob's here.

Intake: 30 mg methadone, 40 mg hydroco,

smoked, Valium 20 mg oral

March 13, Saturday, 2010 (5.75/10)

Drugs. Drugs. Rob's here; we're having a party. THC, diazepam (Rob couldn't handle it), hydrocodone, beer. Worked at Pizza Hut. Rose will be down Thursday.

Intake: 20 mg hydroco oral, 10 mg diazepam oral, smoked

March 14, Sunday, 2010 (3/10)

Ugly feelings all day today. Didn't want to go to work but pushed myself into it nonetheless. I've noticed that whenever Rob visits I get really down and depressed. I'm in a very deep hole now, can't see the light anywhere. I think it has a lot to do with this last week and all the money I just fucking wasted, wasted, wasted, and the thought that it keeps me in this hole, this fucking hole. God, how can I ever feel good about myself again? I've been so unhappy for so long now that I wonder if I'll ever be happy again? I'm so sad, I'm so lonely, and I'm becoming more suicidal by the day. I thought that getting all this extra employment would be the way, but it hasn't helped because now I work all the time to just basically waste the money I make on drugs and other stupid shit.

God, I wish I had a girlfriend.

(Matt, you're pathetic)

Intake: Ø day 1, smoked

March 15, Monday, 2010 (3/10)

John is being a dick. Need to move out soon it seems.

<u>Intake Ø day 2, drink, smoke</u>

March 16, Tuesday, 2010 (3/10)

Depressed as fuck. Trying to make it out by using Amitriptyline; hope it works.

<u>Intake: 30 mg codine, smoked, drank</u>

[Note from the FUTURE! This is the last time I saw Joey as of 4-1-10. He gave me a single T3; that's my goodbye kiss.]

March 17, Wednesday, 2010 (started out a 2, ended at a 5)

Worked 12 hours on the clock today. McDonald's is "tolerable" to a point, but it is also a meat grinder type of job. I dislike it, but it's morning work that matches my evening work, so it's a good situation overall. I need to keep at it and pull myself from this hole.

Pizza Hut is going very well. I genuinely like the people I work with—cool and good people. I'll have an easy time at this job.

The day started poorly being that I was temporarily banned from the computer this morning. I was so depressed at McD's that I could hardly even work; it was almost a nagging physical pain, very very deep. Don't know where this is coming from, but it is intense. Took full dose (100mg) of my TCA, it seems to have worked in the past.

In my twilight days of being 24 years old, I am a man on the brink. I could go either way, and I hope and strive for the positive path in life: love, happiness, health.

Rose is coming tomorrow, can hardly wait.

Intake: Ø no smoke nor drink

NEXT PAGE IN JOURNAL, NO DATE RECORDED

I leave it blank because this page represents the symbolic turning of a new leaf.

MARCH 18, THURSDAY, 2010 (8.8/10)

Beautiful, warm and sunny, a little windy but no one ever criticized the genius of Gorbachev for his birthmark. We'll just call it a perfect day.

Rose was here! My heart sang with joy! We saw Pat, went to Lake Winnebago out on the point and took some photos. Endless talking the entire time, each point matched and we enjoyed the hell out of it. Out for coffee, went to Appleton too, to see Aaron D. We smoked; a very strange girl and a semi-comatose guy were there, too. My "mutant meter" went off immediately, as did Rose's. We joked about it on the way back to Oshkosh.

Then to a wonderful dinner at Tortilla Flats. I had a few margaritas, and a shot of Popov to make the wait staff squeamish. Once again there was constant dialogue between us, ceaseless.

Right before Rose left tonight, I was hoping to put my arm around her for just a little while, but it backfired—not embarrassing considering I have a very firm grasp of our relationship—but, you know it would have been nice to have been held by a beautiful girl you adore. (It's really almost 1950-ish corny: "Gee Dad, could I bring Sally home after the drive-in?")

I think about Rose not obsessively, but I think of her often and always in very positive terms. Adoration—best word I have in my lexicon for it. Love? Love. Fits and doesn't at the same time. She matches me quite well.

The future is always hazy to me, like a fog, but Rose fits in prominently to what I do see ... in some way.

The day went too quickly, as is always the case. Last day of 24. My God, has it all gone so fast?

`Intake: I promised Rose I'd be *sober,`

```
        I drank, but didn't get drunk,

   smoked without getting baked, and the big one:

        NO OPIATES, Ø day 2, smoked


        *sober means no opiates.
```

MARCH 19, FRIDAY, 2010 (4.75) 25 YEARS OLD TODAY

Celebrated my birthday today by working 14 hours. I've noticed that McD's is really adding to my depressive symptoms—I'm always tense there, and I'm there 30+ hours per week. I can't wait to be in a position to leave that job. The second half of my day at Pizza Hut is so much better—it's hardly like working. I like the Pizza Hut gig in relative terms; still hate the position and profession.

Rob and Logan were here briefly tonight, went to some rave of some sort. Rob was high out of his mind on amphetamines, very intense.

Had an amazing conversation with my mother last night on the phone. She opens up to me more and more with each conversation. She sounds as down as I am right now in life. "A bad couple of years, ma?"—"Which were the GOOD ones?" she'd say.

Hateful depression continues almost unabated. Going down now a little more because TCA is beginning to kick in, but it's not substitute for a happy life … Wow, I am really down, no two ways about it. Any kind of reflection I do these days is almost universally negative and unproductive. Help? Help. Not sure. Get out of town, get a car, something.

<u>Intake: Ø day 3, smoked.</u>

MARCH 20, SATURDAY, 2010

(3.75/10) FIRST DAY OF SPRING, 39° OUTSIDE

Slept in, to 9:30 AM! HAHA, 3 months ago that would have made me cringe! Deeply, spiritually depressed, but I write this half drunk and stoned, so it may seem cheery to whoever is reading this.

"My pride is dying; I think I'm all done lying."–The White Stripes

Five hours at Pizza Hut, which did cheer me up more than solitude in this FOUL place.

Wendell, the older black maintenance guy at McD's, saw me walking and gave me a ride to the bank today. I want to make it a goal to play a game of cribbage with him. Cool guy.

I'm trying to address the depression in the next few days.

This journal may end in the next year due to depression inspired suicide.

<u>Intake: Ø day 4, smoked, drank</u>

MARCH 21, MONDAY, 2010 (5/10)

Worked 8 at Pizza Hut. Depression and tension lifting with TCA taking credit.

Intake: Ø day 5, smoked

MARCH 22, MONDAY, 2010 (5/10)

Worked 7 at McD's. Afternoon off drinking/relaxing. Depression all but totally gone now.

Intake: Ø day 6, smoked

MARCH 23, TUESDAY, 2010 - (5.75/10)

Worked 8 hours at McD's; had the night off. Picked up my Vicodin, which I was so focused on getting these last few days, there has been nothing going on anywhere else. Joey doesn't have anything, [and] I can't get from Cindy anymore because she had the doc write her only 40 a month (down from 180, too bad, had some fun times with those).

Aaron came over to trade, and he just tried wheeling and dealing which secretly pissed me off because he was already getting an amazing deal.

Wanted to talk to Rose—no answer. Neither did my mom answer her phone, so I've sat silent and lonely for the last 6 hours or so.

Depression all but gone, using Elavil (formerly referred to as TCA, amitriptyline) because my depression was so severe, I was utterly suicidal. I'm still able to confront the specific issues that were making me depressed and can see the depression, but it does not create the physical/emotional effects—the internal tension, the lack of wanting to leave bed. I'm not going to stop the Elavil for the next several months; perhaps it will stabilize my life further.

I think I may romantically love Rose, and I believe I will begin to make a more serious overture to her once her relationship with Sebastian is over, or closer to over. I may never get the chance.

Intake: 60 mg morphine snort,

40 mg hydroco oral, smoked

MARCH 24, WEDNESDAY, 2010 — (4.95/5)

Tap me on the shoulder, and I'll open up like a flower. Hit the right mix of morphine and hydrocodone this morning before McD's; I was buzzing around McD's like a hummingbird! Made the girls laugh, had a fast day of it.

Pizza Hut went well enough, but there is the first sign of trouble. The schedule that was posted on Sunday had me at 28 (down from 34 last week), and today's schedule has me at 20.5! Unbelievable.

I'm really upset about that. Think I may have a friendly word with the manager about that tomorrow. Who changes the schedule mid-week?

Relationship with Rose has changed ever so slightly. She is pulling away from me now, wrapped up it seems with Sebastian, on the mend with him. Where will the future pages of this journal find me and her?

Light flavor of depression still on the lips. Looking deep into the soul, mind. Lonely now, again, deeper now, worse in subtle ways. Elavil has kept me standing on the deck of the boat during this storm, but I'm still being racked by the storm.

What's going on? Where are we going?

Intake: 70 mg hydroco, 30 mg morphine oral, smoked

*the master hit: 40 mg hydroco/30 mg morphine oral

MARCH 25, THURSDAY, 2010 — (5.5/10)

Bad day at McD's. Vicodin fueled negative, aggressive energy. I just clammed up at work all day. This job is making me tougher, I can feel it, like the Military.

Upset that I wasn't able to work at Pizza Hut tonight. Trying to focus on positive of having 50 hours a week, period, in this economy. It's a better place than where I was on Jan. 1, and that's saying something. Also, feel good for dropping $100 towards probation yesterday. Joey has disappeared, and I have 5 paychecks in April, so I hope to put a lot more down this next month—I'm thinking 5 or 6 hundred dollars, leaving 300 to pay off in May, boom, free. Do it Matthew. Please don't fuck this up; you're so close.

I feel more like I'm losing my Rose. I had a very sterile, Sebastian-monitored conversation for 20 minutes tonight. I mourn her also, that I didn't make my lucky chance permanent, seeing how alike and compatible we are—I love the girl. I could be by her side for the rest of my life, and love and fulfill and support her every day, happy. She will remain a friend and confidant for as long as I can breathe! I will try my best to not influence her with advice against her lover. I want her to be happy, to know her is enough, but I think I could make her happy if I was close to her, in a better state of mind and affairs.

I'll explore this more in the future.

Intake: 60 mg morphine oral,

90 mg hydroco oral, smoked

March 26, Friday, 2010 (5ish/10)

Eleven hours today: 4.5 McD's, 6.5 Pizza Hut.
Lost. Very lost.

I look old and spent for 25. Where did my youth go?

Depressed.

Despondent.

Disappointed.

Discouraged.

Discontent.

Help. Where is love? All I ever wanted in life was love.

Intake: Ø day 1, smoked

"All I ever wanted in life was Love." Matthew wasn't just being
melancholy or overly dramatizing his mood here; he truly
only ever wanted love. Often he would insert visions of love as
he spoke of the future: "Ya ma, someday my wife and I will be
sitting on my porch surrounded by our grandkids and watching the sunset. I'm going to look back at all this and laugh with
them." His visions always seemed to involve a rocking chair,
sunset, wife, and kids. Conversely, his peers often dreamt of
fast cars, big houses, and busty, blonde wives, in that order. He
never even got the darned sunset. His dreams were eclipsed
at age 15 by a toe infection.

I wonder if that kindly old doctor has any idea that the pain he helped Matt avoid as a teen snuffed out all those unborn souls. I will never be able to hold my grandkids, present them pictures of Matt showing off his naked butt as a toddler, watch as they go through the boxes I saved: his baby shoes, favorite books, trophies, and drawings. All those future souls were lost; all that is left is a collection of pill bottles and receipts scattered through the boxes from his apartment in Madison. I also have his American Flag, which he valued highly, a lock of Paulina's hair, and a music box that plays "Oh Little Town of Bethlehem." Physical pain is nothing compared to the pain of knowing I have lost how many babes in how many mangers.

— Matt's mom

MARCH 27, SATURDAY, 2010 (5.5/10)

Spoke with Rose for almost 2 hours this afternoon. We have this amazing connection that grows and flexes with time. So much for my though that I was losing her. I have her in a way, moving more towards her and always talking with her. She is my match.

Talked with Mom, also Good conversation, made my day along with my convo with Rose. I want to visit home in May, for a few days.

Focused on the future, I have no choice now. I'm getting old quick, need to get out, back on track.

Worked 6 hours at the Hut today. Seven days a week continues.

<u>Intake: Ø day 2</u>

MARCH 28, SUNDAY, 2010 (5.5/10)

March is almost over. Once again this last month has just zoomed by. Time seems to be going faster with each passing day.

Depression has almost abated. I still feel a little tinge of depression in my soul; I'll never be able to do away with that until I change my situation sufficiently.

Jobs are going well. I still think they really like me at Pizza Hut, despite the cut in hours (due to business being slow, I'm convinced). McDonalds is a hell hole, just a terrible place to have to go to daily. I try not to let it get me down; it's money after all, money I desperately need to escape this rotten place. Perhaps I should look at it in this way now—as long as I'm putting the money where it needs to go, I should be less depressed.

Think I may finally be coming to terms with my drug use and the impact it's having on my life. I'm 25, and I'm not doing anything worthwhile. I work or I sit at home depressed. If any one factor holds more responsibility than the others it is certainly the drug use. I haven't called Joey at all; I'm doing well resisting that urge. Payday is Thursday and Monday next, so the plan for April is this: $100 from every paycheck goes to probation, that's $500, and then $250 extra wherever I can get it, so $750 will go to probation out of the $900 I believe I owe. This plan, if duly executed, will see me off probation by the first or second week of May.

My secondary plan, after getting off probation, is to gather $200 for my driver's assessment. In order to do this I will need to stop smoking MJ no later than April 15, due to the fact that they could spring the whole "Mr. Edwards, come right this way and pee in my magic cup." Don't need that. I can get my assessment the week of May 27, so looks like I'll go home to visit in June.

After returning in June I'll have to really zero in and focus, get $1000 together for a semi-decent car before August, which would put me out of here in late August/early September. I'm going to be posting this on a sheet by my bed as well as on Facebook.

Now I have the sheet in BOLD black staring me in the face every day. Today was a good day overall.

I'm finally putting a plan into plan in order to be happy with myself.

Intake: Ø day 3

Keep it up.

March 29, Monday, 2010 — (5.75/10)

Seven hours at McD's followed by 8 hours hanging with Pat and his pit-bull Lily. Went a little out of Oshkosh to a "designated wildlife area" as they call it down here—basically, just straw fields with trees, some beautiful red sprouts (willows?), and straw all around with Winnebago Mental Health Institute looming in the background.

A little on the cold side and yet I declare that this must be our last cold day of the season. April first is Thursday and they are calling for 70°! Awesome.

Trying very hard to stay with the positive energy, working well so far.

```
Intake: Ø day 4, smoked
```

March 30, Tuesday, 2010 — (5.5/10)

Been so busy with work that I'm writing this a few days later.

I remember a brutal shift at McD's, followed by Pat once again taking me out to the wildlife area with Lily, much warmer this day, and we saw all manner of wildlife. We saw a bald eagle swoop in to the field from a distance and grab something, probably a mouse, and take it to its nest miles off. Amazing.

```
Intake: Ø day 5
```

MARCH 31, WEDNESDAY, — 2010 (5/10)

Worked 6 AM to 2 PM at McD's and 5 PM to 11:15 PM at Pizza Hut.
Came home exhausted; straight to bed without drink nor smoke.

Intake: Ø day 6

APRIL, 2010

April 1, Thursday, 2010 — (5.85/10)

The day I dream about all winter has finally come! April 1st [is] here, and yet I will read these pages later and forget how much I longed for this very day.

God, how beautiful it was out today. I awoke at 5 AM for my "short" shift at McD's. The walk to work at 5:30 AM revealed many more motorcycles than cars on the road. Perhaps everyone is as happy as I?

Hung out with Cindy at her place. She took a shower and left me alone with her Percocet ... *BUT I TOOK NONE!*

I've developed a "No" voice!

You are working towards something bigger.

Paid $150 to probation today!

Plan's on course.

I love Rose.

I will see Irina soon, too.

<u>Intake: Ø day 7</u>

Why does the so-called "former" addict share drugs? Is it to share the shame of addiction? To demonstrate that others are as fallible as herself? Perhaps it's a twisted form of love, like a mother who stuffs her children with unhealthy sweets to make them smile? Perhaps the one who enables the addict needs to feel needed?

The people who appear to be most qualified to understand and guide an addict on their path to recovery sometimes turn out to be deadly. This "flip side" of addiction presents a real quandary for loved ones seeking safe surroundings for their addicted family members and friends.

— Matt's mom

April 2, Friday, 2010

Setback today. Going to buy an 80; haven't done it yet, but for some reason the process started in my mind is unbreakable. I was doing really well; my "No" voice has been super strong. In the past few days it has guided me through situations in a positive manner that I would never have thought of as possible even 30 days ago. This is different. I have found my trigger!

It's unfulfilled love.

I was chatting with Rose online a little while ago. I have recently identified my love for the girl, my longing to be with her. She was telling me that (as of right now anyways) she and Sebastian are fine, great, whatever. The very second she wrote this I felt fire in my stomach—very familiar, a love fire, full-on hot emotion tore my stomach right open. Once the fire reached my mind it completely and utterly destroyed my wonderful "No" voice. That's crazy because I have been mesmerized by the strength of that "no" voice—Gone, fucking POOF! Within minutes I was opening a beer, at 10:30 AM ON A WORKDAY! Fifteen minutes later I was on the phone with Satan himself, Joey, and was striking a deal that would see my last $80 gone from my pocket. Unbelievable. I haven't gotten the pills yet, so perhaps I haven't felt the shame yet. I am actually quite excited because I think I have found the key to unraveling this whole drug business.

I need to examine this romantic fixation. I need to identify why this bothers me in such a way as to make the rational and controlled individual pass away into dust.

…8 hours later…

Work went well at Pizza Hut. I am really into that job. The work is fast paced but the people, all of them, are kind-hearted and nice. I can joke with them all night and just have a very nice time. Today, one of the younger supervisors, a really nice guy named Trevor, gave me $25 on a loan when I found out that my bank has $20 taken out of my account for some odd reason. Haven't had that happen once since I've been here, and it feels nice to be surrounded by good-hearted people.

I've decided to recoup my money by getting rid of my Vicodin Monday. I just can't be spending money like this, period. It's the only way to make the wrongs of today into right.

Examine this romantic fixation more tomorrow.

Intake: 80 mg oxyco IV

This entry made me ponder how much love and companionship play into addiction. Can anyone successfully maneuver this world without having a close relationship, one that allows for love at a risky distance? The human heart is bountiful when ignited by our spirits and miserly when congealed from instinct. Is loving "from a safe distance" another form of remaining an animal, not fully human, absent of spirit? Are all addictions just attempts at escaping an animal-like existence? Obviously, Matt was seeking the spirit to live, but his shame and isolation may have created a dead-short for this needed electricity. If Matt had that dreamed-of-wife and children or at least someone to tell his stories to besides his journal, would he have also found a reason to persistently say No?

— Matt's mom

April 3, Saturday, — 2010 (5.5/10)

Stuck around home all day today, at least until I went to Pizza Hut for the night shift, 5 to 1-ish. I'm really starting to form a bond with the other guys I work with. The job is very cool, very laid back and relaxing. I can eat whatever I want, and even when it's really busy I don't feel too pressured. Very nice.

I've been sticking to my Elavil lately, anywhere between 100 and 150 mg per night. I'm no longer depressed, but at times I still lack motivation to do certain tasks; getting better by the day, I believe.

Thinking a lot about the impending move, but to where I still do not know. Madison seems most likely, but I have been playing around with the idea of just moving right back to Colorado, skip step one and continue on. It is a daunting thought, and I need to put this feeling out of [my] mind in order to continue.

Intake: Ø day 1

April 4 [sic, as this is 5], Monday, 2010 — (6.5/10)

Exciting and interesting day today. Started at McD's, got paid today—$460, my single largest paycheck since I've been in Oshkosh. I can't imagine I worked that much during the last 2 weeks of March.

Enough money to pay $100 to rent, $100 to probation—my goal for this check was $150, but I paid an extra $50 last week, so I'll still be on track! I also have $100 in hand in case Kevin Wants to sell me that [camcorder]. Hope so; that would make a perfect week for me!

Told Rose I was toying with Colorado. She tried very hard today, via [Facebook] letter, [to tell me] that I should move to Madison. Perhaps she has feelings about me? Maybe I'm not crazy to follow her down there? Wouldn't that beat all? I would love to be with her.

Rob called. I cemented in my plans to move to Madison with him as my roomie.

I'll follow her ....

Intake: 45 mg hydroco oral, smoked

April 6, Tuesday, 2010 — (5/10)

Worked McD's today. Took 8 vikes during my lunch break, and was then in a very tense, ornery, and shitty mood for the second half of my day. Vikes and work don't mix at McD's.

Andrea gave me a ride to pay another $120 to probation—$635 to go. I'm $25 ahead of my goal so far, and I still have 3 more checks to go. I'm getting my license back and I'm getting a car. I'm moving to Madison. I'm going to try—with every inch of talent, drive and love—to be with Rose. I want to marry her, and be happy for the rest of my life.

Hung out with Pat later on at night. Joey came over and filled us in, in grand fashion, about the inside scoop with this murder that happened 9 blocks from my home. A 20-year-old guy and his

18-year-old girlfriend killed a 22-year-old girl in order to steal her stash of oxies, 80's. None of this is known to the public, but word travels fast on the "drug wire," the social system of junkies and dealers. These people make it their business to know about crime and police actions. Strange feeling to know these things.

Intake: 70 mg hydroco oral, smoked

April 7, Wednesday, 2010 — (5.5/10)

Intake: hydroco 90 mg oral, 20 mg MS (morphine sulfate) IV, smoked

April 8, Thursday, 2010 (4.75/10)

Stupidity. Called in to Pizza Hut. Just needed a break.

Intake: 50? Mg MS IV, 50 mg hydroco oral, smoked

April 9, Friday, 2010

Stupid day, both yesterday and today. Missed work for all but 4 hours today (should have been 16). Stayed home using drugs. Oh yeah, even bought drugs, $60 worth. Stupid.

Talked to Geoff. Seems I'll be living with him this time next year.

Intake: 20 mg MS IV, 50 mg methadone oral, smoked

Break the habit starting tomorrow.

April 13, Tuesday, 2010 — (5/10)

Few issues, working, taking it easy. Love Rose; trying to find the proper route to explain it.

Work is going better. Still sucks, but alright. No drugs, but drinking—cope.

Intake: Ø day 3

April 14, Wednesday, 2010

Worked 13.5 hours on the clock today.

I'm moving to Madison; this is a solid and realistic goal. It's the plan—do it by July or August—doable.

I'm staying positive, despite the setbacks of the past week. I'm looking forward to having my driving ability back and getting out of this town.

Intake: Ø day 4, *2 mg alprazolam oral

*Ran into Satan himself. [Joey] gave me a ride home, gave me some Xanax.

April 16 and 17, Saturday, 2010 (7/10)

I finally found a group of guys JUST LIKE ME! Ended up spending several hours with Trevor, Jon, Dillon in Jon's basement, just drinking and smoking—we all told "our" stories, my tale of jail and drug abuse was mesmerizing. I get to be a very good storyteller when I get high. It was so refreshing to be out in a group of people, people like me no less! Very exciting indeed!

Earlier yesterday I went 10 blocks out of my way to help a middle-aged black woman carry her groceries home.

Sent home early from work tonight for vomiting. It was the damned Dexedrine I was given. No more of that.

Intake: methadone, Xanax, Klonopin, Dexedrine, smoked

April 18, Sunday, 2010 (5.5/10)

Sat home today. Danski stopped by, pissed me off pretty bad with his hustling, seems to me that his habit is getting pretty bad. I can't deal with him anymore; it's only going to injure him further.

Travis from Pizza Hut stopped by and so did Alicia, to pick up some study aids.[24]

Hung out with Andrea this morning; her birthday is on Tuesday. Cleaned the restrooms.

Got my vikes this morning, and haven't taken a one! Managed to flush 52 down the toilet in 12 hours!

<u>Intake: Ø day 1, smoked</u>

April 19, Monday, 2010

<u>Intake: 40 mg hydroco oral, smoked</u>

April 20, Tuesday, 2010 (5.5/10)

<u>Intake 50 mg hydroco oral, smoked</u>

April 21, Wednesday, 2010

I'm beginning to lose hours at McD's due to this road construction out front; 25 hours cut by 1.5 hours today, sent home early. At

24. "study aids" - a euphemism for uppers/stimulants. Alicia was a college student; she most likely wanted some 'help' staying awake to write a big paper or study.

this critical moment the city itself is trying to eat me. Still left with close to 50 hours this week, just keep going, I guess.

I'm in an emotional blinder zone lately. The days have been going by so quickly, I'm just working and then resting, etc.

Glad I'm not depressed. Elavil nightly; meeting goals that I've set for myself.

The future holds more promise than the present....

Intake: 75 mg hydroco oral, smoked

April 22, Thursday, 2010 (5/10)

Had an unsuspected afternoon off. Took the last 11 vikes I had on this prescription, so it's off to see the doctor in next 3 weeks.

Intake: 55 mg hydroco oral, smoked

April 23, Friday, 2010 (5.5/10)

I find it tough to write my journals lately. I think it's just this phase. Working or resting, I find it hard to motivate [myself] to even leave home when I have free time.

Drug situation still exists, although at a much lesser level than before. I'm almost done paying on probation, and then it's onward to a car and moving to Madison.

Rose and I are in good touch, but I feel this current situation is precarious—it could change to less at any time. I have no idea how she feels, but I feel it's more negative on romance.

McD's sucks. Pizza Hut is awesome. I've made friends with some guys (most actually) from Pizza Hut, just one more positive.

Things have been okay mostly.

Intake: Ø day 1, smoked

April 25, Sunday, 2010 (5.5/10)

Got home at 5 AM from Paul's place. I wasn't too drunk or stoned, but I believe that mixing the two had something to do with this—I slept until noon! Rose called, spoke with her for a while; I miss her so.

Only Pizza Hut tonight, kick back, went quickly. I really like that job; the people who work there are all laid back, in stark contrast to McD's.

I've been set back a little cash that I was going to pay probation. Drug-related; don't care to reveal this to my future self. Shameful.

Intake: Ø day 1, smoked

April 26, Monday, 2010 (5.5/10)

The days all seem the same again, a blur. Work rest, work, rest, work, rest…ad nauseum!

Pizza Hut is still going well, and McDonalds's is still a hell-hole, but it seems that I'm finding a "place" amongst the other crew members. I'm not great with attendance (missing maybe 1 from every 10 shifts), but I'm great everywhere else.

Reflection has been spotty lately, not much deep thinking going on. I feel less passion to get to Madison, but my plans are still on track. Skipped a $150 obligation to probation just because— shouldn't have, but I'll be off soon enough anyways.

Why do I get excited about doing something, make a plan to do it, do it for a few weeks, and then lose momentum? Unbelievable; my own weakness amazes me even today.

I feel that my Elavil keeps the depression at bay, but looking back on the month I feel like it almost dulls my finer emotions—it keeps EVERY feeling at bay.

Things have been very domestic—fine, things are moving along just fine right now.

Stable.

`Intake: Ø day 2, smoked`

APRIL 28, WEDNESDAY, 2010 (6.5/10)

Worked 16 hours on the clock today. Pizza Hut, as always, was very cool, busy, but a lot of fun.

Went to Paul's place after work. Sat up talking with every one (Jake, Ted, Gary), drank a few beers, smoked a bowl, ate some Dexedrine—all kinds of drugs. Need to get back to focusing on my goals, which are materializing, although at a slower rate. I've spent money on drugs lately, which is horrible.

Tired, didn't get to sleep until 7 AM on 29th, a VERY LONG DAY!

Intake: 25 mg oxyco IV, 8 mg buprenorphine oral,
10 mg dextroamphetamine oral, smoked

APRIL 29, THURSDAY, 2010 (5.75/10)

Slept, woke up, and worked 6 hours at Pizza Hut, BUSY, but a lot of fun no less.

Stopped by Cindy's place. She gave me a ride up to the bank to cash my check ($230). It was beautiful and warm, a great mid-spring day.

I'm happy I've made so many new friends through work, finally!

This is the bright spot; everything else has been neutral; don't know why passion has run out of my life.

The guys at work (Hut) are all really into amphetamines, and they have been generous with me, so I'm into speed again, but I don't love and adore the drug, so I don't believe I'll have issues with it. It drives me to better things overall.

Focus, Matt. Where are your dreams lately?

Intake: Ø day 1, dextroamphetamine 10 mg oral

MAY, 2010

MAY 2, SUNDAY, 2010 (5ish/10)

Came home early morning from Paul's, hung out with him from 2 AM until around 6 AM. Nice guy, really like talking and chilling with him. Even though he's gay (and I'm most certainly NOT), I feel none of the weirdness normally felt with gay guys in my realm—a good friend.

Got in the house; locked out of the computer, phone disconnected—didn't know why—turns out John was a little upset about, once again, small things. Just his character. We talked; he went back to being nice. I formally decided with him that I would have a move-out date of August 1—90 days away. I NEED TO SERIOUSLY GET MY SHIT TOGETHER now if I'm going to be in Madison by then.

Probation should be done but isn't. Big Push in May to get this done.

Intake: random amounts of speed, Suboxone, oxycodone, etc., smoked for use last few days

MAY 5, WEDNESDAY, 2010 (5.25/10)

Bought heroin from The Devil Himself today and yesterday—$40 yesterday, tonight it's half as much in size, $20 more in price! He's been doing nothing but ripping me off lately! Got my appointment with the doc, next week on Wednesday—hydros then + Valium (said I would never use that again after my "suicidal" March. Thinking now I feel that I can use it in concert with the hydroco no problem, moderation, continuation of Elavil essential throughout. Sick, I'm sick to even put that thought through my head after last time.

Drugs. I can't seem to kill this habit. It is what I would consider "under control" at this point. I spend 1/3 or less per paycheck, with 1/3 to rent, and 1/3 to probation. Still bad, I still feel guilty because at this point my drug spending equals $400 per month or better. I include beer and weed in that total—BAD. STOP. PLEASE. Hateful habit.

I've missed a lot of journal time lately. Busy, different frame of mind, need to snap out of that soon.

Intake: heroin = (equal to) 30 mg oxyco IV, smoked

May 6, Thursday, 2010 (5/10)

Short shift at McD's. Walked to Cindy's place to find Kell alone at the house. She looks older since I last saw her (November, '09). According to both her and Cindy she is very sick lately—horrible stomach pain with vomiting. She looks sick, not her vibrant and glowing self. Neither of them will tell me what the doctors think, but they hint at something serious; hope everything is okay.

Of course, I smoked with Kell, and I sat watching CNBC— very gloomy day for the DOW shed 700 points in 10 minutes. This happened several hours after I was watching. I took a nap a little later on and awoke to NPR coverage of the "crash." All those points were mostly regained, losing only 387-ish by the end of trading. Still a very jolting shot.

Felt shitty at Pizza Hut for the second half of my day—a combination of smoking, napping, and then going to work. I have been alone now for so long that it's becoming hard to see an angle out of it, or a time.

Intake: Ø day 1, smoked

May 7, Friday, 2010 (5/10)

Cold, rainy, and dreary outside today. Forecast calling for snow tonight when last week it was in the 80s.

Worked my last shift at McD's for the week, thank God. I've decided to 'break out' of Oshkosh next week Monday and Tuesday. I'll be going up home with Kell for a little 24-hour visit. I'll have to have Kell call me out of work for a "family emergency" on Monday. No Pizza Hut night those 2 days, so I'll end up not having to work at all until Wednesday night. A short little vacation with a doctor visit/refill on Wednesday morning so I can relax, release with a good dose of a good opiate.

I feel a sadness begin to creep in ever so subtly. This town? My life? Both. I'll be breaking out for good in just about 85 days. I can't even imagine it. Yet.

Good connection with Rose, a positive thing.

It's the opiates, man. Gotta figure this out.

<u>Intake: Ø day 2, smoked</u>

P.S. It did snow today, big flakes that started falling around 8 PM.

May 8, Saturday, 2010 (5.75/10)

Rest, All day, Rest. I woke, then smoked, then back to sleep—all the way until 3 PM or so—God, I needed it! I'm becoming secretly run down with all this work. My weekends are my re-coup period when I catch up on all my rest.

Can't say enough about how well Pizza Hut is going. Everyone there, without exception, is very nice. I can tell that they like me personally and professionally. I'm surprised because I haven't felt liked in a very long time; it's strange.

This next week will be interesting.

<u>Intake: Ø day 3, smoked</u>

MAY 16, SUNDAY, 2010 (5/10)

Woe to my neglected journal entries! So much happened this last week! I was home for about 20 hours, long enough to witness my mother file for divorce. Cindy and Kell took me up, but Kell was gone for the event. I'm glad my mother finally made the move to divorce; that was a bad situation all together—2.5 years of trouble. My poor mother, lonely again.

Slow hours at work this week. Pizza Hut is down. I missed McD's a few hours, which means low paychecks the next time around. I need to think Madison, 2.5 months yet and then I'm there. Get into that mode, Matt. Do it.

Lost one of my good friends through drugs. Dude is crazy, thought he had my whole script coming to him for just helping me buy it.

Told Rose that I love her—got the bride wall. Sad day for me. Unrequited love, the worst love of all.

Where to go from here.

Intake: 50 mg hydroco oral, 40 mg Diazepam, smoked

No more Dicking around, I finally had to take care of myself. In contrast to Matt's addiction, Dick's included abuse. He didn't hit me because he recognized that I didn't back down from direct onslaught, stared my enemies in the face, owned guns, used them regularly, and wasn't afraid to shoot any wild animal that threatened me or my kids — and I had the backing of The People's Court. Matthew often joked that his mom was Judge Judy; I wasn't afraid to parse the facts and call in the bailiffs when reading verdicts. In truth, Dick often remarked (during his projectile vomiting of emotional and mental abuse) that I should just shoot him so I would go to prison. He really wanted me to get so infuriated as to do something that reckless. In his alcohol-driven delirium he actually imagined if I killed him he would somehow win, somehow get everything and see me in court at his own murder case! My house was attached to his ego, and he had to own it, even if that meant dying. How irrational is that?

Parts of him were not crazy, just devious. He was also afraid to physically assault me because of his plan to own everything I had. If he was found to be physically abusive, he wouldn't have a chance to take everything I owned. In one of his sober rants, he let it all go — how he was going to get my house and alimony because Wisconsin was a no-fault, community property state. With vibrato and chin in the air, he mused that he would be a respected and independent man once again; he wouldn't need me to survive. This disclosure wasn't the drunken rambling I was familiar with; this was his *reason* for being drunk. He revealed his whole addiction dilemma; he was afraid that he couldn't conquer the new world of work, couldn't make the grade, and wasn't able to take care of himself without a bene- factor. I was that benefactor and he hated me for it.

Without comment, I glided to the phone, summoned an attorney right in front of him, organized appointments, and provided necessary information. He sat there, didn't say a thing, watched me hang up the phone, and then proceeded to explain how I couldn't make it without him. I felt sorry for him at that moment, sober yet insanely drunk. He was so very lost, so very restricted by his stage personality. He was so soused on pride and ego that when the curtain fell and no one clapped, he remained standing at center stage waiting for his roses. I did love Dick; I did. I didn't want the play to be a tragedy. I wanted to star in a love story or at least a comedy. But, I wasn't about to be the victim in a "who done it." So, I broke my contract.

Days before Matt arrived, I signed the papers. Dick knew this, but his alcoholism prevented him from making any plans; he could only plan for his next drink, paralyzed by habit. He did call Cindy, though. Kell and Cindy decided to assess the situation, hoped to talk me out of it. I guess Cindy was his agent or something, charged with fixing the cancelled next show's contract. Kell was in full agreement with my decision.

As people arrived, I explained. Then, the sheriff came and served the papers. Still, Dick didn't move. He was told to leave, by the sheriff nonetheless. He argued with Cindy and Kell that he had 48 hours, and he took every one of them. He even slept in my bed until his hour was up. What insanity! More insane — the sisters believed I hadn't done enough. They stayed after the sheriff left and we debated what to do. I was supposed to get him into treatment, which he refused explosively. I was supposed to pray for him, which only made him quote all those verses on wives obeying husbands. I was supposed to take it, I guess. I was supposed to love him through his addiction.

Some may judge me for being a hypocrite: "Love the addict until your last cent is gone." However, you can love someone and not allow them to hurt you. You can even love someone who doesn't love you back, which was the case here. The problem is abuse. Addiction seems to magnify the real emotional issues in a person.

Matt's issue most likely stemmed from low dopamine levels. His brain was given different receptors and levels, and the opiates/opiods available in our medical culture complicated his biology. Once he tasted the ambrosia, he was lost on the island of Lotus Eaters.

Dick's problem was ego-related. He drank to escape his reality. He hated himself. Drinking just made him hate everyone; he just had so much hate. Living in the same house, we marinated in his bile. After he moved out I gave him ample and repeated opportunities to bury hate and find love, but he wanted nothing to do with it unless it meant staying married to my income.

In the August that followed, I had overwhelming feelings of upcoming doom. I thought my spiritual messages, my premonitions, my waking terrors were related to saving Dick from death. God spoke to me, quietly, and gave me forewarnings that something ominous was going to happen. I thought it was Dick. Crying and pleading with him to listen to me, he remained flippantly condescending, still abusive.

What is someone supposed to do with an abusive addict? Matthew was never abusive — odd, embarrassing, unstable, expensive, time consuming — but never abusive. Addicts' loved ones need to respect themselves and defend their own mental and physical safety. Allowing Dick to abuse me or use me like an election campaign credit card was not helping him; worse, it was like spelunking without a string — I was going too deep into dark underwater caves and had no way to find my way back to the surface. I was drinking, myself, and becoming emotionally unstable. If I allowed Dick to stay in my home, my daughter, my foster daughter, and myself were going to drown. I needed to cut bait and save the ship while there was still enough gas to find shore. I needed to cut and run.

If you are dealing with an abusive or a needy addict, the line is yours to draw. If you allow the addict to abuse you, you feed their cancer. If they are not abusing you — just taking up your time and energy in constant calls and emergencies — you aren't abused; you are loved. If they are using up your money, ask what it is 'really' for. Are they using it to pay for drugs? Try to find a different way to relieve their suffering. If they are suffering, they will appreciate your non-judgmental help. Addicts need advocates. They need relief, and often they just need to be loved, feel loved, feel hope, feel safe. However, if an addict is violent, explosive, emotionally abusive, mentally cruel, you will only make it worse by simpering or complaining and taking it. Call in the bailiff! You will do more to help them recover if you refuse to take even a bit of cruelty.

— Matt's mom

MAY 17, MONDAY, 2010 (?/10)

I did the Valium cave thing again for the last 4 days, with better results than March, except I did get depressed, did tell Rose that I love her (horrible mistake, may have ruined everything). Now, I'm trying to sort that out. Decided to try and come off the Elavil, which has been rough, depressed, horrible.

Had a drug dispute with one of my U.W. buddies; sorted that out last night; feels good to have that out of the way and know that I can chill at the frat house with everyone.

Drug madness lately. It never stops with me. [I've] been using a lot of speed lately, which adds to the rollercoaster effect of every-thing. My Vikes are being filled at a rate of 100 every 10 days now, more than I've ever had. God, need to stop.

Rose, I lost her.

Working a lot as always, but never enough.

`Intake: (nothing recorded except the word 'intake')`

With someone dying every 19 minutes in the US from opioid overdose, who would prescribe this amount? The intakes recorded really astound me.

— Matt's mom

MAY 19, WEDNESDAY, 2010 (5.5/10)

Very interesting night last night. Hooked up with West Side Mike at his place. He had over maybe 8 other people, all black, mostly younger guys. We sat playing spades, drinking, and smoking blunts for the evening—a really grand time. I was the only white guy there, but it was cool as fuck. We'll do it again soon enough. I think I made some new friends. A new cultural experience for sure.

Drugs continue. For the first time since being in Oshkosh I've made some friends.

Intake: 15 mg dexamphetamine, 70 mg methadone, smoked

May 25, Tuesday, 2010, previous week average (5.6/10)

Hot outside today again. Not as hot as yesterday, but still 87° is summer hot. My weather.

Close on probation, $400 away from being free. Lovely. How to get motivated for Madison is a different situation. I hate this place, but my motivation fails me even in the most desperate situations.

I'm still working both jobs, but I take time off whenever offered, a few hours here and there. Both jobs love me, but I find that I lack so much energy to complete all the hours they put me down for. I long for my sheets and my bed, but the house is only comfortable for me when John is out.

Sadness, loneliness never truly leaves me. I've been up and down with the Elavil lately. Tried getting off of it, but feel as if I really need the stuff. Continuing tonight, then 100 mg.

Intake: 3 mg Ativan, 15 mg hydroco

MAY 26, WEDNESDAY, 2010

Missed 8 hours this morning at McDonalds today. Just felt I needed the sleep and rest. Severely BURNED OUT at this point. Never miss a shift at Pizza Hut, but I tend to miss a lot of work at McD's, at least a shift or part of a shift every week. Need it, just need it really badly. I've come to discover that I can only do so much of this stuff, and that equals about 50–60 hours per week. I'm hoping that I can secure 40 hours at Pizza Hut so I can take it down a notch at McD's.

65 more days of this pace.

Intake: Ø day 1

MAY 28, FRIDAY, 2010 (5/10)

Long day today, started at 6:45 AM, worked until 2 PM, minus 30 min. break that was 6.25 hours, 3 hour break (Cindy is going in for emergency surgery; may lose the leg) and then 8.5 hours at the Hut. So, 14.75, we'll say 15 hours today. Long day. Off to sleep.

Intake: Ø day 3, smoked

MAY 31, MONDAY, 2010 (6.5/10) LAST DAY OF MAY!

Strange couple of days these last few have been. I've been work-ing just a shit-ton since about last Thursday … Here's the scoop:

Thursday:	7 am-1 pm McD's	5 pm-1:30 am Hut	13 hrs
Friday:	6:45 am-2 pm McD's	5 pm-1:30 am Hut	15.75 hrs
Saturday:	5 pm-1:30 am Hut		8.5 hrs
Sunday:	5 pm-12:30 am Hut		7.5 hrs
Monday:	6 am-1 pm McD's		7 hrs

Total 5 days: 51.75 hours

Now, that's a lot of hours. Notice how little sleep is between some of those monsters. It's nice to be able to work that much, but it's incredibly hard to keep that pace up for very long before becoming really burned out. I've had a little help lately from Dexedrine, but it's impossible to keep enough around to make it a habit; so much for that. It's a vacation from being sleepy, un-motivated, and tired. When I take speed, my good, nay, my BEST qualities shine brightly; on those days I am always the best employee around.

Next journal item: Melinda. Strange, very strange circumstances surround this 38-year-old beauty who has found a way into my life. I wrote "beauty," but now that I think of it I'm just not sure. She works with me at Pizza Hut, and I've never spent time with her outside of work. She called me yesterday, just broken way up. She had just broken up with her boyfriend, and she was a bit intoxicated. She threw everything against the wall, told me she was wildly attracted to me, was thinking about me quite a bit, had a "crush" on me, etc. She wanted to do something last night, but me being very oblivious and unaware didn't seize the opportunity. I was scared once again! This could have been my opportunity to break my celibacy curse. I wanted to do something today with her, talked with her and made plans for 7 PM, but she never called and I couldn't raise her on the phone. I'm a little bummed. I decided it would be great to hook up with her. I hope I can get ahold of her tomorrow and make it happen; we'll see.

`Intake: 75 mg hydroco oral`

JUNE, 2010

JUNE 4, FRIDAY, 2010 EARLY MORNING

Woe to my neglected journal entries. So many interesting things have happened that I feel bad that I haven't written them down.

I didn't sleep tonight owing to the fact that my last shift ended at midnight. Next one starts at 5 AM, just a little bit from now. It's been still a dead run lately with work. My move to Madison is intimidating to say the least. I feel strange at times thinking about the transition from here to there. I always feel strange about moving, though such is life. Just need to make it happen!

Partied with opiates for about 5 days, paying the price now by feeling a touch of dope sickness. I haven't been tackling a lot of my problems up front lately; just can't; don't have the time, it seems.

Can't wait to get away from this John guy, what an asshole.

Intake: Ø day 2

JUNE 8, TUESDAY, 2010 (5.5/10)

Cold day out today; rainy and dreary. I worked 8 hours at McD's this morning, was looking forward to the evening off, but I was just called in by Pizza Hut. Because of the bad weather, Joe thinks it's going to be busy so he wants another guy on. I decided to go in because I respect the people I work with and I don't like to see them [left] hanging.

Everything else is normal. John got back from his visit home and things are normal. I was worried he was going to go "full metal prick" when he got back, but my forecast failed me. This is good.

Gotta gear up for Madison if I want it to happen. This month I need to get a résumé put together, and then in July I'll get out to Madison and start applying for jobs, get a place all lined up too.

(No intake recorded.)

June 14, Monday, 2010 (7/10)

Today I made my LAST PAYMENT TO PROBATION. I am no longer on probation as of today.

Been partying way too much lately. At the end of this Vike streak, I'll be sick as all hell. I feel so lazy lately, just burned right the hell out.

For July, I need to pool all of my money. I can't crash and burn now, not this late in the game.

This month is my last go around.

I've become QUITE popular amongst my friends and their friends. I'm getting back to the real me. Everyone I spend time with seems to really like me. John had me over tonight; last night Kyle had me over. I've been out to the bars with him more frequently. I feel "liked" for the first time in a long time. Shame it's almost time to leave and start over again.

But Rose will be there.

Intake: about 20 Vikes, smoked

JUNE 16, WEDNESDAY, 2010 (4.5/10)

Missed today and most of last 2 days of work, including a few hours at Pizza Hut. It's the work of the Valium cave!

Probation is paid; now I just need to get my money together for a place in Madison.

Woke up today realizing that I didn't have any more drugs. I've been hitting the Vikes pretty hard lately, filling 100 very Sunday. Now I'll be out until Sunday, and will most likely be getting a little sick from it. Broke; no money for MJ or anything else.

I told myself that in June I would be getting my résumé together, which I need to be doing next.

Depressed just a bit; things have been a whirlwind lately for me. I covet the rest.

Intake: Ø day 1, smoked

June 19, Saturday, 2010 (6/10)

Beautiful day out today. I mowed our huge lawn here on NY Ave. just to be a nice guy, a good workout.

Got my last Vicodin fill yesterday. From now until the final week of July, I won't have any more Vicodin coming. That's just fine; every time I take the stuff I get a horrible liver ache, which is obviously telling me I'm doing some damage to my liver.

It seems now that I am surrounded by friends and people who like me. I will miss the group of guys I've met here, but I believe now that I am rehabilitated enough to make new friends in Madison. I'm expressing myself like I used to. Slowly, I'm gaining back some things I've lost. Putting this Oshkosh chapter behind me will be a big step.

I've just reconnected with Landon on FaceBook after 7 years of not seeing or talking with him. Dan, his father, a man I've always admired, died the other day in a motorcycle accident. Tragic.

Landon has invited me out to Oregon to visit, said he would pay my way out. I'm going to do it ASAP.

Intake: 25–50 mg hydroco, smoked

June 20, Sunday, 2010 (6–7.5/10)

To make the biggest splash you have to belly flop—M.E.

Been looking at rooms in Madison lately. I'm encouraged by what I'm finding—laid back people, prices around $400/month, right downtown no less. I'm moments away from calling one prospective roommate, fingers crossed.

Spoke with said prospect; not sure about the situation, but feel my chances are high.

Spoke with Rose. She said she's done with Sebastian, this time for good. Gave him some clothes and her old car and he's out!

Spoke with Rose yet again. She did it! She followed through and shrugged it off. She is in a lot of pain—Sweetheart, I can only wish for now!

Three work friends came over. Smoked, drank, had a good time of it.

Intake: 65 mg hydrocodone oral, smoked

JUNE 23, WEDNESDAY, 2010 (5.5/10)

Double shift today; went smoothly enough.

I've been looking hard at apartments in Madison. Thought I had one lined up, but it seems that it may not be. In any event, I should be able to come up with something I can get into.

(No intake recorded.)

June 25, Friday, 2010 (9/10)

Spoke to LANDON L. today for the first time in 8 years! Unbelievable, his father was killed 10 days ago in a motorcycle accident. I spoke with Landon all night, 4 hours, and he told me just the most tragic story about the last 4 years in his family.

I always looked up to Dan and Britta L. Dan was this mellow and yet intense medevac vet from the Vietnam War. He flew choppers for a living. Britta was this eternally patient and kind woman, just a great lady all the way around. A perfect marriage it seemed to me.

Four years ago Dan had an affair, and was caught. Britta divorced him, and he screwed her over financially—left her destitute, homeless. He went to Arizona with his girlfriend, and 10 days ago he was killed in a motorcycle accident. Landon went to Arizona to execute his father's estate. He's having severe problems with his father's girlfriend; she was belligerent at his Dad's house the other night. I told him to call the cops immediately. Hope he heeded my advice.

He's coming into about $200,000 of which most will go to his mom. I think he'll walk with about 50K of that. We're making plans to spend time together in Oregon!

Strange days.

`Intake: Ø day 3, smoked`

June 26, Saturday, 2010 (7/10)

Another good day at Pizza Hut. We inducted a new member into our fraternity last night—Carson, a really cool kid who is waiting tables for us. We took him right in, and so far (using all my available ability in perspective) he's cool as shit. Another member of the frat!

Bought some oxies from Satan Himself today. I snorted, which is rare, and one of those pieces (I gave him $40 thinking I was gonna get a 40 and ¼ an 80) was fake shit. Burned the piss out of my nose, got no noticeable high of any kind. I called him and faked him out that I was having an allergic reaction. He sounded freaked. Hopefully he won't give me fake ever again.

Sierra S wandered into Pizza Hut tonight with 2 friends. She was looking real good to me, so I went to the bar where she was at, talked with her, told her to come on over and have a good time. I'm really looking to get laid tomorrow; it seems like it will happen (fingers crossed!). I got a good kiss at the bar, a number, and some hope. MILF, chick is very fine, but she's also 40-ish, so it's all new for me. I'm confident in my abilities in LOVE. Let's see.

Intake: 20 mg oxyco snort, smoked

June 27, Sunday, 2010 (4/10)

Amphetamines cast a long shadow. Yesterday and Friday, hell, starting on Thursday afternoon I was on ever-increasing amounts of dextroamphetamine. Today was my first day off the shit. Noticeable depression, slight, but in contrast to the last few days, it's horrible.

Bored and lonely. Wake up at 5 AM for Hell's morning shift tomorrow. Another week begins. Best way to describe it is as a washing machine.

I want out really badly, out of the semi-seclusion. I would like to be able to drive to another town when I please.

I just tell myself that it's the chemicals playing with my head, has to be. Interesting how chemicals can play with a man's soul.

<u>Intake: Ø day 1, smoked</u>

June 29, Tuesday, 2010 (5.5/10)

I listen to my AM radio and every day I hear worse and worse news. Today earlier, I heard the news tell me that within the next 5–10 years over 50% of my countrymen will be obese. Horrible. Conservative Radio (i.e., Rusty Humphreys, Mike Savage) is predicting the collapse of the system, our system—it my just happen.

Worked 5 AM to 1 PM at McD's today. Tired as hell from only 4 hours sleep, but our new "frat" brother, Carson, wanted to stop over after 11 and I always oblige my friends and guests.

Had Satan Himself talk me into buying 50 mg of liquid methadone. Also came up with about a half-inch of a bottle purported to be Cherritussin—I don't feel a thing even after drinking 2 beers and smoking a bowl. Twenty-five dollars gone this time, but even if I had gotten what I thought, the money would have been gone anyways, into the hopeless drug pit.

Naftali, a guy looking for some roomies, sent me an email offering me the room! I have plans to see him next week, at which point I will pay him and forget worrying about a room! I didn't think this guy would give me the room; haven't heard from him in like 10 days. Grad student in Philosophy. Intriguing; he's from NY City; did some college there. I haven't ever seen the guy, so in my imagination he looks kinda Jewish. The first and last name strikes me as Israeli, Jewish. COOL! A new experience. He's offering a room right in the city for like $380 per month, so about 4 bones a month. I'll need to get a job that pays better than 9 or 10 per hour, 40 hours, and also another part-time gig for a back-up and extra cash.

Only Ukraine and Irina I'm thinking about lately. I'll meet her again.

John was in rare asshole form today. I've said over and over again that no matter what, I will leave this damn place on the last day of July. Today he served me a "move-out" notice for the 31st of July.

Very severe looking; just completely conceived to be shitty. I'll be happy that I'll never have to see his trashy ass when I get to Madison. I'll have to couch surf for 2 weeks in August before I move down, and find a garage to temp[orarily] store my room stuff.

I get up and down feelings lately, from one second to the next. I am anxious as hell for Madison, but I'm going. I just need to not fuck up with drugs between then and now, and I'll be fine.

<pre>
Intake: 25 mg methadone liquid*, smoked,

30 mg codeine*

*If it was real at all that is.
</pre>

JULY, 2010

July 2, Friday, 2010 (5.5/10)

Now things are closing in. I am going next week to secure a place for myself in Madison. It will be with that Naftali guy, right in town too—pretty amazing. I'm starting to become very nervous about the whole deal, just my usual jitters about moving. I hate the moving process.

(No intake recorded.)

July 7, Wednesday, 2010

Making bad moves this close to the goal is a hell of a thing. Spent about $200 on drugs yesterday and [the day] before. Can't let it get me down. I have possession of Valium again; we'll see how this shakes out.

(No intake recorded.)

July 8, Thursday, 2010 (5/10) Valium Cave

Got a cellphone today, $137.00. Bought some weed and some crack cocaine, was tossed some oxy 10s (2), eating Valiums all day. Going tomorrow to see new place in Madison.

Alarmed that I blew 2 checks on drugs like this.

```
Intake: oxyco 20 mg oral, 1 rock, 6
0 mg valium oral, smoked - No More.
```

JuLy 1ȣ, SuNDAy, 2010 (5.5/10)

Wow, neglected journal. I've been away from these pages for 10 days.

Haven't talked to Joey in a while. I go back to the doc on Wednesday for refills, hopefully, and I've been dealing directly with Bob for REAL liquid methadone. Not under control, but still financially sustainable. Need to cut it out. I've heard that Madison is a notorious drug center; maybe I won't make it?

Can't wait to leave this house and John. I HATE him lately, asshole. I want to leave him alone in this place, and I'll be able to in 13 days (or less); we'll see.

Such is life. I'm nervous. I've given control of about 70% of my finances to Paul, who I trust through and through. This is my 'moving' money. Making sure I'll have enough for first and security and I want a second month paid for by the time I get there, just in case a job is hard to find (it shouldn't be).

Moving very quickly now; no time for my beloved journal. Try to make more time in the future for it.

```
Intake: Ø day 1, smoked
```

July 28, Wednesday, 2010 (3—8.5/10)

Today's good news caps a week of nothing but failures and surprises. I was really bad into the drugs for the last 8 days or so, and I was pretty ashamed at the money spent. Yesterday, I was so depressed I was contemplating death. Today I confirmed a room in Madison!

No intake recorded.

Before confirming his room, Matt and I boxed a good match by phone almost daily. He couldn't get a realtor to accept his lease agreement without a cosigner. I firmly disagreed with cosigning anything that I couldn't pay for easily. He tried every angle and emotion to convince me, and I deflected each punch with logic. If he couldn't convince a realtor even with first month, last month and a security deposit, he couldn't convince me, either. To boot, he wasn't a college student; was 25, and was a year-long renter. He had to do this on his own because I wasn't cosigning. So, he submitted his applications with an explanation matching his position.

When he called this day, he was jubilant. Through the phone, I patted him on the back and reassured him that he was of age and man enough to get his own darned lease! We laughed and talked about his new roommates and new outlook.

We also talked about the divorce. Kelly and Cindy were decidedly pissed. Dick talked them into hating me. Matt couldn't believe how quickly they turned and how easily they believed his lies.

I was also oblivious to Matt's tactic of lying by omission. He didn't try to make me hate someone, make me attack someone to take their possessions, or anything negative. He only made me believe everything was hunky dory. His jobs were great, though he hated McDonalds desperately. As far as I knew, his health was fine, and his friendship with Rose was the best. Never a hint was given about his opiate nightmare.

I remember coaching him on how to win her affections. He didn't believe she would ever love him like he loved her, but I disagreed. Reassuringly, I let him know that a girl wants the man to make the first move. We went on for over an hour about what women want and need to feel romantic and safe with a man.

The conversation ended with peace and love. Matt was joyful about his room, I felt at peace that he was finally moving forward, and we both felt love in the air.

AUGUST 11, WEDNESDAY, 2010 (3 TO 9 MIXED/10)

Moving to Madison on Sunday. [Last] week I was found in a local park, semi-ODd and heatstroked. Went to the hospital and then went to jail. I was locked up in isolation for 6 days. Laura Welle never filed the paper work for my early release![25]

I emerged on Monday afternoon only to find that I was kicked out of Cindy's place and that none of my Pizza Hut friends ever want anything to do with me anymore! Can't get a hold of a single one! Untouchable now for this so called "crime." I'm very upset. Lucky that Kyle H is a good-hearted and kind individual and took me in for the next few nights.

Everyone, at the slightest sign of trouble, walked away from me. Got that "R" tattoo yesterday. Rose will love it!

So many problems, but my big plans are intact. I'll be gone from here soon enough.

Jobs in Madison look good; may already have one.

Intake: Valium, Vicodin, smoke

Cindy called me, just frantic. She explained how he was taken to the hospital, landed in jail, didn't have his PO in town as she was on vacation, and then went on and on and on about his drug use. She felt he needed to go to treatment. I hadn't heard the word treatment from her ever. Why now? After reading through the journals I can't believe she didn't ever

25. Matt's probation officer

once tell me Matt had a drug problem. She said he swiped her pills, but never let on anything about needing serious help, so I was skeptical. That, and Matt was so normal sounding. He didn't sound like he had back in '07. We talked at length, too. Never a thing said about methadone, needing a fix, druggy friends, nothing. Cindy was super angry at Matt for doing this, but why? She told me he couldn't stay with her anymore. What did he do that was so bad? Almost die? It didn't add up.

I did my sleuthing and found the correct person in Winneconne Probation. The young woman was very apologetic, almost fearfully so. I explained how I believed my son needed to go to treatment, and she *disagreed!* She went on about her day, how bogged down in paperwork they all were, and how she had finally found the time to search through Ms. Welle's files for the release papers. She didn't say anything about drugs in his system. She said the doctors agreed he had had heat stroke, and he was detained because the system showed him in arrears. She poured out apology after apology. She was getting him released pronto. I asked again if he could instead be put in a rehab. Nope. Nothing doing, and not necessary. He was in the process of being released, so too late and he didn't need it, anyway.

Within hours Matt called me. He was an emotional blaze of three things:

1. He got robbed.

2. He died.

3. Cindy kicked him out.

This satanic drug guy was in the park with him talking after Matt filled some script. He was jogging, which Matt did enjoy and did often, when he sat on a bench to rest in the close-to-100° heat. Next thing he remembered was the rescue squad slapping him. The paramedics told him that a woman had seen him lying on the bench looking gray, tried to wake him, and got no response. She called 911 as she thought he was dead. He *was* dead. His heart had stopped beating by the time the medics arrived, but they were able to get it going again.

What really upset him was that this Satan fellow saw him collapse from the heat and then picked his pockets for pills. He left him to die.

— Matt's mom

MADISON

On August 12, I too Matt home for a few days before the "big move." We had a really relaxing yet emotional few days before going back to gather and transport possessions. By this point, Matt looked aged. In fact, I commented about the deep creases dividing his checks; he looked like Keith Richards. But, he never once behaved slightly slurred, sleepy, detached, or disconnected. He was chipper and normally energetic.

We discussed in depth what the heck went on in the park, and he explained: His Valium was for the pain he experienced from all the hemorrhoid surgeries, which I still scoffed at. "The Devil" was a man who got kids hooked with free drugs and then ripped them off. He hated this man within his very bones. The medics saved his life; they told him his heart had stopped.

Kelly and Cindy were instrumental accomplices to his drug use. Painfully, he divulged how each of these trusted watchdogs spurned him when he needed help. Neither wanted anything to do with him after he went to jail and almost died. All they seemed to care about was if Dick was being taken care of, and what I was going to lose in the divorce. Unconscionable but true — they were both more concerned about a coffee pot left at the river cabin and a chainsaw my dad had given me than how badly drunk Dick was or how deeply addicted Matt was. Kelly even refused to return a table and chairs I had loaned her, and refused a visit from me.

They kicked Matthew and me out of their lives. He hadn't done anything to either of them and neither had I, but I wasn't allowed to divorce Dick for being an abusive alcoholic while they were allowed to spurn Matthew for almost dying due to drugs. I was relieved Matt was leaving Oshkosh.

Matt continued explaining his recovery in all sincerity. By leaving Oshkosh he would be able to break free of all the dealers, the drugs, the fair-weather relationships. He and I talked in great detail about the new landscape of Madison, and I warned him about its reputation, its location in the drug highway, and its big city crime. This would have been the time for Matt to reveal the past year's darkness, but he didn't. Instead, he assured me he had a hand on the stick shift and was driving in low gear. He felt he had the power and the drivetrain necessary to handle any temptation. He assured me that he only took pills prescribed to him. Never even slightly did he indicate he was using IV drugs.

After a day home, we went to wish grandma happy birthday in the nursing home. Matt was saddened by her condition; she didn't recognize any of us. The day went by normally; it was even deeply moving and nostalgic. That afternoon, I let him take the Jeep to go visit his favorite spots: Rock Dam and Spectacle Lake. He said, "Mom, these places mean a lot to me; I want to see them one last time before moving to Madison." Things were normal, but at times the atmosphere was tinted in sepia.

While driving back to Oshkosh, Matt recounted a terribly disturbing dream, one of many he had had over the last 3 years. The first he had in jail, others he had over the winter, and this one was the same except for one big thing: His great-grandma Beulah was usually present in his dreams, but she never spoke. Odd. She was a warm and deeply Christian woman who loved Matt dearly. Grandpa Chet was always in his dreams, and he was the one who spoke directly to Matt as a seer. Matt would ask him questions. In jail he asked Grandpa if he would be set free, and Grandpa shook his head. This came true; Matt wasn't set free and had to complete his time and probation. In another dream, Grandpa and Matt were carrying a casket with Beulah in it. They talked as Matt asked him for advice. He often dreamt of Grandpa carrying a casket with Beulah, but she never spoke. In this new and very troubling dream, Beulah was not in the casket. Matt spoke to Grandpa as if she were, but grandpa was talking to Matt about his future and warning him, and when Matt asked who was in the casket, he shook his head in sadness. Matt awoke in jail pondering who *was in the casket.*

As he retold the dream, he stopped to look at me with sincere concern and sadness. He explained that every time he dreamt of grandpa, the dream came true — the 5 days in jail (he was released the morning of his 6th day), the court's decision, and other dilemmas. I didn't try to assuage his fears; instead we pondered the metaphysical and what it all meant.

Conversation darkened even more as we neared Oshkosh. We had to stop by Kelly's, and I wanted to explain things to her. She was highly agitated about a coffee maker that Dick wanted. Supposedly, I wasn't even allowing him a way to drink coffee. Exiting on to Jackson Street with the largest garbage dump in Wisconsin right at the ramp, we continued past the state penitentiary. Its depressing entrance matched our conversation. Then, came the state mental health agency, the sheriff's department, and a barrage of strip joints and adult toy shops. This ended and the city began after several miles, just enough time to make a few calls and ask Kelly if we could come over and visit.

She wouldn't even allow me in her house. Matt talked her into letting him say goodbye to her, so we could at least come by. A good half hour passed as I waited outside. Thankfully, she came out and we had a chance to talk. Dick's lies were astronomical. Once someone would show me the tapestry, I could easily prove each thread to be fabricated. She was disappointed with Dick, and was also sorry for treating me unfairly. We made amends.

After packing Matt's belongings in the trailer, we headed toward Madison. Once we left the county, something happened to Matt. He became giddy, almost as if he was Scrooge who'd awakened from a bad dream to find himself back in his bed and still alive.

As we crossed the county line, Matt turned to me and said the most amazing thing: "Ma, know what? Kelly isn't what you think. She goes on and on about me being a druggy and being a slouch, but do you know why I went back in alone before we left? She wanted to give me a few Percocet. She thought I might need them in Madison! I wanted to tell you that. I took them, too, ma. Don't worry though; I don't need them. I just wanted you to know how crazy the whole place is and the whole 'family ties' business. Ma, they lied …." He went on about all sorts of things like his first day there with Cindy, her habit, their disdain for him, etc. Especially hurtful was when Cindy wouldn't let him stay with her after he collapsed in the park and went to jail for unpaid fines (which was erroneous). He couldn't figure out what he'd done to her.

He was deeply injured by the friends at Pizza Hut. No one would answer his calls or even talk to him when he stopped by. He was a marked man, and the only thing he'd done was almost die in public.

I guess dying by accident is rude and insulting. Matt went on about mistakes he'd made with drugs while there, but he made it sound like it was in the past. Then, he received a text message. It was Joey, and Matt was alive with moxie. "Ma, you know who that was? It was Satan trying to sell me heroin. He was the one who left me for dead in order to steal my script! He came into my house and stole from me, too. Ma, I never want to see him or anyone like him again!"

"Seriously, kiddo? He just texted you to buy drugs? Just block his number!"

"Got something better. Watch this!" he laughed. Then he began typing and narrating: "This is Matt's mom and I am sending this to all his contacts. My baby boy is not doing drugs anymore. He almost died and I am working hard to find the man who was there. If you contact Matt to sell drugs, I am going to have you arrested. Leave my baby alone!"

"Whatever. You are such a cutup. Really, what are you going to say?"

"No ma; really. That is exactly what I sent him. Wanna see? I'm serious! I am done with the drug crap and pushers!"

I was stunned, eyes staring, and mouth open. "You didn't, did you? You really sent that? Hilarious!"

Then he went on some more about this horrible guy and his new life without Joey's influence. He hated the guy.

Laughing, comparing looks to see how obviously we were related, and problem-solving the Rose romance, we drove almost to Madison. Just as we could see the city ahead, Matt asked me a serious question: "Ma, am I looking old and ugly? I used to look pretty good, if I don't say so myself."

"Sweetie, you will always be the most handsome guy I know, but you have aged. What's up with the creases in your cheeks? How did that happen?" Wrong thing to say. I shouldn't have been so honest. Matt became hunched with defeat and regret.

"Ya, I know. Too bad." He got really silent.

"Come on; you're still quite good looking. Old happens to all of us. So what if you don't look 18 anymore. Women don't care about looks. They want someone who will love them deeply and consistently. You're any girl's best bet for that." He was unmoved.

"Ma, if anything ever happens to me, I want you to have my journals. They will explain everything."

"Posh, I don't want them, then. Nothing had better happen to you. Stop it. You're being all weird and serious. Come on; look; it's Madison. You made it out!"

"No seriously; they will explain *everything*."

I pulled the Jeep and trailer over on the interstate. Looking him in the eye, I asked, "What would they explain? What are you saying? Is something wrong? Please, let me know."

"Nothing is wrong…" he paused and looked out the other window. "It's just that I'm a bit nervous and I wanted you to know that I write everything in those journals. They are for you. I love you, and I want you to look at them if anything should happen. It's just that you need to know they aren't full of thoughts and feelings only. They are everything I do. Just don't worry, but know that I want you to have them if something ever happens, okay?"

AUGUST, 2010

August 17, Tuesday, 2010 (9/10)

What a week. The last few days have seen just about all my progressive dreams fall into place. I have a wonderful little place on Elizabeth St. in the heart of Madison. Rose is about a 20-minute walk from me, closer to the capital, which is magnificent to view from any angle, day or night.

Within 24 hours of being in town I landed a full-time job that pays $11 per hour! Just landed another one too—mornings, at least $10 per hour. Hope they both work out.

Rose is here!♥

We're getting along quite famously (although it's platonic; my love for her is unrequited.)

Walmart in Madison filled my scripts 2 weeks early!

Elated

Satisfied

Life is good!

Roommates also cool as hell!

Intake: 50 mg diazepam, 45 mg hydroco, smoked

August 19, Wednesday, 2010

Rose and I are going to have breakfast this morning, and then it's off to work again at 2:30 PM at Essen Haus. I hope they like me. I think I could really clean up at this place. Things are going well.

Intake: hydroco, valium, smoke

August 21, Friday, 2010 (7/10)

Got off work early today. It was rainy out. [I] met a street musician who happened to be a junkie and homeless too. He traded me some shoot-able percs for some Valiums and we just chilled out. Interesting experience to say the least. A good guy with a lot of problems. I like people like this, as long as I can sense that they are peaceful at heart. I didn't mind having him over, and I told him to call me if he had some good hook-ups, which it seems he does.

Essen Haus is still going very well. I'm writing this on the morning of the 21st, so I'm about to see what breakfast service is like. Striving to make a good impression; [I] think it's working.

Rose should be back tomorrow. I haven't been able to get her on the phone lately; probably going through a lot of shit with Sebastian and the divorce.

Just loving Madison…. What a relief from Oshkosh.

```
Intake: 60 mg hydroco oral, 25 mg oxyco IV,4
        0 mg Valium, smoked
```

August 22, Sunday, 2010 (6.5/10)

All the days in Madison have been good. Worked breakfast yesterday and today at Essen Haus. Things seem to be going well there.
I feel competent and strong in the kitchen at Essen, and I feel the
main guys like me. From Tuesday up until today I worked 36 hours,
which before taxes yields $396, enough to pay a full month's rent
and utilities. Impossible still for me to imagine making so much
money, $11 per HOUR! Yay!

Made my first heroin connection in the city today. Went down to
State Street and found a homeless black man, who for $2 in turn
introduced me to a second homeless black man, who for $7 dollars
introduced me to "The Man," but even he didn't have the shit. I
walked 7 blocks with this last guy to meet up with yet another black
man who took us about 10 minutes outside the city. All told, I had
to pay $21 extra for this $50 bag of white. This $21 was [for] getting
info from beggars, gas money. I even had to give up $10 for that

ride out of town and a bump to black man #4 out of my bag. Now, for all that trouble I have a direct phone #, but the dope isn't the best. I think I may search better sources next time.

Intake: $100/ heroin IV, 45 mg hydro oral,

10 mg diazepam oral

August 11, Wednesday, 2010 (8/10)

What great times. Madison is wonderful. I had yesterday and today off. Spent first half of the day reading books and relaxing. Chased down some heroin—$65 wasted of course—and then I watched *Bodysong* with the neighbors (who are cool as hell), and then Rose came over.

Rose is my light. I spent the evening with her having a few beers. Such a pleasure talking with her. I have a deep, spiritual connection with her, but she will not become romantically involved with me … yet. I'm not so worried about the romance, as long as I can be close to her; it's enough.

I'm intoxicated with my situation here in Madison. Everything is beautiful; everything is easy and friendly and interesting.

I must be in OZ!

Intake: 45 mg hydroco oral,

1 hit heroin snort, smoked

August 27, Friday, 2010 (5/10)

Noticed the first hint of fall the other day—depression slowly creeping back in. Spent second half of day with Rose watching a movie and going grocery shopping. Spent the last of my Oshkosh money on weed, a shitty portion of heroin, and groceries. Now I'm stuck without dope until next Thursday or Friday when my scripts go to fill, and then I can begin to handle fall and winter.

The job at Essen Haus seems to be going well. Looking forward to my paychecks this upcoming week from them.

Still, feel like I'm in a very dark place.

```
Intake: heroin 1 hit, smoked
```

August 28, Saturday, 2010 (6/10)

Today would have been much better except for the fact that I felt like shit from AS for most of the afternoon/evening. I thought it would be less, but things got kicked up for some reason. I had a 2-week habit, and it feels like I'm coming off a 1- or 2-month kick. Depression is back, hence re-starting my TCA. We'll see!

Spent today afternoon drinking with Rose. Went to James Madison Park and just lay in the sun, then walked to a bluegrass festival in Orton Park. Watched *Bodysong* with Rose, finally.

Kicking sucks.

<u>Intake: Ø day 1, smoked</u>

August 30, Monday, 2010 (5.5/10)

Depressed lately, TCA hasn't quite kicked in. Another day or two and I'll be much better, at least that is the consensus among the different parts of my brain.

Work has been stressful to say the least. I worked with Adam alone for the first time; what a complete and total asshole that guy was…. Made me look pretty bad in front of the owners, but he has no control over himself. As long as I can continue working with Gerardo and Bob on Sat. and Sun. morns and Wed. and Thur. nights, I should be okay.

Spent the second half of the day/evening entirely with Rose, always a great time. Depression seems worse during the daylight hours for some reason.

Waiting for Thursday…. Payday and pharm come Thursday.

<u>Intake: Ø</u>

Poetry As it Hits the Page

by Matthew J.D. Edwards

A feeling passed before me
quickly, flitting away from attempt
to grasp, to understand
it was akin to remorse
deep, utterly pungent
I cannot possess this feeling
akin to remorse is not remorse
because I enjoyed those days
you and I, striding together
through the landscape of youth
privy to the warmth of the sun
I still return to find our places of peace
Find them I do, under heaven and stars
You, my love, your presence lingers
as I can still see you
dancing in the tall grass
fading gently, your ghost into the forest runs
weary am I as I kneel in the sand
no longer those days do we inhabit
I am left with this passing feeling
and the landscape
under the influence of September wind.

DEATH

Thursday came only for an hour or so. His heart stopped some-time around midnight the evening of the 1ˢᵗ of September. He died after spending the night chatting with his roommate over a glass of wine and laughing with the neighbors on their porch.

Rose called repeatedly the next morning, but got no answer. She finally texted his roommate David, worried that he had stood her up and had a shift to work that night. David knocked on his door — no answer. So he opened it. Matthew was lying on his bed with his journal, a needle, a spoon, and a glass of water next to him. He was gray, obviously dead.

AFTERMATH

The investigation began immediately. His journals, cellphone, wallet, clothes, and drug paraphernalia were kept as evidence and studied. They studied his journals, cell messages and numbers, and interviewed his roommates and Rose. His Facebook page and email were accessed. Everything of personal value to both Matthew and me became cold evidence for official eyes only.

Begging — even weeping and pleading — did no good; the straight-backed and clean-shaven investigator had a job to do. He was tasked with finding who had sold Matt the drugs and putting all involved in jail for homicide. Interestingly, his name was also Matt. Matt was both understanding yet practiced at sterile replies. I wanted the journals and he wanted to complete his directive: prosecute criminals. Why didn't the "officials" care about a grieving parent and a dead man's last wishes? I soon found out why no amount of letters written to the governor, to the state's attorney general's office, to the head of Madison Police Department, and numerous other agencies made a bit of difference.

No one cared.

Detective Matt and I had a few too many conversations for his liking, so he finally explained (without neglecting his directive) how drugs and police interact — it's hopeless. Even if the seller were found and put in jail, many more fill the supply line, straight from Afghanistan. His income came from doing what he was told, and he knew that his whole drug-fighting vocation would not affect the drug trade by one electron. He also knew that the bigger problem was prescription drugs. Tutoring me in Drugs 101, he explained how addicts begin on prescriptions and then turn to the cheaper street drugs. My son died because the street drugs vary in strength, and he probably found something fairly pure, something he couldn't gauge. Matt the investigator was doing this job for the income and pride in service, just like the rest of us. The whole legal system was bent on completing the task, fulfilling directives, and getting paid. It was a little economy, and this economy didn't pay grieving loved ones. I was dealing with robots whose motherboards followed statutes, not logic.

In the end, Detective Matt found a heart somewhere behind his badge. He succumbed to my logic: "If no one has been caught after 9 months, the likelihood is small that a conviction will ever occur, and I want to read what happened to my beloved son." In May of 2011, the journals, the clothes he died in, his cell phone, and $44.78 were released to me. The case was closed.

WHAT CAN WE DO?

Was Detective Tye correct? Is Matt's case closed? Evidence keeps building as people keep dying, and Matthew's tragedy is performed by new actors for new audiences everywhere. How many people see Matt as the villain? How many are miscast as the villain in performance after performance?

The CDC's (Center for Disease Control and Prevention) report, Prescription Opioid Overdose Data, summarized a study done the same year Matthew died:

> "As many as 1 in 4 people who receive prescription opioids long-term for non-cancer pain in primary care settings struggles with addiction." The CDC report further states, "Overdose deaths involving prescription opioids have quadrupled since 1999, and so have sales of these prescription drugs. From 1999 to 2014, more than 165,000 people died in the U.S. from overdoses related to prescription opioids."

If we lined up their caskets, they'd stretch for 219 miles, but Matthew died of heroin so these statistics do not even include him. The CDC's Heroin Overdose Data report states:

> "Heroin-related overdose deaths have more than tripled since (the year Matt died) 2010."

Mortality numbers from heroin and prescription opioids are rarely combined, yet the U.S. Department of Health & Human Services states, "Opioids are natural or synthetic chemicals that bind to receptors in your brain or body. Common opioids include heroin and prescription drugs such as oxycodone, hydrocodone, and fentanyl." Why do statisticians divide opioid deaths into prescription and non-prescription categories when:

> "The molecular structures of heroin and oxycodone are almost identical. There are many prescription opioid narcotics which are similar to heroin …. [and these drugs] come from the same place heroin does — the opium poppy."

Would you accept a prescription for heroin? How can we continue to prescribe and accept opioids as anything else? How many more people need to suffer addiction and/or death before we change our semantics to reflect the CDC's finding that "1 in 4 people" will become addicted after long-term use of opioid pain relievers.

What is "long-term use?" Matthew's first pill at age 15 began his addiction, yet Detective Tye closed his case with the word "heroin" marked as the cause of death. Who killed Matthew? Mr. Heroin? Mr. Oxy? Mr. Vike? Dr. Who? Or was it the man on the Madison street who was the focus of Detective Tye's investigation? How can this one man be more culpable with his one act of selling Matt his final dose of heroin than all the others who prescribed drugs, sold drugs, shared drugs, looked the other way, or turned the other way? Why can't we blame the product? Any other product that killed that many people would be pulled from the market immediately.

Who or what kills the hundreds of thousands who become addicted to opioids, both legal and illicit? The bar charts on the following page represents real human faces and hearts.

Are there human lives in these numbers or only criminals deserving of their fates? According to the Madison Police Department, Matt's death was a crime. According to Wisconsin state law, what Matthew did was a crime. In fact, everyone in the second chart was a criminal because heroin is illegal. Prescription opioids are not.

National Overdose Deaths
Number of Deaths From Prescription Opioid Pain Relievers

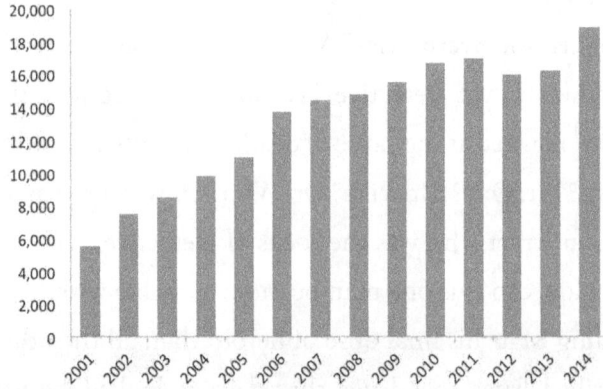

Source: National Center for Health Statistics, CDC Wonder

National Overdose Deaths
Number of Deaths From Heroin

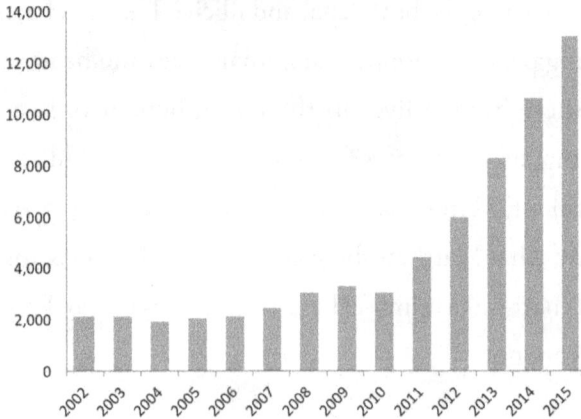

Source: National Center for Health Statistics, CDC Wonder

What is your hope after reading Matthew's words? Would you put him in jail? Would you charge him for treatment? Would you put him on a list and make him wear a metaphorical scarlet A?

Prescription opioids kill many more than faulted, unstable, hard-to-love, troubled, or rejected people? In 2014, did 30,000 US citizens die of opioid use because they were mentally and emotionally faulted, suicidal, destined to fail at life, or just plain stupid? Can they be disregarded as having social problems, families who failed them, and sub-standard communities to live in to the point they were destined to die of something illegal?

In 1985, the year Matthew was born, more people died while riding bicycles than from "opiates and related narcotics." From 2000 to 2014, nearly half a million Americans died from drug overdoses." It would alarm citizens everywhere if the pedal bike mortality rate stayed comparable to that of opioid mortality. The outcry over 500 thousand pedal bike deaths would be deafening. We would warn everyone not to ride, take away children's bikes, and even make biking on highways and side-roads illegal. Would we blame this on bad families, rotten communities, inadequate policing, and mental illness? Would we say that cyclists have a disease? Would we look to see how people acquire bikes, explore what motivates them to ride again after the first ride, and investigate who told them that riding a bike was not risky if you only do it once or for a short period?

American society did not degenerate and lose all moral compass and self-control in the space of 25 years. People who get opiates/opioids are widely stratified individuals, but they are all worthy of knowing the truth and telling their truth without shame or fears of being punished by the legal system. We must ask different questions, listen to their stories, and not label them as weak degenerates. Addicts deserve unconditional love, forgiveness, and help.

This is not a legal problem. Plenty of laws state that dangerous substances must be banned or heavily controlled. This is not a disease. One in four people are not born with a defective brain. Addiction is an ironic tragedy:

Act I — It hurts so you must pay money to the doctor.

Act II — Pain is not part of life so you must pay for chemicals.

Act III — It hurts differently now so you must somehow find more chemicals until your money is gone.

Act IV — You are shameful. Doctors or judges must lock you up and charge you for that service.

Act V — You are a criminal. You must live on the edges of society until you die.

End credits — Pharmaceutical Companies, Doctors, Police Departments, Judges, Employers, and Friends and Family.

How do we help stop this play from showing again and again? Hope is not likely to be found in more laws. Enforcing a law is more difficult than getting it enacted, and the legal system cannot possibly respond with the necessary change in opinion needed by the millions who suffer while feeling and being treated like criminals. Laws often benefit the legal system's bottom line more than the people they are intended to serve.

Education is what's needed for the masses who trust medical science without question. Only education will foster a sympathetic response for those caught in this snare, and only awareness will bring about a dead-stop on profits made by the individuals and corporations who hand out heroin without the same warnings required for open-heart surgery.

If people knew the ease with which one can become addicted from taking just one pill, would they accept their first prescription? I would not have allowed Matthew to take that first Vicodin. I would have scolded the doctor for thinking the pain was so unbearable that he needed something notoriously dangerous, and would have told everyone that our little clinic was prescribing heroin.

That was then. Now, our complacent population is accustomed to pain-free or reduced-pain medical care. We need to confront the pharmaceutical industry, change the bleached and scientific terms used to disguise synthetic heroin, and demand litigation for damages. Class-action law-suits educate a different set of people.

I am not certain how to change our society or our approach to opinions and practices, but I hope Matt's words inspire you to think about the problems, the addicts in your life, and your role. Thank you for reading Matt's story. He could not speak openly, and died without the hope of telling his children or grandchildren what he experienced. Stand in the gap for him and those like him. Be his prodigy. Help him tell as many people as possible that he was a good man, an honorable man, a courageous man, and a valuable man. Confront those who claim to know what an addict thinks and feels. Reopen the case on heroin/opioid addicts by asking for a retrial, an impartial jury, untainted/unbiased witnesses, and a voice for the accused? Tell others what Matt couldn't.

GET IN TOUCH

Matt's mom, Jane is working to change minds and hearts regarding opiate addiction. Invite Jane Funk to speak to your audience.

Email: mattsjournals@gmail.com
Telephone: 715-545-2256

Please visit this book's Facebook page: *What I Couldn't Tell You,* facebook.com/mattsjournals to share your thoughts. Or send a Tweet to @mattsjournal1. Visit our Twitter page at Twitter.com/Mattsjournal1, or view this book's website at WhatICouldntTellYou.com.

Your comments on the subject of opiate addiction or reactions to Matt's journals are welcome. And please help spread the word about addiction by posting an honest review of this book on Amazon.com.

In 2014, The Biscuit Factory TV produced a feature-length film about Matt and his journals. *Written Off* is available by contacting the producers Molly Hermann and Rob Lyall at biscuitfactory.tv or The Biscuit Factory, LLC, 917 West Broad Street –Suite 200, Falls Church, VA 22046. Please visit written-off.com to watch the film's trailer and see Matt and Jane tell their stories. Molly and Rob are using this film to change minds, too. Contact them to request a showing for your school, organization, or group.